International Perspectives on Chicana/o Studies

"This exciting and timely anthology provides great insight into the growing international appeal of Chicana/o Studies, a field previously believed to be of merely regional and local interest within the United States."
—*Guisela Latorre, The Ohio State University, USA*

"Leen and Thornton's volume represents a major new contribution to Chicano/a Studies in English. While offering a clear and focused investigation of Chicano identities and culture, it is sensitive to the contingent, evolving and multifaceted nature of those identities and their cultural manifestations. Unusually international in approach and with a wide range of excellent contributors, the book covers areas as diverse as literature, art, film, institutional programmes, everyday life practices and wider matters of cultural identity and identification. It is essential reading for all those interested in the field."
—*Philip Swanson, The University of Sheffield, UK*

This volume examines how the field of Chicana/o Studies has developed to become an area of interest to scholars far beyond the United States and Spain. For this reason, the volume includes contributions by a range of international scholars and takes the concept of place as a unifying paradigm. As a way of overcoming borders that are both physical and metaphorical, it seeks to reflect the diversity and range of current scholarship in Chicana/o Studies while simultaneously highlighting the diverse and constantly evolving nature of Chicana/o identities and cultures.

Various critical and theoretical approaches are evident, from ecocriticism and autoethnography in the first section, to the role of fiction and visual art in exposing injustice in section two, to the discussion of transnational and transcultural exchange with reference to issues as diverse as the teaching of Chicana/o Studies in Russia and the relevance of Anzaldúa's writings to post 9/11 U.S. society.

Catherine Leen is a lecturer in the Department of Spanish at the National University of Ireland, Maynooth, specializing in Mexican and Chicana/o literature and cinema and Argentine and Paraguayan cultures. Her recent publications include works on Sandra Cisneros and Guillermo Gómez-Peña.

Niamh Thornton is a senior lecturer in Hispanic Studies and Film at the University of Liverpool. She is a Latin Americanist with a particular focus on Mexican film and literature and a key interest in the representations of conflict. She has also written about queer representations and cyberculture.

Routledge Research in Cultural and Media Studies

For a full list of titles in this series, please visit www.routledge.com

International Perspectives on Chicana/o Studies

"This World Is My Place"

Edited by Catherine Leen and Niamh Thornton

Routledge
Taylor & Francis Group
New York London

First published 2014
by Routledge
711 Third Avenue, New York, NY 10017

and by Routledge
2 Park Square, Milton Park, Abingdon, Oxon OX14 4RN

First issued in paperback 2017

*Routledge is an imprint of the Taylor & Francis Group,
an informa business*

Library of Congress Cataloging-in-Publication Data

International perspectives on Chicana/o Studies : "this world is my place" /
    edited by Catherine Leen and Niamh Thornton.
        pages cm. — (Routledge research in cultural and media studies ; 56)
    Includes bibliographical references and index.
    1. Mexican American arts—Study and teaching.   2. Mexican
Americans—Study and teaching.   I. Leen, Catherine, editor of
compilation.   II. Thornton, Niamh, editor of compilation.
    NX512.3.M4I58 2013
    704.0368'72073—dc23
    2013018828

ISBN 13: 978-1-138-09784-1 (pbk)
ISBN 13: 978-0-415-83335-6 (hbk)

Typeset in Sabon
by Apex CoVantage, LLC

Contents

Figures

Acknowledgments

This volume is the fruit of multiple encounters and exchanges across the Atlantic and beyond and thanks are due to many. Grateful thanks to the contributors, artists, and writers whose hard work and generosity made this book possible.

Catherine Leen would like to thank the Fulbright Commission of Ireland for supporting her research at UCSB in 2007 and especially Francisco Lomelí and his family for their warm welcome. Thanks also to the Workshop and Conference Support Fund at the National University of Ireland Maynooth for their support in organizing the International Chicana/o Studies Colloquium at NUIM in 2010, and to all at the Department of Spanish, NUIM. Thanks also to Catherine O'Riordan of the Graphic Studio Gallery, Dublin, for her invaluable advice and enthusiasm for this project. Special thanks to Niamh for coediting this book. On a personal note, sincere thanks to the Leen and Bermingham families for looking after little Hazel in the final stages of the preparation of this manuscript, and love and thanks to Eddie for his constant support and encouragement.

Niamh Thornton would like to thank Catherine for collaborating on this project, which involved many border crossings, from the North to the South of Ireland, but also across many different time zones as we reached out to our scattered contributors. I wish to extend a special love and thanks to Dario for his wizardry with images, and much love and thanks to Liz, as always, for being my rock and supporting me intellectually as well as practically throughout this process.

Introduction

This volume presents a snapshot of international approaches to Chicana/o Studies as we enter the second decade of the twenty-first century. It has long been assumed that this particular discipline is only relevant to U.S. readers, particularly those residing in the Southwest region of the United States, but, in fact, Chicana/o Studies has become influential across borders and features in the teaching and research of universities worldwide. This interdisciplinary, humanities-based volume approaches the internationalization of Chicana/o Studies through cultural production, with essays on literature, art, mass media, and film. While the book explores new critical approaches, transcultural and transnational exchanges, and new art forms or writing, it also seeks to establish a dialogue with the groundbreaking work carried out previously in the field. It is for this reason that the title of the volume references a poem by Bernadette García from the celebrated 2002 collection of essays *This Bridge We Call Home: Radical Visions for Transformation*.

García's poem describes the frustration of a Latina student whose White male professor dismisses the poetry of Alice Walker as "other" and distinctly inferior: "He said it he did *It has its place but I'd be very disappointed if you wrote like that*" (Anzaldúa and Keating 2002, 390, italics in original). Appalled by his condescending and Anglo-American attitude, García writes mockingly that this professor considers the world to be his place, when in fact this exclusive, male-dominated ivory tower is, for her, an outmoded and fast-disappearing space (Anzaldúa and Keating 2002, 390). While García's view that academia or the world in general has changed so radically as to accommodate people of all ethnicities equally may be somewhat optimistic, nonetheless, her confident assertion that her work is as valid as that of any Western writer and that the world has become a more inclusive and diverse place are matters that speak to the central themes of this volume. Issues such as bilingualism or multilingualism, racial tensions, generational divisions, and the interchange between vastly different cultures have become concerns that affect communities far beyond the U.S. Southwest or other areas in the United States where there is a strong Mexican presence. While the essays collected here emphasize the diversity and transnationalism of Chicana/o

Studies, they also reflect on how the place of Chicana/o Studies in academia around the world has evolved.

Chicana/o Studies has grown exponentially as an academic discipline within and beyond the United States since the first departments of Chicana/o Studies were established at UCLA and UC Santa Barbara in 1969. Recent decades have seen the establishment of a thriving biannual conference organized by the Instituto Franklin, Universidad de Alcalá, at various locations in Spain. These conferences have been attended by scholars working in the area of Chicana/o Studies from countries including Argentina, Mexico, Austria, Ireland, France, Spain, Germany, and Poland. In 2011, the Instituto Franklin also founded HispaUSA, an organization devoted to the study of Chicana/o culture whose activities include the publication of the *Revista Camino Real,* a journal that publishes "articles that reflect the different sensibilities and peculiarities of the Hispanic world in the United States" (Instituto Franklin 2011). Other conferences with a strong Chicana/o emphasis have been held in recent years in Germany, Russia, and Turkey, and María Herrera-Sobek edited a special issue of the *Journal of American Studies of Turkey* in Fall 20000 that was dedicated to Chicana/o culture. While writers such as Sandra Cisneros enjoy worldwide success, the work of other writers and theorists such as Helena María Viramontes, Cherríe Moraga, and Denise Chávez feature strongly in international conferences and are the subject of a number of critical studies and PhD theses, as well as being included in the curricula of undergraduate and postgraduate courses as far afield as Russia and Argentina.

At the heart of this volume is the idea of place, whether expressed in examples of transcultural cooperation and engagement or through the continued exclusion of Chicanas and Chicanos from political or cultural agency through the creation of borders that are very much a reality, even if they do not appear on a map. Chicana/o Studies has always been a field marked by tensions over place. As a dispossessed people, Chicanas/os were forced to redefine ideas of nationhood and belonging in an often racist or indifferent society. As the Chicano Movement consolidated, however, it became apparent that the issue of staking a place *within* it would also become problematic. The author and educator Tomás Rivera, who was a pioneer in synthesizing Mexican literary influences with his experience of living in the United States as a person of Mexican descent, insisted on solidarity as a key unifying force. Santiago Daydí-Tolson notes that: "Rivera himself uses the singular to refer to the collective when he talks about the Chicano in general and says that 'this is the kind of character I tried to portray in my work'" (Daydí-Tolson 1988, 137). The difficulty that arose from the insistent focus by Rivera and his generation on community and solidarity was that many voices were excluded from this vision, especially those of women. Paradoxically, this exclusion had the positive outcome of inspiring a strong tradition amongst Chicana writers to speak of the oppression they suffered as a result of the patriarchal nature of the Chicano Movement. Anzaldúa compares the pressure that Chicana women endured to conform to their society's *machista* expectations to having to wear a mask to hide one's real face: "When our *caras* do not live up to the image that the family or the community wants us to wear and when we rebel against the engraving of our bodies, we experience ostracism, alienation, isolation and shame" (Anzaldúa 1990, xv).

The tradition of writing against the oppressively male politics of the Chicano Movement has led to the emergence of committed feminist writers, such as Cisneros and Ana Castillo, whose use of language is a powerful tool that cuts through the decades of racism and sexism directed at Chicanas. Although Cisneros has achieved worldwide acclaim and her books have been translated into numerous languages, she is not immune to the pressures that a patriarchal society imposes on women, and she has spoken frequently about how her male relatives have bridled at her open discussion of issues such as violence toward women as a betrayal. Outside Chicana/o society, Castillo notes that the work of Chicana writers is still considered suspect because it is judged according to Anglo-American norms:

> What makes the Mexic Amerindian woman's literary expression questionable (and indeed ours is often under suspicion as legitimate literature) is essentially the same mechanism that has always kept us invisible as human beings and suppressed our contributions to the changing process of society. (Castillo 1995, 165)

The continuing struggle of Chicana writers and artists to counter ethnic, gender, or class prejudice is reflected in a number of the chapters in this volume, including Ellen McCracken's study of the increasing presence of female writers in Chicana/o literary space, Imelda Martín-Junquera's exploration of Pat Mora's *House of Houses* as ecofeminist literature, Mario García's reading of Mary Helen Ponce's *Hoyt Street—An Autobiography* as autoethnography, and Catherine Leen's examination of the reappropriation of religious iconography as a metaphor for the empowerment of women in both Chicana and Irish art.

A further topic to consider is the much-cited notion that in our globalized, transnational world, in which we are all supposedly connected through the Internet, borders have ceased to matter. Since Chicana/o writers, filmmakers, and artists have always negotiated the complexities of living "in the hyphen," as Ilan Stavans puts it, they are uniquely placed to reflect on a brave new world that at times seems to eradicate cultural distinctiveness in a globalized culture that ignores or seeks to minimize difference (Stavans 2001, 4). Citing Renato Ortiz, Nestor García Canclini notes that there is a marked tendency to homogenise cultural specificity "by exploiting the coincidences in thought and taste in all societies" (García Canclini 2001, 93), yet he adds that the fact that even global conglomerates have to bow to local particularities means that rather than disappearing, "ethnic, regional, and national identities are being reconstructed in relation to globalized processes of intercultural segmentation and hybridization" (García Canclini 2001, 94). Thus, not only does this mean that cultural specificities remain extremely important despite globalization, but that these differences can be exploited to create hostilities between people and to maintain the only too real physical borders that have been reinforced in recent decades through U.S. government policies that have increased the militarization of the border, such as Operation Hold the Line (1993), Operation Gatekeeper (1994), Operation Safeguard (1994), and Operation Jump Start (2006) (Romero 2008, 75). Other negative consequences of U.S. intervention in the borderlands are the persecution of immigrants and the crime resulting from the intensification of maquiladoras along the border, topics that are discussed in the essays by María Herrera-Sobek and Nuala Finnegan. The overcoming of metaphorical and ideological borders and the increasing internationalization of Chicana/o rituals and artistic expression are discussed in chapters by Cristina Elgue-Martini, Tatiana Voronchenko, Francisco Lomelí, and Niamh Thornton.

As a way of overcoming borders that are both physical and metaphorical, this volume seeks to reflect the diversity and range of current scholarship in Chicana/o Studies while simultaneously highlighting the diverse and constantly evolving nature of Chicana/o identities and cultures. Although the chapters take in a wide range of genres and issues related to Chicana/o culture, they are arranged into three sections that reveal synergies and multiple parallels across disciplines and critical approaches. These sections are not mutually exclusive but suggest the principal concerns of this volume: "Critical Paradigms: Continuities and Transitions," "From the Regional to the Global," and "Visual Culture and Activism." As Alicia Gaspar de Alba observes: "In the current social arena, the constant movement of people and ideas across hemispheric borders position contemporary Chicano/a experience and cultural expression as part of an incipient transnational imaginary" (2003, xvii). It is our hope that this volume, which in myriad ways foregrounds the many points of contact between Chicana/o cultural expression and cultures outside the United States, will reveal new insights into the field and confirm its relevance to twenty-first-century global exchanges.

WORKS CITED

Anzaldúa, G., ed. *Making Face, Making Soul, Haciendo Caras: Creative and Critical Perspectives by Feminists of Color.* San Francisco: Aunt Lute Books, 1990.
Anzaldúa, G., and A. Keating, eds. *This Bridge We Call Home: Radical Visions for Transformation.* New York: Routledge, 2002.
Castillo, A. *Massacre of the Dreamers: Essays on Xicanisma.* New York: Plume, 1995.
Daydí-Tolson, S. "Ritual and Religion in Tomás Rivera's Work." In *Tomás Rivera: The Man and His Work,* edited by V. E. Lattin. Tempe, AZ: Bilingual Review Press, 1988.

García, Bernadette. *This Bridge We Call Home: Radical Visions for Transformation.* New York: Taylor and Francis (Routledge), 2002.

García Canclini, N. *Consumers and Citizens: Globalization and Multicultural Conflicts.* Minneapolis: University of Minnesota Press, 2001.

Gaspar de Alba, A., ed. *Velvet Barrios: Popular Culture & Chicana/o Sexualities.* New York: Palgrave Macmillan, 2003.

Herrera-Sobek, M., ed. *Journal of American Studies of Turkey* 12 (Fall 2000: Special Chicana/o Issue).

Instituto Franklin de Alcalá. *Revista Camino Real: Investigación en Estudios Norteamericanos.* 2011. Accessed March 22, 2013, https://www.institutofranklin.net/en/publications/revista-camino-real.

Romero, F. *HyperBorder: The Contemporary U.S.-Mexico Border and Its Future.* New York: Princeton Architectural Press, 2008.

Stavans, I. *The Hispanic Condition: The Power of a People.* New York: Harper Collins, 2001.

Part I

Critical Paradigms
Continuities and Transitions

Critical paradigms are a good beginning. They allow the reader an opening into Chicana/o Studies and its theoretical frameworks. In this section, cultural production is taken as the key to understanding how Chicana/o identity is played out, explored, defended, and projected for an implied Chicana/o and non-Chicana/o audience. For Gloria Anzaldúa: "Culture forms our beliefs. We perceive the version of reality that it communicates. Dominant paradigms, predefined concepts that exist as unquestionable, unchallengeable, are transmitted to us through the culture" (1999, 38). Culture, then, is how we understand who we are. Anzaldúa continues in her book to challenge how women have been: "subservient to males" (1999, 39), and complicit in transmitting the rules of these more powerful men (1999, 38). That is, they carry the burden of responsibility for upholding cultural values while simultaneously finding ways of resisting those who oppress them.

The authors in this section explore how women navigate these apparently contradictory positions, as well as providing insights into significant trends and patterns in Chicana literature. Notably, all three examine the work of women writers, which itself suggests a dramatic shift from the male-dominated world of the early Chicano Movement and a sea change from the lack of attention to Chicana writing noted by Ellen McCracken in her chapter. Another significant development since the 1960s has been the publication of groundbreaking critical and theoretical works on Chicana/o Studies, such as Cherríe Moraga's *A Xicana Codex of Changing Consciousness: Writings, 2000–2010* (2011) and Arturo Aldama and Naomi Quiñonez's *Decolonial Voices: Chicana and Chicano Cultural Studies in the 21st Century* (2002), by international publishers, yet Anzaldúa's writing continues to inform the work on critical theory by scholars represented in the field. The variety of literature examined in this section and the identification of genres as diverse as chapbooks, Chica Lit, ethnographic autobiography, and the ecofeminist novel are also richly suggestive of the continuing evolution of Chicana literature and the continual reinvention of its central themes and modes of expression.

Ellen McCracken takes a look at publishing and its evolution from chapbooks, a pamphlet-style publication of small print runs, to Chica Lit, a category that is determined with high-volume sales of works generally issued by a big publishing house. Chapbooks exist on a small scale and vary in quality. Some were accompanied by detailed illustrations, whilst others were a collection of photocopied pages. With the arrival of e-books, they have taken on a different quality as unique, bespoke texts that become covetable objects (Carter 2011, n.p.). For some, the chapbook was an end in itself, while for others it was an alternative means of circulating their writing (often poetry). In McCracken's chapter, it is clear that many Chicana writers issued their work in this format for specific reasons. They lacked access to alternative means of publication, because of the inherently conservative nature of much book publishing and the consequent marginalization of Chicanas in publishing up to recent times.

If chapbooks can be construed as ephemera that were distributed informally or by small publishing houses, the recent phenomenon of Chica Lit is also seen as ephemera, but in the different sense of being lightweight, easy reading, centered on romance with a largely female readership. McCracken tackles the questions of gender in relation to authorship and readership in tandem with the thorny issue of who is writing and for whom. She traces the trajectory of the move from chapbook to the Chica Lit phenomenon, taking in other significant developments on the way, as a means of approaching Chicana/o cultural and social change through publishing.

Gender is also at the forefront in the other chapters in this section as Chicanas experience double marginalisation, due to their sex and culture. Imelda Martín-Junquera and Mario García consider texts that position the author clearly within the narrative, albeit in distinct ways. Martín-Junquera examines Chicana literature from an ecofeminist perspective with a particular focus on Pat Mora's *House of Houses* (1997), a memoir which voices her family's experiences in the first person. Set against the backdrop of significant historical events, such as the Mexican Revolution, and reflecting on the protagonists' subsequent move north of the border, it uses the house and garden as evocative tools to convey the family's stories.

Ecofeminism is a powerful means of approaching this text because of the narrative connections between people and the garden made by Mora, but also because it lends itself to an exploration of how to link this space with the female characters. As Martín-Junquera observes, ecofeminism is not a critical tool that has yet gained much currency in Chicana/o Studies despite much growth in this approach in other fields. She explores the resonance of this space and provides a model for future studies of this kind.

Continuing this exploration of the particularities of women's experiences growing up in this interstitial space, García closely examines Mary Helen Ponce's *Hoyt Street—An Autobiography* (1993). He provides a brief historical overview of Chicana/o history to contextualize his account. Then, drawing on theories of transculturation as articulated by the Cuban anthropologist Fernando Ortiz, he explores how Ponce's autoethnographic approach attempts to understand her own childhood and coming of age.

In a country like the United States, where to belong is to acculturate and assimilate, Mexicans have been seen to be resistant and eager to keep outside of mainstream culture. García uses Ponce's text as a way of exploring the multiple strategies employed by each new generation to figure their way into and through the various ways of being Chicana/o, Mexican, and North American. This study is tinged with gendered expectations that make women responsible for upholding traditions and cultural practices and transmitting these onward to the next generation.

García explores the very real discrimination that Ponce experienced on growing up and reflects upon how she negotiated these struggles as a child. In addition, he highlights the emotional anguish that these struggles inflicted upon a generation told that their Mexicanness was a failing and who had to find ways of maintaining a sense of self despite this negative message. This generation is the one that formed the Chicano Movement, and Ponce's text provides García with an invaluable means of exploring who they are and the historical, social, and cultural conditions that impelled them to challenge the negative stereotypes of their culture and peoples imposed upon them from outside.

McCracken, Martín-Junquera, and García's chapters variously explore publishing, *terroir*, and growing up, and provide useful critical paradigms for the future study of other texts and contexts. For all three authors, culture and its expressions are not fixed but a series of ongoing and ever-changing adaptations, reconfigurations, and negotiations. Foregrounding the experiences of women, on whom much responsibility has been placed to maintain rigid traditions irrespective of their validity and relevance, allows for an expanded exploration of what culture means and takes into account alternative perspectives and voices.

WORKS CITED

Aldama, A., and Quiñonez, N., eds. *Decolonial Voices: Chicana and Chicano Cultural Studies in the 21st Century.* Bloomington: Indiana University Press, 2002.

Anzaldúa, G. *Borderlands/La Frontera: The New Mestiza.* San Francisco: Aunt Lute Books, 1999.

Carter, H. "Chapbooks: Ancient Form of Publishing Enjoying Renaissance 500 Years On," *The Northerner Blog* in *The Guardian Online,* March 4, 2011. http://www.guardian.co.uk/uk/the-northerner/2011/mar/04/chapbooks-publishing. Accessed February 20, 2013.

Moraga, C. *A Xicana Codex of Changing Consciousness: Writings 2000–2010.* Durham, NC: Duke University Press, 2011.

1 From Chapbooks to *Chica Lit*

U.S. Latina Writers and the New Literary Identity

Ellen McCracken

In the beginning, the venues for U.S. Latina writers were chapbooks and occasional publications in the journals or newspapers of the Chicano Movement. The Chicano journal *El Grito* dedicated only one special issue to women's writing in 1973. A few small presses raised funds to publish small collections of the new women poets. In striking contrast, in June 2002, after a bidding war among five mainstream publishers, 32-year-old Alisa Valdes-Rodríguez received a $500,000 advance from St. Martin's Press for *The Dirty Girls' Social Club,* a novel she wrote in six days. This chapter will consider how the early publications of Latinas in journals and chapbooks have evolved into the half-million-dollar advance.

At the height of the Chicano Movement in the early 1970s, a handful of Chicana poets were beginning to make their mark. Anna Nieto Gómez called for "humanity and freedom between men and women" as the prerequisite for *"la revolución verdadera"* [the real revolution] in her poem which appeared along with Leticia Hernández's *"Mujer"* ["Woman"] in the April-May 1971 issue of *Hijas de Cuauhtémoc [Daughters of Cuauhtémoc]* published at California State University, Long Beach. In her September 1971 *"La Nueva Chicana"* ["The New Chicana"] published in *El Camino [The Way],* Ana Montes invokes the no longer silent Chicana who has "cast off the shawl of the past to show her face: and spreads the word *"VIVA LA RAZA."* Leticia Hernández's 1971 poem "Hijas de Cuauhtémoc," connects contemporary Chicanas to their pre-Columbian mothers and the Adelitas of the Mexican Revolution (see García 1997, 19, 73, 109, and 141). Nineteen-year-old Lorna Dee Cervantes traveled to Mexico City with her Chicano theatre group for the Quinto Festival de los Teatros Chicanos [Fifth Festival of Chicano Theatre] in 1974, where she gave her first poetry reading and had the first publication of her poem "Refugee Ship" in a major Mexico City newspaper that year. She taught herself printing and published the literary magazine and press *Mango* from 1976 to 1982, releasing Sandra Cisneros' chapbook *Bad Boys* in 1980 (see Ikas 2002, 27–28).[1] Other major Chicana poets such as Lucha Corpi, Alma Villanueva, Bernice Zamora, and Ana Castillo began to publish in the mid-1970s.

As Marta Sánchez (1986) and others have argued, Chicana writers of the early Movement period focused on poetry because of time and money pressures, and the desire to rapidly communicate a message. The early poetry functioned similarly to the *corridos* of previous decades by recounting information about a figure or event important to the community and immediately disseminating the message. A poem could be quickly written and published in a small journal or newspaper, or publicly declaimed in the Latino tradition of oral recitation. Poetry required less time and resources than novel writing or play production. But poetry could also be marginalized. Carlota Cárdenas de Dwyer's 1975 anthology *Chicano Voices,* published by Houghton-Mifflin, had 34 contributions by men and only three by women, and included the work of five men and only two women in the chapter on *"La Chicana"* (even the imposter Danny Santiago had a story he had published in *Redbook* included in this anthology).[2] Building on the early Movement poetry of urgency, Chicanas continued to write and publish verse in subsequent decades. But read by fewer people, poetry does not produce the profits for publishers that fiction does. Despite the important role that poetic discourse played in the early feminist writing of the Movement period, Latinas would make their mark in mainstream publishing circles with the exciting new fiction that blossomed in the post-Movement period.

It is important to note that the so-called Boom of Latina fiction did not suddenly appear from nowhere. Critical redeployments of narrative were central to the Chicano Movement and from the start involved the recuperation of oral traditions, *corridos,* history, journalism, fiction, narrative poetry, mural art, theater, film, and political narratives such as the utopian recovery of Aztlán. The Chicano Movement initiated a large-scale renarrativization of the master account of U.S. history, this time from the perspective of the repressed subjects of the melting pot. Women published political essays and short stories early in the Movement, and volumes of fiction by Estela Portillo, Berta Ornelas, and Isabella Ríos (Diane López), appeared in the 1970s. Throughout the 1980s, an emerging group of new Latina narrativists published their longer works of fiction with small regional presses. These included: Castillo, Cisneros, Denise Chávez, Corpi, Judith Ortiz Cofer, Mary Helen Ponce, Nicholasa Mohr, Rosario Morales, Aurora Levins Morales, Carole Fernández, Carmen de Monteflores, Gina Valdés, Sheila Ortíz-Taylor, Alma Luz Villanueva, Margarita Cota-Cárdenas, Helena María Viramontes, Patricia Preciado Martin, and Beverly Silva. There began to form a community of women writers who are, in Ramón Saldívar's terms, "counterhegemonic to the second power" because they "critique the critiques of oppression [by men] that fail to take into account the full range of domination" (1990, 173). They contest what Angie Chabram-Dernersesian terms "the preferred male subject" of Chicano and Latino nationalism (1992, 83).

In this post-Movement period, the new cohort of Latina writers benefited from the inroads made by the struggles of the early Movement. Several have commented on the financial aid they received to attend college and the grants they were awarded to pursue writing in the late 1970s and 1980s. Little by little, they began to come together across geographic distances to support and critique one another's writing. Lorna Dee Cervantes points to her own initial interactions with writers such as Cisneros, Castillo, Viramontes, and Vigil beginning in 1976. These were a new group of Chicana writers who were the first to be educated in the public schools and therefore more liberal than their Catholic-school-educated counterparts (see Ikas 2002, 32–33).[3] Small clusters of writers such as these served as the space of fomentation of the new fiction that would appear in the 1980s. Julia Alvarez recounts her frustration at only being able to find male Latino writers in the bookstores when she first began to connect her writing and her ethnicity. Finally, in 1983, the anthology *Cuentos: Stories by Latinas* opened a space of incipient community for her, and the publication of Cisneros' *House on Mango Street* the following year marked the beginning of her connection to writers such as Castillo, Ortiz Cofer, Cervantes, Moraga, Viramontes, and Chávez. Alvarez notes:

> Suddenly there was a whole group of us, a tradition forming, a dialogue going on, And why not? If Hemingway and his buddies could have their Paris group, and the Black Mountain poets their school, why couldn't we Latinos and Latinas have our own made-in-the-U.S.A. boom? . . . At last I found a comunidad in the word that I had never found in a neighborhood in this country. By writing powerfully about our Latino culture, we are forging a tradition and creating a literature that will widen and enrich the existing canon. So much depends upon our feeling that we have a right and responsibility to do this. (1999: 169–70)

Cisneros similarly recounts the isolation she felt as she struggled to complete *The House on Mango Street* when she returned to Chicago in 1978, and the strength she experienced when she finally connected to other Latina writers: "She [Cisneros] hasn't read Virginia Woolf yet. She doesn't know about Rosario Castellanos or Sor Juana Inés de la Cruz. Gloria Anzaldúa and Cherríe Moraga are cutting their own paths through the world somewhere, but she doesn't know about them yet. . . . She's making things up as she goes" (2009, xv). Sometimes she invited other writers who shared her sense that art should serve their communities to hold workshops in her apartment and together they published the anthology *Emergency Tacos,* referring to their predawn visits to the 24-hour *taquería* after finishing their collaborations. She credits literary critic Norma Alarcón, founder and editor of the journal *Third Woman,* with showing her examples of writers who served others rather than principally themselves, such as the Mexican writers Elena Poniatowska, Elena Garro, and Rosario Castellanos. She speaks of being unable to trust her own voice, censoring herself, unsure of her own way: "Until you brought us all together as U.S. Latina writers—Cherríe Moraga, Gloria Anzaldúa, Marjorie Agosín, Carla Trujillo, Diana Solís,

Sandra María Esteves . . . until then, Normita, we had no idea what we were doing was extraordinary" (2009, xxiv). From her position as a professor at Indiana University, Alarcón's support and publication of new Latina writers dispersed across the country helped the new literary movement to coalesce.

In addition to the small clusters of Latina writers who came together in the late 1970s and 1980s, larger societal pressures helped to foment the boom in publication of fiction by women. Two primary forms of multiculturalism developed in relation to the militant movements that demanded an end to the myth of the melting pot. First, what might be termed populist multiculturalism, or multiculturalism from below, confronted dominant U.S. ideologies and social practices that urged immigrants to abandon their culture and become anglicized in order to attain the American dream. Grassroots groups of disenfranchised ethnic and racial minorities rejected this pressure to assimilate, and militantly struggled to be accepted and recognized on their own terms as proud subjects of difference. Large demonstrations, labor organization, hunger strikes, street theater, murals, literature, political essays, journalism, minority publishing ventures, and new university courses worked together to contest the theory and practice of the melting pot. The response of U.S. institutions to this social unrest can be termed hegemonic multiculturalism, or multiculturalism from above. That is, in an attempt to contain and even to profit financially from the large-scale protests of minorities, hegemonic institutions searched for ways to pacify and limit the social unrest. Universities established and funded departments of ethnic studies and multicultural centers, allocating small, sometimes token institutional spaces to minority groups. Nonetheless, these arenas never entirely contained the continuing social protest. When Chicana/o students went on a hunger strike at the University of California, Santa Barbara, in the mid-1990s, university officials attempted to contain it by creating a space for the protest, setting up tents for the strikers and providing health personnel to monitor their medical condition.

Mainstream publishing houses, many owned by large media conglomerates, also fomented multiculturalism from above, primarily because they desired to make money from these social movements. One by one, they offered book contracts to selected Latina writers in the late 1980s and 1990s, understanding that there was now a large audience of minority and nonminority readers interested in ethnic fiction. In the late 1980s, Cisneros became the first Chicana writing fiction centering on Chicana/o themes to receive a contract from a large commercial publisher, Random House, and a relatively small number of other Latina writers obtained contracts from mainstream publishers shortly thereafter, including Alvarez, Garcia, Castillo, Montserrat Fontes, Sandra Benítez, Chávez, Villanueva, Viramontes, Ponce, and Demetria Martínez. In perspective, this commercial "boom" of only 11 U.S. Latina fiction writers in the 1990s is grossly out of proportion to the country's demography—35.3 million in the 2000 census and 51.9 million in 2011. These publishing conglomerates were in reality only tentatively dipping their feet in to test the new market, unwilling to put large-scale editorial and marketing resources behind these writers. And perhaps most objectionably, in my view, this multiculturalism was accompanied from above by an approach to marketing the writers and their books as postmodern ethnic commodities.

Responding to demands for minority recognition and seeing in these demands the chance to make money, mainstream publishing houses began in the 1990s to market this handful of Latina writers as "minority commodities," attempting to reabsorb writers and texts into mainstream ideology as desirable elements of postmodernity that can be purchased and, to some degree, possessed. Folkloric representations of Mexican womanhood appear on the cover of Cisneros's *Woman Hollering Creek and Other Stories* (1991) and the reissue of *The House on Mango Street* (1994) by Random House (Knopf). Bright, folkloric colors retint the neighborhood depicted on the cover of Alvarez's *How the Garcia Girls Lost Their Accents* (1991), with childish block lettering on the clothbound edition and crayon-colored dancing letters on the paperback. The bright colors scream out on the cover of her 1997 *Yo!,* this time with an ostensibly unmotivated exotic Middle Eastern woman gazing at us as she reclines half nude with pillows, scarves, and an exotic plant. Norton's cover for Castillo's *So Far from God* (1993) depicts New Mexico Hispanos in a religious procession in a folkloric manner, almost as if they were tiny dolls in a doll house, walking past a home with no roof, surrounded by earth and hillsides that have been retinted fuscia. Newspapers and magazines followed suit with similarly exotic depictions of U.S. Latina writers, continuing the fuscia tint in the *Los Angeles Times* review of Castillo's novel, and including Cisneros' story "Woman Hollering Creek" in its Sunday magazine "Tales for a Summer Day" with a folkloric depiction of the protagonist Cleófilas wearing a fuscia peasant dress, her head nearly touching a TV set, and a stereotypic picture of a Mexican campesino in pink trousers and a burro on the wall behind the bed (see McCracken 1999, 11–39; Kingsolver 1993, 1; and Cisneros 1990, 5).

All of these depictions are polysemous and open to various interpretations by diverse viewers. At the end of Alvarez's *Yo!,* and more extensively in an essay in *Something to Declare,* the author points to the centrality of the figure Scheherazade as the first muse of her writing, perhaps the motivation for the Middle Eastern woman on the cover of *Yo!.* How many readers in fact connect this brief allusion to the cover illustration, and for how many does the cover remain a stereotypic, unmotivated image? For some readers, the art by Nivea González on the cover of Cisneros's novels may represent an important dissemination of the work of a talented Chicana artist, not a folkloric depiction of Mexicanness. But when Random House uses another painting by González on the cover of a novel by a male writer from the Philippines, F. Sionil José, the publishing house engages in what I term minority metaphoricity, the belief that one minority can easily substitute for another, that if one minority group's fiction sells well with a certain artist's work on the cover, another entirely different global reality can profitably be sold in the same way. Despite the idealist frame of hegemonic multiculturalism through which these writers' work is marketed, contestatory elements of the texts themselves rupture the romantic veneer of the cover and the publicity. For consumers who move beyond displaying these "minority commodities" on their coffee table to carefully reading the contestatory messages inside the books, the folkloric images on the covers are transcended.

The radical legacy of Latinos' struggles for recognition and full civil rights in the 1960s and 1970s has raised questions about Latinas publishing with mainstream presses. Do they betray the ideals of the Movement by leaving the grassroots Chicana/o presses that supported them early on, in order to enter the mainstream? Do they structure their works differently in order to attract a wider public? Do they feel obliged to foreground their ethnicity in certain ways in order to keep the interest of publishers and readers? On what basis are decisions made about whose work is published in the mainstream and whose is not? Has Latina literature reached a commercially degraded plateau when 32-year-old Valdes-Rodríguez composes a novel in six days in a Starbucks cafe and, as I mentioned in the introduction, receives a $500,000 advance for it after five big publishing houses engage a bidding war?

A Cuban American from New Mexico and former pop music critic for the *Los Angeles Times,* Valdes-Rodríguez tried unsuccessfully to sell a book she had written on Latina/o music ("Alisa Valdes-Rodriguez and Her Amazing Rants" 2003; Banks 2002; Wilson 2000). When her agent returned it, reporting that publishers would rather have a novel, she quickly wrote *The Dirty Girls' Social Club,* which spawned the bidding war and the record half-million-dollar advance. I would speculate that Valdes-Rodríguez's familiarity with the rules of hegemonic multiculturalism allowed her to play the game so quickly and so successfully in order to produce a literary commodity more attuned to the mass market. Valdes-Rodriguez is in a situation similar to Terry McMillan, who, despite her mass-market successes *Waiting to Exhale* and *How Stella Got Her Groove Back,* complained that academics and intellectuals were not taking her work seriously. Thirty years after the intense and quickly circulated poetry of the Movement, have Latinas/os now attained a similar temporal effect (the quickly written, circulated, and read) with the genre of the best-selling novel? What is such a novel's relation to the political, gender, and ethnic issues of our day? And, where it did not cost much money to get a poem published in the early Movement, has the reverse extreme occurred now so that ethnic writing pays quite handsomely once one discovers the formula of the best-selling minority commodity?

If writers such as Cisneros, Alvarez, García, Castillo, and Viramontes represent the first group of U.S. Latinas to break ground in the early 1990s by publishing innovative fiction with mainstream commercial presses, Valdes-Rodríguez embodies the logical conclusion of this trajectory in which the literary text is now almost completely structured by the demands of consumerism. While writers in the first group of novelists negotiate and sometimes internalize the demands of mainstream publishers as they attempt to write works of art, Chica Lit writers such as Valdes-Rodríguez, Mary Castillo, Caridad Piñeiro, and Michele Serros aim for the widest audience possible and follow formulas for commercial success. Admitting that she set out to be a "Latina Terry McMillan," Valdes-Rodríguez has argued that she gives her publisher what it wants, but does something more important at the end that transcends the publisher's constraints. She argues that she should be seen as a "Latina Stephen Hawking" rather than a McMillan (Valdes-Rodríguez 2007, n.p.). Despite the occasional instances in which she asserts writerly independence, Valdes-Rodríguez strongly shapes her literary production according to market demands. While the gains achieved by multicultural-ism from below underlie her novel, and there are occasional references to and criticism of these political movements, hegemonic multiculturalism pre-dominates in her novel.

Valdes-Rodríguez resents to some degree that that she can only make money by performing as a Latina. She notes that her publisher rejected the second novel she submitted because it had an Irish American saxophon-ist as protagonist instead of Latina characters. The autobiographical novel emphasized her Irish heritage from her mother's side—an ethnicity with less cultural capital today than her Latino side (Valdes-Rodríguez 2007).[4] Valdes-Rodríguez wants to have it both ways—she both plays on stereotypes of Latina/o ethnicity and debunks them. She strives to set the record straight on who Latinas are, emphasizing their heterogeneity. She argued extensively with her publisher about an appropriate cover for *The Dirty Girls' Social Club,* refusing to let them use images of donkeys, cactuses, and mantillas on a book about wealthy Latinas with high-powered careers.

Nonetheless, spectacles of ethnicity begin on the paratextual front and back covers of *The Dirty Girls' Social Club.* Drawings of faceless women with exaggerated hourglass figures stand in the stereotypic female pose that Erving Goffman termed "the coy knee bend" (1976, 45). Holding cham-pagne glasses that have childish bubbles floating above, the women wear horizontally striped dresses that blend them into the pastel stripes of the background. These figures do not evoke the professional status of the Latina characters Valdés-Rodríguez is striving to portray in the book. Instead of the rejected images of donkeys, cactuses, and mantillas, the cover now uses ste-reotypic sexuality to market the book. The cover suggests that ideal Latinas are slender, curvaceous, coy, and dress in bright colors.

In another example of a linguistic spectacle of ethnicity, the implied author makes fun of Chicana/o culture using parody in the discourse of the character Amber, a Californian Chicana who changes her name to Cuicatl and breaks into the mainstream music scene as a *Mexica* singer. Amber's utterances are dominated by common Spanish swear words:

> After the first song, I grab the postcards and address the crowd in Span-ish: "*Chingazos! Chingazos!*" They go crazy. "Listen to me *chingazos,*

Did you see Shakira lately?" Everyone boos. "That's right. She's a *pinche* disgrace. Blond hair. She's a disgrace to La Raza and La Causa . . ." I throw the postcards out and they float down into the sea of brown hands. "They're addressed to her manager, *hijos de puta!* We're telling them we don't want this kind of representation . . ." Then they start to chant "*Que Shaki se joda, que Shaki se joda . . .*" Cheers. "Love yourself. Love your brown Aztec self, Raza!"(95)

Here the Cuban American writer employs parody to create ethnic spectacularity at the expense of Chicanas/os. While Valdes-Rodríguez seeks to debunk stereotypes about Latina/os, she sometimes employs them to create humor and to make the book a more desirable postmodern commodity.

The implied author of Valdes-Rodríguez's novel strives to present an insider ethnography to mainstream audiences about the culture of ethnic Others. She explains the nuances of her culture, attempting to teach more accurate views of Latina alterity. The authorial persona, Lauren, addresses readers directly:

A lot of you probably don't speak Spanish, and so don't know what the hell a "*sucia*" is. That's okay. No, really. Some of us *sucias* can't speak Spanish, either—but don't tell my editors at the *Boston Gazette,* where I am increasingly certain I was hired only to be a red-hot-'n'-spicy clichéd, chili pepper-ish cross between Charro and Lois Lane, and where, thank God, they still haven't figured out what a fraud I am. (2003, 4–5)

Chatty, colloquial language—designed to make readers feel part of a group of friends—takes a distance here from stereotypes of Latinas, precisely as it invokes these motifs to flavor the novel.

Plagiarism, parody, and pastiche are noted narrative strategies of postmodernist fiction. Fredric Jameson (1983) argues that pastiche replaces parody in the commodified texts of late capitalism. While Valdes-Rodríguez engages in some parody in the novel, she also employs pastiche and perhaps even unconscious plagiarism. Naming one of her characters "USNAVYS," because of the woman's parents' deep esteem for the U.S. Navy, she in effect quotes without attribution the title of the novel by Puerto Rican author Pedro Juan Soto, *USMAIL,* in which parents named the character after the U.S. mail truck, which always had something important to deliver. She quotes Cisneros with the phrase "man-man" (Valdes-Rodríguez 2003, 207; and Cisneros 1991, 117), again without attribution, and repeats the common instant message phrase "laugh out loud" again and again as the novel ends. She does not engage in historiographic metafiction's technique of metaplagiarism, in which the author deliberately plagiarizes and denounces him or herself subtly to readers, inviting them to discover the stolen intertext (see McCracken 1991).

Valdes-Rodríguez's characters offer readers what Lisa Zunshine (2006) terms a variety of opportunities to try on mental states that seem potentially available to them but different from their own. How would it be to lead the glamorous life of a columnist for a major city newspaper or be a Chicana rock star? What mental processes might you go through if you were a talented, professional writer and unexpectedly found yourself attracted to a Dominican drug dealer? Would you put the best face on your husband's brutal attack, as Sara does, arguing that her husband was trying to hug her when she fell down the stairs and that he did not in fact push her? The variety of vicarious identities available to readers allows opportunities to try out behaviors, lifestyles, and mental states without suffering the real consequences of such activities. Like the images in glossy women's magazines or free samples of food in a store, one can dabble in certain styles and tastes without committing fully to them. In another instance of this phenomenon, the cover of Piñeiro's *South Beach Chicas Catch Their Man* (2007) shows the backs of four slender women in evening attire sitting on barstools for readers to emulate so that they too can vicariously "catch their man" when reading the book.

Valdes-Rodríguez also aims to attract readers with the utopian theme of group friendship that withstands geographic and temporal distance, personality differences, and the prevarications of contemporary life. The members of the group are all economically successful Latina women in diverse careers and with several subethnic and racial backgrounds, offering readers from different economic and ethnic backgrounds utopian models with which to identify and experience pleasure. Valdes-Rodríguez consciously markets this utopian theme of community as she breaks down the border between life, fictional representation, and cyberspace. She notes that she tries to keep alive in cyberspace the group-of-friends theme that worked so well in her first novel. She has created a cyber group of "reader-friends" which in late 2007 numbered 600 and had emailed over 80,000 messages. The *sucias* in the Yahoo group dialogue with one another and even give the author advice on projected novels. She sent three prospective novel scenarios to the group and it chose her least favorite one for her next novel. Market-driven, she noted that she would comply with her cyber group's preference (Valdes-Rodríguez 2007, n.p.).[5]

In contrast to quickly-read Chica Lit are such nuanced, layered, and multidimensional novels as Alvarez's *In the Time of the Butterflies,* Cisneros' *Caramelo* (2002), and Junot Díaz's *The Brief Wondrous Life of Oscar Wao* (2007). They engage in innovative postmodernist strategies in which the secure boundaries between fiction and truth are called into question, as they create what Linda Hutcheon (1989) terms historiographic metafiction. While commodified ethnicity plays some role in their work, it does not predominate as in Chica Lit. Despite their depth and nuance, they sell well and garner places on the best-seller lists. Alvarez's novel was made into a movie and Díaz's won the Pulitzer Prize in 2008. Although they are marketed as multiculturalism from above, this was not the raison d'être of their creation.

Should U.S. Latina writers have eschewed the various degrees of commodification that mainstream publishing requires? While I strongly support the tremendous accomplishments of the smaller presses such as Arte Público, Bilingual, and Spinsters/Aunt Lute in bringing a wide range of Latina/o writing to the public—U.S. Latina/o literature would not be what it is today without them—this literature must also reach the broader audiences that mainstream presses afford. In 1987 when I was asked to write an article on *The House on Mango Street,* I could not find a copy of the book in any of the five college libraries or the numerous bookstores in the New England town where I taught. How could this intellectually vibrant university town not have a copy of Cisneros's classic 1984 text? This marginalization changed in 1991 with Random House's release of her new book and the subsequent reissue of *The House on Mango Street,* now available in nearly every bookstore in the country, and even Monarch Notes, Cliff Notes, Sparknotes, and MAXnotes for students seeking shortcuts. *The House on Mango Street* has sold over 2 million copies without Cisneros having tried consciously to write it as a postmodern ethnic commodity, and in 2009 was rereleased in a special twenty-fifth anniversary edition (Rutten 2002)[6].

The hard feelings and legal disputes that resulted when Cisneros left Arte Público are tragic. On a visit to the University of California, Santa Barbara, Cisneros autographed a library copy of the Arte Público edition of *The House on Mango Street,* and wrote biting comments in the published text. Underlining the entire last line of the book with the "delete" editing sign and her initials, she wrote: "interpolations by ed. Nick Kanellos without my permission! Sandra Cisneros" (1984, 102). In the last line on page 86, she deleted the word "using" and similarly wrote: "Interpolations here & elsewhere without my permission."[7] The press had been a loving, although perhaps overbearing, midwife for the birth of her fiction, but needed to let her move on, just as we release our children when they no longer need our everyday nurturing, hard as this might be. Minority presses such as Arte Público continue to publish scores of new writers, as new generations build on the accomplishments of Movement activists in even larger numbers. But battles must be fought as well at the mainstream commercial presses to make space for and put money behind this important new writing.

How might we characterize new Latina narrative 30 years after the Movement? Some writers are linking ethnicity to broader themes or moving beyond this narrative focus. Stella Pope Duarte's *Let Their Spirits Dance* (2002), published by the Latino series Rayo at Harper Collins, narrates her family's loss of her brother in the Vietnam War and their contemporary journey of recuperation to the memorial wall in Washington, D.C. In this important historical juncture of emerging globalization, several Latina writers have moved beyond Movement nationalism to hemispheric issues of *Nuestra América* [Our America]. Alvarez uses historiographic metafiction to renarrativize the Trujillato from the perspective of the martyred Mira-bal sisters in *In the Time of the Butterflies;* her 2000 novel *In the Name of Salomé* rescues from historical oblivion a nineteenth-century Dominican writer and her daughter who at age 66 participated in the Cuban Revo-lution, drawing women's writing from the Caribbean into the agenda of the U.S. mainstream; and her 2001 novel *A Cafecito Story* urges privileged North Americans to understand the ecology and politics of the new organic coffee production in the Third World and the role we can play in the ulti-mate success or failure of these grassroots ventures. Graciela Limón, who has published eight novels and continues to work with Arte Público Press, proffers a hemispheric ethnic identity in several of her books, such as the compelling novel *Erased Faces* (2001), which narrativizes a Chicana's jour-ney to Chiapas, where she participates in the Zapatista uprising, learns the details of the centuries of exploitation of the indigenous women and men there, and falls in love with one of the women *guerrilleras* in the struggle. Cisneros's dense and nuanced epic of transborder Mexican and Mexican American culture, *Caramelo,* carefully honed over nine years of writing, coexists with the rapidly produced and consumed texts of Chica Lit, just as occurs in other mainstream literary publication in the United States and throughout the world.

The early Movement chapbooks, newspapers, and small journals have given way to venues such as expanding minority presses, university presses, and mainstream publishing conglomerates, along with literary agents, and even movie contracts for Latinas. With some 70 Latina writers publishing longer works of fiction on Latina/o themes in the last 25 years, and the breakthrough advance of $500,000, we can envision a continuously renew-ing and growing body of Latina novels that retain their critical perspectives at the same time as they receive the attention and respect of the cultural arbiters and the literary mainstream, and are simultaneously avidly read by ordinary people throughout the United States and in translations worldwide.

NOTES

1. Cisneros notes that Chicano poet Gary Soto helped her get this first book published (see Mirriam-Goldberg 1998, 50).
2. Anglo writer Daniel James published a novel *Famous All over Town* (1983) under the Chicano pseudonym "Danny Santiago." In 1984, the American Academy and Institute of Arts and Letters awarded the novel a distinguished fiction prize, and when the true identity of the author was revealed, admit-ted that it might not have given the award had it know the author was a 71-year-old white male masquerading as a Chicano. The editor at Simon and Schuster who worked with "Danny Santiago" noted that James used Chicano slang in his letters to him, pretending even outside the novel to be Chicano (see Ramos 2005, n.p.).
3. Cisneros, however, attended Catholic schools and the Jesuit Loyola Univer-sity in Chicago.

4. In August 2008, however, the author announced on her blog that she was beginning revisions on her upcoming novel *The Husband Habit,* "the first chick-lit novel I write where the ethnicity and/or race of the lead characters is ambiguous and unimportant to the story. I'm not saying Vanessa *isn't* Latina; I'm just not saying she *is,* either. She is just Vanessa, every-woman, an American chef. I have doubts as to how much of Vanessa's days would be filled with ponderous questions of ethnic identity, if indeed she even had one"). Here the author attempts to have it both ways with respect to ethnicity—the character could or could not be Latina—and to extricate herself through this ambiguity from her publisher's insistence that she focus on Latina ethnicity because this formula sells well.

5. In late August 2008, her blogsite tally was 313,433 hits. For the author's new website, see http://www.alisavaldesrodriguez.com/.

6. Cisneros recounts that she found the subject matter and voice of *The House on Mango Street* in an epiphanic moment as a graduate student at the University of Iowa. While many of the middle-class students in her class had no trouble identifying with Gaston Bachelard's thesis that the house is the symbol of one's inner sense, she, in contrast, saw her family's small bungalow in the Chicago barrio as an embarrassment, a prison that she was ashamed of. She soon realized, however, that precisely this class and ethnic marginalization offered something that her classmates could not speak of. She was an authority on ethnic poverty and in a unique position to fictionally narrate this experience (see Mirriam-Goldberg 1998, 41–44).

7. Kanellos made similar changes in other writers' creative works, notably an ungrammatical modification of the last sentence of Roberta Fernández's *Intaglio* (1990). Wanting the writer to use less untranslated Spanish, he added a new last line to the book with a mistake in subject/verb agreement: "Each of us tell it as we see it" (1990, 154). The press transposed several epigraphs of the stories in the book sometime between the proof stage and the final printing, destroying the montage Fernández intended.

WORKS CITED

Alvarez, J. *How the García Girls Lost Their Accents.* Chapel Hill, NC: Algonquin Books, 1991.

———. *In the Time of the Butterflies.* Chapel Hill, NC: Algonquin Books, 1994.

———. *Something to Declare.* Chapel Hill, NC: Algonquin Books, 1998; New York: Plume, 1999.

———. *Yo!.* Chapel Hill, NC: Algonquin Books, 1997.

"Alicia Valdés-Rodríguez and Her Amazing Rants." *Lukeford.net,* 2003. http://www.lukeford.net/profiles/profiles/alisa_rodriguez.htm. Accessed March 7, 2013.

Banks, R. "Latina Novel Gets $500,000." *Associated Press,* July 2, 2002.

Cárdenas de Dywer, C. *Chicano Voices.* New York: Houghton-Mifflin, 1975.

Castillo, A. *So Far from God.* New York: Norton, 1993.

Chabram-Dernersesian, A. "I Throw Punches for My Race, but I Don't Want to Be a Man: Writing Us—Chica-nos (Girl, Us)/Chicanas—into the Movement Script." In *Cultural Studies* (81–95), edited by Lawrence Grossberg, Cary Nelson, and Paula A. Treichler. New York: Routledge, 1992.

Cisneros, S. *Caramelo: Or Puro Cuento.* New York: Knopf, 2002.

———. *The House on Mango Street.* Houston: Arte Público, 1984; and Twenty-Fifth Anniversary Edition, New York: Random House, 2009.

————. *Woman Hollering Creek and Other Stories.* New York: Random House, 1991.

————. "Woman Hollering Creek." *Tales for a Summer Day. Los Angeles Times,* July 1, 1990. http://articles.latimes.com/keyword/sandra-cisneros/featured/5. Accessed March 7, 2013.

Díaz, Junot. *The Brief Wondrous Life of Oscar Wao.* New York: Penguin, 2007.

Fernández, Roberta. *Intaglio: A Novel in Six Stories.* Houston: Arte Público, 1990.

García, Alma M., ed. *Chicana Feminist Thought: The Basic Historical Writings.* New York: Routledge, 1997.

Goffman, E. *Gender Advertisements.* New York: Harper & Row, 1976.

Hutcheon, L. *The Politics of Postmodernism.* New York: Routledge, 1989.

Ikas, K. R. *Chicana Ways: Conversations with Ten Chicana Writers.* Reno: University of Nevada Press, 2002.

James, D. *Famous All over Town.* New York: Simon and Schuster, 1983.

Jameson, F. "Postmodernism and Consumer Society." In *The Anti-Aesthetic: Essays on Postmodern Culture* (13–29), edited by H. Foster. Port Townsend, WA: Bay Press, 1983.

Kingsolver, Barbara. "Lush Language: Desert Heat: *So Far From God* by Ana Castillo." *Los Angeles Times Book Review,* May 16, 1993. http://articles.latimes .com/1993–05–16/books/bk-35724_1_ana-castillo. Accessed March 7, 2013.

Limón, G. *Erased Faces.* Houston: Arte Público Press, 2001.

McCracken, E. "Metaplagiarism and the Critic's Role as Detective: Ricardo Piglet's Reinvention of Roberto Arlt." *PMLA* 106, no. 5 (October 1991): 1017–1082.

————. *New Latina Narrative: The Feminine Space of Postmodern Ethnicity.* Tucson: University of Arizona Press, 1999.

Mirriam-Goldberg, C. *Sandra Cisneros: Latina Writer and Activist.* Berkeley Heights, NJ: Enslow, 1998.

Piñeiro, C. *South Beach Chicas Catch Their Man.* New York: Downtown Press, 2007.

Ramos, M. "The Strange Cases of Danny Santiago and Amado Muro." *La Bloga,* August 5, 2005. http://labloga.blogspot.com/2005/08/strange-cases-of-danny-santiago-and.html. Accessed February 28, 2013.

Rutten, T. "The Vanguard of Ethnic Voices in Popular Literature." *Los Angeles Times,* July 12, E-1, E-4, 2002.

Saldívar, R. *Chicano Narrative: The Dialectics of Difference.* Madison: University of Wisconsin Press, 1990.

Sánchez, M. E. *Contemporary Chicana Poetry: A Critical Approach to an Emerging Literature.* Berkeley: University of California Press, 1986.

Sionil José, F. *Three Filipina Women.* New York: Random House, 1992.

Valdes-Rodríguez, A. *The Dirty Girls' Social Club.* New York: St. Martin's Press, 2003.

————. Panel discussion at Santa Barbara Book and Author Festival. Santa Barbara, CA. September 29, 2007.

————. "Knee-Deep in Re-Writes." *Official Website of Alisa Valdes.* http:// alisavaldesrodriguez.blogspot.com/. August 22, 2008. Accessed August 27, 2008.

Wilson, M. "The Language of Genocide." *St Petersburg Times,* Nov. 3, 2000. http://www.sptimes.com/News/110300/Floridian/The_language_of_genoc.shtml. Accessed March 1, 2013.

Zunshine, L. *Why We Read Fiction: Theory of Mind and the Novel.* Columbus: Ohio State University Press, 2006.

2 Healing Family History/(Her) Story

Writing and Gardening in Pat Mora's *House of Houses*

Imelda Martín-Junquera

Although Pat Mora has been studied from a multiplicity of points of view highlighting the postmodern character of her publications, her intimate link with nature has not, until recently, found much interest among scholars focusing on Chicana literature. These include a remarkable study, "Intersections of Nature and the Self in Chicana Writing" by Benay Blend (2000), who focuses on Mora and other Chicana writers' ecofeminism, and another by Patrick Murphy, who considers Mora's poetry in *Literature, Nature and Other: Ecofeminist Critiques* from 1995.

Critical neglect of this aspect of Mora's work can be attributed to a wider pattern in Chicana/o Studies. The number of studies analyzing Chicana/o literature from an ecocritical perspective has proliferated in recent years, becoming an increasing trend during the first decade of the twenty-first century. Before the year 2000, very few academics had paid attention to the vision of the environment portrayed in Chicana/o literature; and the intersection between race, class, and gender dominated the literary scene under the umbrella of ethnic studies. The first journal article applying an ecofeminist perspective to Chicana literature appeared in 1998 by María Herrera-Sobek. This has been followed by others, such as Carmen Flys Junquera's study on environmental justice in her publications on Rudolfo Anaya's novels.

As a poet, essayist, and novelist, Mora has extensively explored the relationship of the human being with the environment, especially of women and the environment. Her children's books represent a vivid example of this tendency in her writing as she exemplifies in *The Desert Is My Mother/ El desierto es mi madre,* an illustrated long poem published in a bilingual edition, which enhances the caring and nurturing qualities of the desert in comparison with those provided by a mother. Patrick Murphy understands that Mora's ecofeminism "contains a specific type of cultural politics that refutes not just patriarchy in general, but Chicano patriarchy in particular" (53–54). Apart from her open critique of the patriarchal attitudes present in the structure of Chicano families, Mora also takes very seriously the educational purpose of literature as well as the protection of the environment, thus combining all in her children's and young adult's fiction. She clearly points out in her literature the need to liberate women from cultural restrictions.

Her website, http://www.patmora.com, constitutes a summary of her writings as well as stating clearly her commitment to contributing to educate the new generations in an environment of respect, tolerance, and understanding. The preservation of culture and tradition is also deeply embedded in Mora's poetry. In her works, she constantly brings awareness of how identity is forged through understanding heritage and developing natural bonds with the land.

House of Houses (1997) represents Pat Mora's attempt to rewrite the history of her father's and mother's families (the Moras and the Delgados) as well as her own, from her point of view and from a gendered perspective. She dramatizes the past that she never knew, bringing her ancestors back from the dead in order to come to terms with her own inheritance. She places all of them in the family house, creating a family memoir that she considers a nonfiction book. Mora seems to fulfill a dream with this narrative: joining together different generations of family members who have contributed to her personal development, to her identity both as a Mexican American woman and as a female writer. She builds her narrative in what Gretchen Legler calls "postmodern pastoral" (1997, 229), or how women writers aim at establishing a dialogic relationship between the human and the natural world through ecological and feminist theories.

Mora writes her memoir creating a narrator that functions as her alter ego who celebrates life, ethnicity, family, and nature. She brings the ecological desired harmony between humanity and nonhuman nature in her narrative; balancing care of her family and the garden, treating both as active subjects, instead of considering them passive objects of study; she provides agency for the women in this family and for the plants of her garden by initiating conversational relationships between them all.

Maria Antonia Oliver-Rotger suggests that Pat Mora creates a time and a space of the mind with a garden as a neuralgic center where four generations of women blossom and flower (2003, 329). The house, the garden, and Oliver-Rotger's identification of the female characters with flowers call for an ecofeminist analysis of the narrative, an approach that explores closely the implications of this identification both for women and nature. Although this equation has divided most feminists, who see it as the justification for female oppression and as a tremendously essentialist vision of femininity, others such as Val Plumwood, on the contrary, have "a critical ecological feminism in which women consciously position themselves with nature" (1993, 21).

As the writing progresses, the garden functions more and more as a metaphor for the process of writing, both needing special care and giving fruits as seasons change:

> After helping to dry the breakfast dishes, I wait under the cottonwood for Aunt Chole, determined to write the story, for stories, like plants, need attention and protection, this garden, for example, an accumulation of

nurtured possibilities. The fruit and shade trees, flowering plants and herbs, survive in this desert oasis because of the attentiveness of the family, its seeds, plantings, cuttings, pinchings, feedings, prunings, and endless, endless watering. (Mora 1997, 156)

The analogy of the writing process with gardening strengthens the ecofeminist claim that women can take advantage of their closeness with nature to heal the world, to cure the wounds inflicted on the environment by human beings. At the same time, this activity brings about the integration of women into the world of culture but without severing the connection between women and the natural world, in fact, highlighting it, as Ynestra King does when she writes:

> We can use it as a vantage point for creating a different kind of culture and politics that would integrate intuitive, spiritual and rational forms of knowledge, embracing both science and magic insofar as they enable us to transform the nature-culture distinction and to envision and create a free, ecological society. (1989, 23)

Here King insists on one of the tenets of ecofeminism: the dissolution of the binary opposition nature-culture, advocating a closer approach to nature. This branch of ecofeminism attempts to bring men back to an intimate contact and fruitful relationship with nature. Ecofeminists point out that the ecological crisis we are undergoing has a patriarchal root: the separation of men from nature, considering nature and the Earth as a whole as a group of resources to be exploited by humans. Decentering the human being also brings a better awareness towards understanding the destruction of the environment and the possibilities of providing solutions to it. Mora's contribution to this dissolution of the binary opposition between nature and culture comes with the analogy between writing and gardening and how both processes are imbricated in the narrative, acting as therapy to heal the wounds inflicted by the history of immigration in her family.

Along with the process of rewriting her family history comes the reconstruction of the family home. The house represents Pat Mora's mind, the family memories stored in her head, knocking on the doors of imagination in an attempt to come alive, like the house Charlotte Perkins Gilman creates in *The Yellow Wallpaper* (1899), which stands for the restrained mind of the protagonist. Perkins Gilman has been considered the leader of feminism activism in the United States during the turn of the nineteenth to the twentieth century. This text, condemned to oblivion during the first half of the twentieth century, was recovered by the second wave of feminists in the 1970s. These activists brought to academia women's literature that had been excluded from a canon established under patriarchal authority. Today considered a classic of nineteenth-century feminist literature, *The Yellow Wallpaper* uses the first person to narrate the symptoms of postpartum depression of a woman confined to the highest room in a rented house by medical prescription and how her perception of enclosure changes along the narrative. Diagnosed by her own husband with hysteria, the woman defies his open prohibition of avoiding intellectual activity and writes her diary, thereby sharing her descriptions of the room where she is locked with the reader. The room paradoxically happens to be an old nursery covered with yellow wallpaper from which the narrator contemplates a woman trying to liberate herself. She longs to walk in the garden she can see from the window, to be in contact with nature and breathe fresh air, but she is not allowed to. At the end of the story, she understands the woman is her own reflection, her inner self who attempts to break free from the role of submissive wife and mother; the woman who creeps over her own husband, abandoning the room and the house. The room, in fact, represents her own distorted mind trapped inside a house, which is the clear representation of her body; a body that has undergone childbirth, has experienced it as traumatic, and receives the wrong treatment from her husband and doctor. Writing proves, then, the best therapy, the means to obtain freedom, a fact that the protagonist learns and soon puts into practice.

Writing is a liberating experience for Mora and Perkins Gilman, an activity that opens the doors of their houses to mental freedom and challenges the claim that "Third World women are oppressed both by national and international injustices and by family systems that give husbands, fathers and brothers absolute priority" (Kelly 1997, 116). Although not exactly Third World women because of their upper-class condition, both narrators are undoubtedly oppressed by patriarchal laws, exemplifying Kelly's statement about women and power: "The unfair sexual distribution of power, resources, and responsibilities is legitimized by ancient traditions, socialized into women's own attitudes, enshrined in law, and enforced when necessary by male violence" (Kelly 1997, 116).

The main difference between Perkins Gilman's character and Mora's narrators is physical confinement. While the former has to remain in the room upstairs and contemplate the garden from a barred window, Mora's narrator moves with complete freedom around the house and the garden, around the mental space she is creating: "Inside, I roam, explore the chambers of my heart, this wish house, oriented long ago to catch the breeze and long afternoon shadows" (Mora 1997, 18). Where doubt, fear, and alienation dominate the first narrative, harmony, love, and caring populate the second. Both women reach freedom; they liberate themselves from their mental constraints and invent a new feminine physical and psychological space. In Mora's text these characteristics seem to evolve directly from a matrilineal tradition, from the "true gynotradition" Mora establishes in her narrative when the women in the house gather to celebrate Mother's Day in May. It is certainly a day when all the women indulge in praising each other and expressing how their union means the strength of Mora's dream house: "'She's so smart because she's female. Face it, my dears, females are smarter. We have to be, to survive.' Aunt Chole, Lobo, Aunt Carmen, and Mother's daughters and granddaughters nod as do her grandmothers and great-grandmothers" (Mora 1997, 144).

Among the multiplicity of voices, those of the women are heard loudest; they haunt a male-dominated Mexican tradition and rise victoriously as storytellers and perpetuators of the most valuable family secrets preserved silently in the family pictures that Pat Mora shares with her readers, making them an active part of the narrative. Oliver-Rotger affirms that Mora is constantly aware of the presence of the reader throughout the novel: "She has written with a strong sense of audience, trying to capture the interest of the people from the region she usually writes about" (2003, 320). In fact, Mora stresses in the narrative the times she sits down with any of her relatives, pen and paper in hand, waiting for them to find the voice that will transform them into main characters of the family memoir, in the pillars to sustain the house of houses. Mora's nonchronological account shows the characteristics of oral storytelling, satisfying the listener's curiosity but maintaining a certain level of intrigue and suspense.

Mora realizes after her long mental journey into the family's past that the house of houses stands on strong pillars of trust and permanence: it is a timeless reality that does not rest on a physical space either. Thus, both are eternal and infinite, like the history of her family perpetuated by her children and the memories she is recuperating along the narrative: "That's what I want, Lobo, not to lose any of you, to lure you, the living and the dead, into this unlocked house, as flowers lure us into the garden" (Mora 1997, 20). Mora is not alone in figuring her family's story through national grand narratives. Julia Álvarez (*In the Name of Salomé* 2001) and Sandra Cisneros (*Caramelo* 2002) have also created their own historical narratives, their family memoirs that imbricate personal and national history. Their own stories contradict official history, which gets constantly revisited, destroying myths of freedom and repression embodied in relevant historical figures. Similarly, *House of Houses* revises the archetypal characterization of revolutionary leaders such as Pancho Villa and the received representation of the dictatorship of Porfirio Díaz in Mexico. Both the Mora and the Delgado families, who have suffered the oppression of Villa's followers, talk about their flight to the United States to escape from Villa's hands. Embedded in the re-creation of these personal and historical narratives, immigration plays a central role in the narrative as Mora's ancestors cross the border illegally and settle in El Paso under the same conditions, although her maternal ancestry and her parental one come from completely different backgrounds and social classes.

These three writers insert their family memories, producing "feminine collective autobiographies," as Oliver-Rotger (2003, 320) understands and analyzes them. For her, these narratives represent an attempt to give voice to formerly silenced subjects, very much in consonance with the idea of providing agency to nature. Thus, Mora's house is made of words, haunted by narrators and different discourses of the past mingling and dissenting from those of present times, interrupting and irrupting at ease to contribute to the process of building the house of houses, that is to say, the story of stories: "In my dream house, as in my dreams, we are together, the family spirits, the soul of this adobe" (Mora 1997, 43).

What distances Mora from Álvarez or Cisneros in this memoir is her ecofeminist treatment of history following the reconnection with the land that Gloria Feman Orstein contemplates in ecofeminist arts:

> If the severing of our intimate connectedness to the Earth, the sky, the dead, the unseen, and our ancestors was the accomplishment of the Enlightment, then ecofeminism calls for an endarkenment—a bonding with the Earth and the invisible that will reestablish our sense of interconnectedness with all things, phenomenal and spiritual, that make up the totality of life in our cosmos. (Feman Orstein 1990, 279–280)

Mora's house finally becomes a female house; she builds her own house, a space that belongs to her, contrary to the idea of ownership that the narrative shows: a very patriarchal model. Historically, it has always been the male representatives in the family who build, buy, or lose houses. Pat's grandmother, Amelia, constantly complains to her descendants because she has always felt like a guest in her own home when others are around and has suffered rejection from her stepdaughters: "Eduardo works in his Juarez law office, and fortunately the daughters still living at home also work, Nacha and Adelina at a department store, and Lola at the El Paso Chamber of Commerce. During those hours, Amelia's home is hers" (Mora 1997, 52). Amelia, the woman deprived of a space of her own, the wife constantly criticized, the niece who never receives the inheritance she is entitled to from Spain, endures all the hardships and receives her reward while still alive: she is miraculously healed of a cancer she was suffering from. Mora seems to claim a position of honor for this woman repeatedly relegated to a secondary role by her own family. She rewrites her history, placing her as the heroine who defeats cancer without knowing how and gets to spend her last years peacefully surrounded by her descendants. This is consistent with other ecofeminist writers who link nature and the body. Legler articulates this concept, stating that

> nature, I argue, has been inscribed in the same way that women's bodies and sexual pleasure have been inscribed in patriarchal discourse, as passive, interceptive, docile, as mirror and complement. The conceptual links between women and nature suggested by ecofeminists make rewriting one part of rewriting the other. (233)

This rewriting of female stories and female bodies comes hand in hand with the rewriting of nature, especially since Mora makes constant analogies between writing and gardening. Mora's female characters fight passivity and grow in independence over the narrative as the plants in the garden blossom.

The structure of the narrative covers a whole year from January to December in twelve chapters, plus an introductory chapter establishing the different stages for the construction of the narrative and the house at large. The introduction sets the foundations of the house for the reader, welcoming dead relatives and inviting them to help with the laborious task of building the house and keeping the garden. Hard work starts in the following chapter, *Enero friolero/* ["Chilly January"], with the beginning of the year and concludes in the last chapter *Diciembre mes viejo que arruga el pellejo/* ["December, Old Month that Wrinkles Our Skin"], when "Gradually, our breaths become one" (Mora 2007, 291). Mora, who introduces herself and names her ancestors in the chapter devoted to February, finally starts the process of finding her own voice, and consequently, her own identity; after liberating her mind from the ghosts of her past, satisfied she has been able to reconstruct and repopulate the stone house her father built in 1939. Although the Mora family didn't lose their house like the Delgado's, they had to abandon it when they were forced to move to California fleeing from Villa's regime.

Along with the different months, Mora also recovers the traditions associated with them: Christian ones such as Christmas, the Day of the Dead, Lent, Candlemas, and so forth, but, especially, those other traditions related to nature and the seasons. Mora makes analogies with festivities in the calendar and events in her family. April, when Lent finishes and Christians celebrate Christ's death and resurrection, coincides with the time Raúl Mora lives his own Calvary and agony. He is diagnosed with a mental illness that will take him away from his loved ones. May comes with the contemplation of a garden blossoming; all the pains and efforts of the past months make this month the most beautiful of the year. November 2, the Day of the Dead, is an explosion of memories, remembrances, and rituals that get repeated every year, keeping families busy: caring for dead relatives, while trying to follow Christian, Aztec, Mayan, and any other traditions they may have inherited from their multiple backgrounds.

The writer, as Mora discusses in *Nepantla* (1993), is contemplated as a *curandera* who has been given (in Rebolledo's words) "the opportunity to heal historical neglect" (1993, 167). It is for Mora's narrator to

> remember the past, to share and ease bitterness, to describe what has been viewed as unworthy of description, to cure by incantations and rhythms, by listening with her entire being and responding. She then gathers the tales and myths, weaves them together and, if lucky, casts spells. (Mora 1997, 131)

As a writer/healer Mora is also called to become a bridge between the species that populate nature and to establish a link between the human and the natural world, since she has been called by nature itself to do so. She doesn't exploit the dualism of the *curandera,* the powerful attributes as a witch that many Chicana writers use in their narratives and poetry; she concentrates mainly on the friendly and conciliating aspect of the traditional figure. Feman Orestein sees this as a characteristic of how "ecofeminism considers the arts to be essential catalysts of change" (1990, 279). Therefore, the natural world becomes an active entity entering in dialogical relationships with the writer, changing the traditional patriarchal attitudes that have historically contemplated nature as passive matter, thus establishing a relationship of domination. Mora explores what has been called "postmodern pastoral," a literary genre where women writers historize themselves as participants in a natural landscape and politicize that participation (Legler, 2003, 229). A relationship of friendship and care based on "loving perception," as Karen Warren explains in "The Power and Promise of Ecofeminism," is established between the human and the natural world, substituting the one of domination and oppression based on hierarchical structure (1990, 29). Legler explores further the concept of the postmodern pastoral in women's writing, affirming that the tradition of American nature writing has been traditionally androcentric: "In such texts the land has almost always constituted as an 'other,' a 'thing-for-us,' not as a 'thing-in-itself'" (1990, 22). This deprivation of agency is reflected in Mora's language as well, since she undergoes a process of "embodying nature," as Donna Haraway argues, thereby consciously transforming nature through language into an active actor (1988, 581).

Mora constantly crosses borders. Born in El Paso, Texas, her body and mind live for and on a physical and psychological borderland: "I am Patricia Mora, born in El Paso, Texas, daughter of the desert, of the border, of the Rio Grande del Norte" (Mora 1997, 44). Barriers of time, space, life and death, combinations of oral and written forms of literature, all share an imaginary sphere, a reality created just for the sake of the family and the history of a time she didn't live. For Linda Hutcheon this temporal and spatial move is integral to "Postmodernist fiction [which] suggests that to re-write or to re-present the past in fiction and history is, in both cases, to open it up to the present, to prevent it from being conclusive and teleological" (Hutcheon 1988, 110). Thus, Mora sets the inhabitants of her dream house in a timeless space, crossing chronological barriers and reuniting all of them, fusing and confusing the present and the past since the narrative shows the narrator in a constant time travel throughout the chapters.

As I have stated from the beginning, this narrative can be inscribed within the "postmodern pastoral," or how women writers use literature to provide agency to nature by means of postmodern narrative techniques. Among the postmodern techniques Mora uses, Oliver-Rotger highlights the conscious fragmentation of her work. Mora fills in gaps and inhabits all kinds of borders, even literary ones, including remedies, recipes, poems, and prayers to different saints. Diving into her memories, these come mingled with smells, colors, textures, always bodiless essences coming back from the past: "I lean into them as I lean into the purple scent that transports me to our childhood backyard, the tree from my youth, the old Chinaberry, *la lila,* I'd climb; in the spring, climb into the lavender aroma of its delicate flower clusters" (Mora 1997, 133).

Another recurrent postmodern technique that Mora applies to her narrative and where she establishes an analogy between her conversations with her dead relatives and her communication with nature is the blurring of the barriers between life and death. She also uses this technique to remind the reader of the unclear limits between truth and fiction in the narrative, as she insists it is a nonfictional one. Both binaries—life and death and truth and fiction—combine to start a game with the reader; for example, when Aunt Chole doesn't understand the link to mystery and communication with the dead that her niece has created: "I don't understand this talking with the dead. It's one of Patsy ideas. It's okay. It's okay. If she wants to do this, it's okay with me" (Mora 1997, 138). This is the first time the reader learns that not all the characters are alive and that the memoir has been written to re-create the past events that took place in the lives of Mora's ancestors. Thus, the breaking of time barriers constitutes another valuable resource for the reconstruction of personal and family history.

Recounting the deaths of her relatives, Pat Mora always talks about bodies dying, implying their spirits are all sticking around, communicating, and sharing the good and bad moments with the living. "In the adobe skin of this house in which the living and dead dwell, as our dead dwell, move and speak inside the layers of our human skin; my father and I enjoy the petaled breeze drifting through the garden's mimosas and honey locusts" (Mora 1997, 122). Nature connects the living with the dead.

As the dead return to the soil, the garden gains importance in the narrative, their remains blossom and the dead are given new life in the new flower buds that will open with spring: they still live in the new generations. Nature becomes not only a speaking subject but also a desiring subject, another way in which postmodern pastoral is articulated in Mora's narrative. November as a season of contemplation in the novel finds Mora trying to reconcile herself with her past, with the fact that all of her conversations with the dead belong to her imagination and happened during a time when her relatives were alive. Even "the garden folding into itself to dream of spring" (Mora 2007, 263) reminds the reader of the imaginary character of Mora's reunions with her ancestors. Following the metaphor she has established with writing from the beginning of the narrative, Mora returns to this identification around Thanksgiving. She uses a clear analogy to let the reader know that she is reaching the end of her literary adventure:

> We'll retreat from the yard these next few months, let the garden rest as writers retreat from their work for perspective, many the similarities between gardening and writing. Like the gardener, the writer stores

scraps below the surface, allows a complex and mysterious process to transform the compost into nutrients, enriching the muck with which we work, composed of all that lived before, layers of visible and invisible bodies. (Mora 2007, 267)

Mora has succeeded in rebuilding the house of houses, has completed her memoir and she is now ready to send it to a publisher, waiting for acceptance like the gardener waits patiently for the fruits to appear. This paragraph does not only represent a justification of the possible additions to the true events and transformations that her imagination may have introduced to make the text more attractive to the public, it is an explanation of the whole process of building the house, of constructing a personal identity, coming to terms with tradition and heritage. Mora is obviously talking to a reading audience and the analogy between the layers of the soil and her ancestry does not leave room for doubts as to consider the text itself the product, the fruit from the garden of writing; the characters stand for the plants in flower that give way to the fruits in the summer and Mora herself embodies the figure of the *curandera,* the mediator in conflicts, the collector of these ripe fruits with which she builds the house of her dreams: the memoir that heals the pains and frustrations of four generations of Mexican Americans who now rest in peace in the lives of their descendants. The communication between the human beings and nature has successfully been established as they lie together in the same physical and imaginary space represented by the garden and in the pages of the memoir she has completed—creating a true "postmodern pastoral" where the garden and the characters of the narrative maintain an endless conversation.

The conciliating aspect of the *curandera* explored by Mora in *House of Houses* helps improve feminist and environmental values through the similarities with the process of writing, of rewriting history in order to heal the wounds of historical patriarchal impositions and abuses committed on Chicano women.

Thus, the analysis of *House of Houses,* from an ecofeminist point of view and from a gender perspective connecting women and nature, proves rich in its possibilities and serves to open new avenues for the study of the dialogic connection between human beings and the environment in Chicana/o fiction. The completion of the house means the creation of a female space where nature plays a central role and the affirmation of her individual identity. Contrary to the confinement experienced by her female ancestors, Mora feels liberation in the action of drawing new geographies within the domestic realm, within her own invented house where she holds all the generations of her family in the hope of leaving an undeletable heritage to her descendants.

WORKS CITED

Álvarez, Julia. *In the Name of Salomé*. New York: Algonquin Books, 2001.

Blend, Benay. "Intersections of Nature and the Self in Chicana Writing." In *New Essays in Ecofeminist Literary Criticism*, edited by Glynis Carr. Lewinsburg: Bucknell University Press, 2000.

Cisneros, Sandra. *Caramelo*. New York: Knopf, 2002.

Feman Orenstein, Gloria. "Artists as Healers: Envisioning Life-Giving Culture." In *Reweaving the World: The Emergence of Ecofeminism*, edited by Irene Diamond and Gloria Feman Orenstein. San Francisco, CA: Sierra Book Club, 1990.

Haraway, Donna. "Situated Knowledges: The Science Question in Feminism and the Privilege of Partial Perspective." *Feminist Studies* 14, no. 3 (Autumn 1988): 575–599. http://links.jstor.org/sici?sici=00463663%28198823%2914%3A3%3C575%3ASKTSQI%3E2.0.CO%3B2-M. Accessed April 5, 2012.

Herrera Sobek, María. "The Nature of Chicana Literature: Feminist Ecological Literary Criticism and Chicana Writers." *Revista Canaria de Estudios Ingleses* 37 (November, 1998): 91–100. Print & online.

Hutcheon, Linda. *A Poetics of Postmodernism: History, Theory, Fiction*. London: Routledge, 1988.

Kelly, Petra. "Women and Power." *Ecofeminism: Women, Culture, Nature* (112–119), edited by Karen Warren. Bloomington: Indiana University Press, 1997.

King, Ynestra. "The Ecology of Feminism and the Feminism of Ecology." In *Healing the Wounds: The Promise of Ecofeminism*, edited by Judith Plant. Philadelphia: New Society, 1989.

Legler, Gretchen T. "Ecofeminist Literary Criticism." In *Ecofeminism: Women, Culture, Nature* (227–238), edited by Karen Warren. Bloomington: Indiana University Press, 1997.

———. "Toward a Postmodern Pastoral: The Erotic Landscape in the work of Gretel Ehrlich." In *The ISLE Reader: Ecocriticism 1993–2000* (22-32), edited by Michael P. Branch and Scott Slovic. Athens: University of Georgia Press, 2003.

Mora, Pat. *Nepantla*. Albuquerque: University of New Mexico Press, 1993.

———. *House of Houses*. Boston, Mass: Beacon Press, 1997.

Murphy, Patrick D. *Literature, Nature, and Other: Ecofeminist Critiques*. Albany: State University of New York Press, 1995.

Oliver-Rotger, María Antonia. *Battlegrounds and Crossroads: Social and Imaginary Space in Writings by Chicanas*. Amsterdam: Rodopi, 2003.

Perkins Gilman, Charlotte. *The Yellow Wallpaper*. http://www.gutenberg.org/ebooks/1952. Accessed June 1, 2012.

Plumwood, Val. *Feminism and the Mastery of Nature*. London: Routledge, 1993.

Rebolledo, Tey Diana. *Women Singing in the Snow. A Cultural Analysis of Chicana Literature*. Tucson: University of Arizona Press, 1995.

http://www.patmora.com. Accessed November 15, 2012.

Warren, Karen. "The Power and the Promise of Ecological Feminism." *Environmental Ethics* 12, no. 2 (Summer 1990): 125–146.

3 Transculturation, Memory, and History

Mary Helen Ponce's *Hoyt Street: An Autobiography*

Mario T. García

The memory is a mysterious—and powerful—thing. It forgets what we want most to remember, and retains what we often wish to forget. We take from it what we need.

Mary Helen Ponce, "Note from the Author," in *Hoyt Street*

[A]utoethnography . . . refer[s] to instances in which colonized subjects undertake to represent themselves in ways that *engage with* the colonizer's own terms.

Mary Louise Pratt,
Imperial Eyes: Travel Writing and Transculturation

Mexican Americans or Chicanas/os are no strangers to American history. As a largely mestizo or mixed ethnic group of Indian and Spanish backgrounds, one can trace their particular history as far back as the indigenous civilizations of Mexico and what became the Southwest of the United States, as well as to the Spanish conquest of the Aztec empire and other native communities beginning in 1521. The mixing of genes and culture in what the great Cuban anthropologist Fernando Ortiz termed "transculturation," or what Mexicans refer to as *mestizaje,* took place over 300 years of colonial rule. Chicana/o history also includes Mexico's independence struggle beginning in 1810 and concluding in 1821. Independent Mexico stretched from present-day Central America to the California-Oregon border. Not being able to defend its northern frontier—El Norte—against an expansionist United States with its religious sense of Manifest Destiny, Mexico in the U.S.-Mexico War (1846–48) lost close to half of its territory stretching from Texas to California. It is with the conclusion of this war and the annexation of El Norte that the first official Mexican Americans appear as a new American ethnic group, even though they and their ancestors had been in this area for centuries. What I call the Conquered Generation in Chicana/o history (1848–1900) feels the full brunt of conquest, and although admitted as citizens and technically enumerated as "whites," most succumb into a subaltern second-class citizenship, although not without resistance. Only the commencement of mass Mexican immigration at the turn of the twentieth century would, at least from a numerical standpoint, rescue Mexican Americans from historical obscurity. From 1900 to 1930 over one million Mexican immigrants crossed the border and, with the exception of the years of the Great Depression in the 1930s, they are still arriving. In over 100 years, the Mexican American or Chicana/o experience has been characterized not only by this continuous migration, but also by generational changes through the children, grandchildren, and great-grandchildren of immigrants. It is in this historical context that I want to situate my discussion (see García 1981 and García 1989).

First, a word about terminology that involves not only my chapter, but also that of the others to follow. The term Chicana/o is, as far as can be determined, one first introduced by working-class Mexican immigrants in the early twentieth century. Most believe it is an indigenous-influenced pronunciation of *mexicano*. By the 1940s, as part of an interesting example of transculturation, U.S.-born Mexican Americans reappropriated the term, especially in the urban barrios or neighborhoods. In the 1960s, with the militant Chicano Movement of that era, the term Chicana/o was overtly politicized to refer to activists in the Movement. The term Mexican American refers to U.S.-born Mexican Americans, and its genealogy is to be found in the 1930s and 1940s among the children of Mexican immigrants. Later terms such as Hispanic and Latino are umbrella ones to categorize all people of Latin American descent in the United States. In my chapter, I will interchangeably use both Chicana/o and Mexican American to refer to U.S.-born Mexicans.

Under the rubric of assimilation or acculturation, scholars have traditionally studied ethnic groups in the United States. This involves the thesis that immigrants arrive and, although initially facing what historian Oscar Handlin considered cultural shock, in time they begin their linear journey toward Americanization. This process will be further accelerated among their children, such as German Americans, Italian Americans, Russian Americans, Jewish Americans, and even Irish Americans. Although as part of their Americanization these European groups will retain some symbolic ethnicity, such as Columbus Day or St. Patrick's Day, for the most part, they in a generation became full-blown assimilated and acculturated Americans. While this one-way process has been challenged by later scholars from a more postmodernist perspective stressing fragmentation of identity and multiculturalism, the assimilation/acculturation model still has strong support among some in the academy and, perhaps more importantly, among many white North Americans who cannot accept the idea that for other immigrant groups, especially those of color and their descendants such as Chicana/os, this process has been more complicated.

Many North Americans today believe that Mexican Americans, unlike people of European descent, refuse to acculturate; that is to Americanize themselves. This belief—a mistaken one at that—has led to tensions, including the recent adoption by the state of Arizona of Law 1070 mandating police checking of one's legal status but primarily aimed at the Chicana/o community; the further passage of Arizona House Bill 2281 prohibiting the teaching of Chicana/o Studies and other ethnic studies in the public schools; and recent hostilities against Chicana/os for celebrating the Cinco de Mayo marking the Mexican army's defeat of an invading French army in 1862, but transformed by Mexican Americans in the United States into a feast day of cultural pride and ethnic identity. As Ponce notes in her introduction written in Santa Barbara in 1992 where she was a Dissertation Fellow in Chicana/o Studies: "Mexican-Americans need to tell their side of the story in order to put to rest negative stereotypes" (Ponce 1993, x).

The fact of the matter is that Mexican Americans, including immigrants, do change and do acculturate, but perhaps in a more involved fashion. This complexity has to be understood as the result of three major geo-historical factors: (1) Mexico is right next door to the United States and shares a common almost two-thousand-mile border and, as a result, there will always be some evident Mexican ethnic and cultural influence in the United States; (2) as mentioned, unlike European and Asian immigration to the United States, Mexican immigration, influenced by the proximity of Mexico as well as the economic imbalance between both countries, has been mostly continuous since 1900, again assuring a noticeable Mexican ethnic and cultural presence north of the border; and (3) the racialization of Mexicans in the United States, that is, the perception of the racial inferiority of people of Mexican descent that has assured for many their continuing marginalization within the United States and even second-class citizenship, a racialization that also affected some European immigrants but only through the initial immigrant generation.

These three factors have kept most Chicanas/os and other Latinas/os at arm's length from other Americans, not because Mexican Americans have not wanted to integrate and become part of the North American whole, but because other North Americans have not welcomed them. These conditions, then, have resulted not in a traditional assimilation/acculturation pattern where one is transformed from one culture and identity into another in the way that some traditional anthropologists suggest, but instead into what Ortiz, in his classic study of Cuba, originally published in 1947, called transculturation. By this he meant that cultural contact or what literary scholar Mary Louise Pratt calls "contact zones," such as in the case of the history of Cuba with its varied ethnic and cultural groups—especially after the Spanish conquest, when this diversity included African slaves—does not always result in acculturation—moving from one culture to another—but instead in transculturation (Pratt 1992, 6). That is, cultures meet sometimes by force, but instead of one culture fully absorbing the other, there is instead a mixing or syncretism or dialectics of cultures, such as in the case of *mestizaje* in colonial Mexico. Transculturation does not mean that all cultures are regarded as equal since transculturation is the result, as Ortiz notes, of

European or other forms of imperialism. This process should be familiar in Ireland as the result of English imperialism, with the subsequent result of a unique Irish nationalist culture yet one not immune to English influences. In a process of transculturation, cultures mix, although in a state of tension. Moreover, the transculturated subalterns are not simply victims of this process, but they themselves in a creative way adjust, create, and invent a new culture for themselves that is not someone's else's culture but their own. Transculturation is not a passive process but a dynamic one (Ortiz 1995). This is how Ortiz, himself, explains transculturation:

> I am of the opinion that the word *transculturation* better expresses the different phases of the process of transition from one culture to another because this does not consist merely in acquiring another culture, which is what the English word *acculturation* really implies, but the process also necessarily involves the loss or uprooting of a previous culture, which could be defined as a deculturation. In addition it carries the idea of the consequent creation of new cultural phenomena, which could be called neoculturation. In the end . . . the result of every union of cultures is similar to that of the reproductive process between individuals: the offspring always has something of both parents but is always different from each of them. (Ortiz 1995, 102–3)

It is under the theme of transculturation that I want to analyze Mary Helen Ponce's *Hoyt Street: An Autobiography*. In this 1993 coming-of-age autobiography, which is similar to a bildungsroman or what Pratt refers to as "contact literature," Ponce provides one of the richest accounts available of Mexican immigrant and Mexican American culture covering the period of the 1940s. A student of anthropology herself, Ponce provides what Clifford Geertz calls a "thick description" of culture. Of this influence, she has said: "I see myself more and more as an anthropologist who writes fiction, because I am always interested in the way cultures interact" (Ikas 2002, 185). Her story is set in the San Fernando Valley of the Los Angeles basin in the small town of Pacoima, or "Paco," as the Chicanas/os call it. She and her family live on Hoyt Street, where she situates much of her account of growing up Mexican-American. She later received her BA and MA from nearby California State University, Northridge, and her PhD from the University of New Mexico, where her dissertation was on the early twentieth-century writer Fabiola Cabeza de Baca. Her fictional work includes *The Wedding* (1980) and *Taking Control* (1987).

The context of Ponce's *Hoyt Street* concerns the children of what I call the Immigrant Generation in Chicana/o history. This is that generation of Mexican immigrants who arrive in the United States in the early twentieth century to find work on the railroads, agriculture, mining, and sundry other forms of unskilled labor throughout the Southwest. I use the term Immigrant Generation even though there will be subsequent generations of immigrants, because at no other later time will immigrants so totally dominate the Mexican experience in the United States economically, politically, and culturally. There are some exceptions, such as northern New Mexico, that are bypassed by the immigrant trail, but most other places are transformed from earlier nineteenth-century Mexican American communities—the Conquered Generation—into Mexican immigrant ones such as Los Angeles. By contrast, later immigrants after the Great Depression have to coexist with expansive generations of U.S.-born Mexican Americans. The first of such generations I call the Mexican American Generation in Chicana/o history. This is Ponce's generation in part.

Ponce's ethnographic autobiography, or what Pratt terms "autoethnography," examines the transculturation of the Mexican American Generation through her early life up to age 14 and that of her siblings and friends. She calls her story a communal one and a social history of her hometown—what one of her friends called Mary Helen's Macondo in reference to Gabriel García Márquez's mythical town in *One Hundred Years of Solitude*. This generation is characterized by being bilingual and bicultural, as they are, at one level, affected by Americanization programs in the schools and through mass culture, but, at another level, are able to assert their own Mexican cultural roots in the creation of a syncretic and inventive hyphenated or transcultural position. As historical subjects both at the group and individual level, they undergo a form of cultural reconciliation.[1] What I want to do in this chapter is to examine briefly how Mary Helen Ponce and the Mexican American Generation of Pacoima and specifically on Hoyt Street demonstrate these changes.

But before I do this, I want to note that the Immigrant Generation—the parents of the Mexican American Generation—also undergoes change or "cultural learning," but not as dramatically as their children (Huffman 2001, 30). Just being immigrants in and of itself is already a major change. Living in Spanish-speaking immigrant communities, these immigrants were able to relocate not only themselves—their bodies—but also their culture. Through their family traditions and through building community with other immigrant families, the Immigrant Generation was able to ameliorate Handlin's Americanizing cultural shock by living in more culturally sheltered immigrant enclaves. This was true of other immigrants as well and is, in fact, an immigrant characteristic throughout the world. However, this does not mean that they did not undergo some level of transculturation. Some, such as the Mexican women who worked as domestics in U.S. households, picked up a modicum of English, perhaps at their workplaces or in contact with English-speaking North Americans. Certainly, they changed by adapting to new consumer products that they purchased, such as canned foods and household products. In their predominantly Catholic churches, they often had to deal with non-Mexican priests and nuns, since not many clergy accompanied Mexican immigrants, unlike the case with European Catholics. As part of their transculturation, some Mexican immigrants, such as

Ponce's parents, were able to buy their own homes and possess a greater stake in North American society. A few, like Mary Helen's father, even took the step to become U.S. citizens, while most Mexican immigrants did not, as many believed that they would return some day to Mexico—not an unreasonable belief given Mexico's proximity and a land rather than a water crossing. While immigrants retained much of their *mexicano* way of life, still they were not immune to Americanizing forces while they, as historian George Sánchez (1993) suggests, began the process of becoming Mexican Americans. It is this process of "becoming" that involves transculturation, where dual or multiple cultures meet and are transformed into something new. The Immigrant Generation commences this process, although it is still more balanced toward the *mexicano* side, but it would be their children who advance it even more to the extent that it becomes quite noticeable.

Adult immigrants of whatever ethnic background will always be culturally distinct in their immigrant culture, accents, and even appearance. But this changes with their U.S.-born children, who learn English in the schools as well as the history and cultural traditions of the country. They speak English with little or no accent, and their socialization is likewise influenced by North American mass culture such as the movies, music, and dance. This new, more Americanized generation is what I call the Mexican American Generation that dominates the period between the 1930s and the early 1960s prior to the Chicano Movement. By 1940, U.S.-born Mexican Americans represented the majority of Mexican descent people in the United States. The term "Mexican American" is coined in this era and is symbolic of the transculturation of this generation. That is, this generation bridges its *mexicano* parental culture with the English-speaking North American culture of the schools and larger society. Ponce's text reveals these transculturating influences at the grassroots level.

However, before deconstructing how she does this, I want to also say that the Mexican American Generation is important from a political perspective, as I have addressed in my research on this generation. Besides the biological Mexican American Generation that Ponce represents, there is also a political generation that forges the first significant civil rights movement by Mexican Americans in the United States. Led by new political leaders and new organizations such as LULAC and the American G.I. Forum, to name just two of the more prominent ones, this political generation stressed the integration of Mexican Americans into U.S. society by breaking down barriers of racism and discrimination that kept Mexican Americans locked out of the mainstream. They especially waged struggles to desegregate the infamous segregated and inferior "Mexican schools" of the Southwest. They further attacked discrimination in jobs, wages, public facilities, representation in juries, political representation, and stereotyping in the mass media. Although often criticized by later Chicana/o Studies scholars as being assimilationist, the fact is that this leadership supported cultural pluralism and a diverse U.S. society (García 1989). This culturally pluralist perspective through the process of transculturation or the sharing of cultures is evident as well at the community level, as we can see in Ponce's narrative.

Transculturation begins at home. That is, Mexican Americans such as Ponce are first and foremost influenced by their *mexicano* home and community culture. They first learn to speak Spanish and are socialized or acculturated to a *mexicano* identity and culture that is representative of immigrant communities. They are part of the working-class culture of their parents. In Mary Helen's case, her father first worked in the fields and then as a self-employed hauler of wood. This *mexicano* influence is furthered due to chain migration of other relatives arriving from Mexico to temporarily live with the Ponce family (Ponce 1993, 8).

At the same time, as Mexican American children grew up, generational tensions became evident. Parents were not in favor of some of those changes that they believed were diluting *mexicano* cultural influences. Americanization seemed to lead to their children having less respect for their parents and their elders. As their children began to learn English, parents became concerned that they were losing their ability to speak Spanish fluently. Ponce's mother, for example, emphasized to Mary Helen and her siblings the importance of speaking correct Spanish. Food tastes among their U.S.-born children also changed as kids developed appetites for other foods. Ponce notes the changes in dress as well, especially among her older sisters, as the fact that they worked outside the home afforded them more gender freedom and the ability to purchase more stylish U.S. outfits compared to the more modest dresses worn by their mother. Still, despite these developing cultural tensions within families, the home remained as one side of the transculturating experience for Mexican Americans that nourished the Mexican side of the equation. Increasingly, however, the other side manifested itself so that Ponce and other Mexican Americans as they grow up are aware that, as she puts it, they lived in two worlds (Ponce 1993, 71, 121, 208, 266, 330).

There is no question but that the schools were the main Americanizing agents for the children of immigrants of whatever background. This is certainly the case with Mexican Americans, as Ponce's story reveals. It is in the schools where most immigrant children first learned English, although, in some cases, including Ponce's, older siblings already in school had the effect that the younger ones such as Mary Helen entered schools already knowing some English. She notes that before entering kindergarten, she knew English including her ABC's and could count to 100 in English (Ponce 1993, 112). But most other Mexican Americans apparently knew much less, if any, English. Hence, the public schools in the barrios or Mexican neighborhoods from the very beginning had English-only policies in what were literally called "Mexican schools." "At school," Ponce recalls, "we were constantly told: 'Speak English, English only. You're not in Mexico now'" (Ponce 1993, 112). The exclusively Euro-American teachers in Mary Helen's school also served as role models, especially if they were young, slim, and pretty, such as Mrs. Blynders in the eighth grade. Ponce and many of the other Mexican girls wanted to look like their teacher, whom Mary Helen considered to be a "fairy-tale princess" (Ponce 1993, 318).

Although called "Mexican schools," these institutions aimed to deculturize the Mexican American students and to Americanize them. Ironically, certain aspects of the Mexican schools, at least in the case of Ponce, actually helped to preserve some aspects of Mexicanization that ended up producing hybrid Mexican American students. For example, despite the English-only emphasis of the schools, most Mexican American students did not lose their facility with Spanish since it was replenished at home. Most, if not all, spoke Spanish with their parents but used English with their siblings and friends, although Ponce notes that with her friends sometimes she spoke in Spanish (Ponce 1993, 35). Indeed, in one part of her text, she expresses pride that she was bilingual. During her family's annual late summer migration to work in the fields of Southern California, Ponce attended a special school for the children of migrant workers as well as those of the growers. Although the migrant children were made to feel their difference with the White students, when it came to reading Mary Helen proudly displayed her bilingual reading skills. She writes: "It was only when we read aloud that I felt I was as smart as the regular students. I *was* bilingual, able to pronounce with ease the names of such early Spanish conquistadores as Cabeza de Baca, Hernán Cortés, and Ponce de León (who I inferred was a relative). . . . If nothing else, I could read with the best of them" (Ponce 1993, 180). Ponce further notes that in her Pacoima elementary school, songs that the students learned were mostly in English but some were also in Spanish. For example, at Christmas time, the students sang Spanish songs such as "Noche de Paz" [Silent Night]. Other songs such as "The White Dove" were sung in both English and Spanish. And, in her eighth grade class, Mrs. Blynders ordered a music book that included songs about Mexican life and, as Ponce stresses, "in a language we were otherwise told not to use when in school" (Ponce 1993, 319, 311, 322). Such Mexican cultural apertures in the school only served to reinforce a bilingual and bicultural identity for Mexican American students such as Mary Helen and represented part of the transcultural process experienced by these students, rather than a strictly linear Americanization.

Another interesting example of the Americanization of Mexican American students and of the Mexican American Generation as a whole was the tendency for students such as Mary Helen to "Anglicize" their first names in order not to be perceived as "the other" or as "the stranger." Kids changed their names either amongst themselves or sometimes teachers did it for them because they could not pronounce the Spanish names. On this, Ponce writes: "[W]e liked our names in English best, never questioning teachers who, rather than struggle with our 'foreign' names, quickly deduced their American counterparts and entered them on our school records. In time we identified with our names in English and even forgot how to spell our Spanish names" (Ponce 1993, 35). Name changes also represented a generational break with parents who had named and baptized their children with Spanish first names. Their children rebelled against this and, at least at school and among their friends, changed their names. María Elena Ponce became Mary Helen Ponce. Her siblings also did the same. They became Nora, Elizabet, Berney, Joey, Ronnie, and Norbert. Her friends also changed their names. Santos became Sandy. "My good friend Teresa López went from 'Theresa' to 'Tére' to 'Terry' in one week," Ponce observes. She notes that the name Terry represented "the current rage" (Ponce 1993, 220). At the same time, not all of her friends changed their names. The sister of her friend Sandy insisted that she be called Ana Teresa. Moreover, not all teachers changed Spanish names to English ones and her principal at school, Mrs. Goodsome, attempted to correctly pronounce Spanish names (Ponce 1993, 220 and 311). In addition, even though students such as Mary Helen changed or liked having their first names changed, many in turn invented Spanish or bilingual nicknames for each other. Nita became "*la mocosa*" [snotty] because she refused to wipe her nose; Virgie became "*la mioña*" [pissy] because she once had peed in her pants; and Nancy was "*la volada*" [flighty] because she liked to flirt with the boys. Another friend was nicknamed "El Bugs Bunny" because of his buckteeth (Ponce 1993, 199). These examples of reversions to the use of Spanish again reflect a more nuanced process of cultural change that linked the Mexican to the North American to produce something uniquely Mexican American.

Still another example of a transcultural experience was and still is the practice by bilingual sons and daughters to translate for their parents. The Mexican American Generation became literally a translating generation, bridging themselves with their Spanish-speaking parents and to the larger English-speaking world. In the Ponce family, the children, both older and younger, served as translators for their parents. Sister Elizabet translated English-language mail for her mother; Mary Helen translated the English newspaper for her symbolic grandmother, Doña Luisa. At Sunday evening English-language movies shown in the church hall, Ponce provided a running commentary to Doña Luisa and her Spanish-speaking friends. Sometimes, however, Mary Helen could not think of the correct Spanish word and ended up improvising terms that often confused more than enlightened Doña Luisa and her friends; and, in a sense, Ponce in her autobiography further serves as a translator for us (Ponce 1993, 160, 208, 269–71).

Mass cultural influences, along with the schools, represented a major force for cultural changes and cultural innovations. The movies, for example, were perhaps the most significant influence. Young Mexican Americans loved Hollywood films and attempted to look like and act like their favorite film stars. By comparison, they saw their parents as old-fashioned. Mary Helen's older sisters, for example, took to wearing the tight skirts that female stars favored (Ponce 1993, 15–42). Mexican American females, in particular, associated slim bodies with U.S. culture even though some of them, like Mary Helen, were chubby, which they probably associated with being Mexican. As Ponce puts it: "In the movies the slender girl always got her man"

(Ponce 1993, 293). Other starlets that she notes were especially idolized by her and her friends included Hedy Lamarr and "la Rita Hayworth." The mention of Rita Hayworth is of particular interest since she in fact was Mexican, having been born in Tijuana as Rita Cansino. However, it is doubtful that Mexican Americans were aware of this because Hayworth herself seems to have kept this a secret in order to pass as White. A particular favorite of Ponce's older sisters was Joan Crawford. Trina, for example, attempted to arch her eyebrows just like Crawford. Besides going to see movies, Mexican American youth avidly read movie magazines (Ponce 1993, 293, 329–30, 176, 297, 337). While Hollywood films helped to Americanize Mexican Americans, other circumstances associated with moviegoing complicated this process and led to a more transcultural one. For one, Mexican Americans saw English-language films in segregated theaters that only brought attention to their Mexicanness. According to Ponce, theaters that catered to Euro-Americans did not officially deny entrance to Mexican Americans, but it was common knowledge that they were not welcomed there. Moreover, besides attending the only theater in nearby San Fernando that did cater to Mexican Americans, this one also showed Mexican movies. Mary Helen notes that she also liked these films, especially those with stars of Mexico's Golden Age of filmmaking such as María Félix and Jorge Negrete. It was not until after World War II that the other theaters openly allowed entrance to Mexican Americans (Ponce 1993, 303–5). Of this desegregation, Ponce observes:

> Not until after World War II did Mexican-Americans become socially acceptable at local movie houses and restaurants. Men from the barrio, it became known, were also wounded and killed while fighting for their country, the good old USA. It was unpatriotic to turn away nonwhites in uniform, especially those with medals and Purple Hearts pinned to their chests. (Ponce 1993, 305)

However, this cultural duality associated with moviegoing and movie influences only added to the bicultural nature of the Mexican American Generation.

In addition to English-language films, Mexican Americans were also influenced by North American music and dance. Young Mexican American women such as Mary Helen's older sisters joined their White counterparts in swooning over Frank Sinatra. Some also liked black singers, such as the young Fats Domino. Ponce's younger brother, Joey, learned to play jazz on the saxophone (Ponce 1993, 15–42). Their sister Trina and her friends loved to dance to American music. "They experimented with 'slow dancing,' a style popular in the Los Angeles dancehalls," Ponce writes, "which allowed couples to hold each other close and to slide back and forth in time to the sultry music. Now and then the girls jitterbugged, twirling away for hours, until they fell to the floor from exhaustion. Once they had rested, back they went to dancing the very latest and most 'hip' steps" (Ponce 1993, 267). Clearly influenced by black music, Ponce's sisters used slang such as "cool it" and "chick." They referred to guys who dressed sharp as "cool cats" and to others as "squares" (Ponce 1993, 176). At the same time, Mexican Americans were not completely turned off to Mexican music played on Spanish-language radio stations and heard at home. Some even liked it, including singers such as Jorge Negrete (Ponce 1993, 144). In fact, as Anthony Macias documents in his insightful book *Mexican-American Mojo,* Mexican American musicians both before and after the war experimented with synthesizing Mexican and Latino musical forms with North American ones such as jazz and swing (Macias 2008). Musical and dance tastes, along with musical production, only added to a more transcultural reaction to mass culture by Mexican Americans.

Finally, World War II proved to be a major Americanizing experience for the Mexican American Generation. Estimates range from 300,000 to 500,000 Latinos, mostly Mexican Americans, who saw military duty during the war. These men are part of the Greatest Generation. For most, it was the first time they had left their hometowns. They now scattered throughout the states for their military training, in contact for the first time with many other ethnic Americans. Many, of course, saw action in Europe and the Pacific. A great number never returned; and those who did came back either physically or emotionally wounded or both. Despite lingering stereotypes that somehow Chicanos and Latinos do not really want to be part of the United States, the fact is that Mexican Americans and other Latinos have spilled blood in all U.S. wars, including those today in Iraq and Afghanistan.

In her autobiography, Ponce notes the impact of World War II on Pacoima, on Hoyt Street, and on her family. Many of the young Mexican American men in the community either volunteered or were drafted into the military. Those who enlisted on their own preferred the Marines because of the attractive dress uniform, as well as for its reputation of machismo. Brother Berney wanted to join his friends in the service but was declared 4-F or ineligible due to a hearing problem. He felt shame for not being in the war and embarrassed that his friends might think he did not have the courage to fight. Many friends, including boyfriends of her older sisters, went to war. Mary Helen recalls that she and her preadolescent girlfriends were attracted to the military uniforms worn by Mexican Americans, except for the Army one that they disliked. They wished that they were old enough to date the guys in uniform. She writes of the great outpouring of community sentiment at the burial of a Daniel Torres, who received the Congressional Medal of Honor for his valor. Torres was one of many other Mexican Americans who won this highest honor during the war. The war did not just affect the young men, however, as some Mexican American women also served in the military, although not in combat duty, and many more, like her older sisters, went to work in the new defense industries in Southern California and in this way can be considered part of the Greatest Generation (Macias 2008, 25–6, 210, 213–19).

While the war proved to be a major socialization of patriotism and Americanization, it also possessed a transcultural side in that the immigrant parents and, indeed, the entire Mexican community of Pacoima, both U.S.-born and immigrants, participated in supporting the war and in celebrating the U.S. victory. Of this, Ponce writes: "Many families on our street were affected by the war. Those who could afford to bought war bonds; others stuck gold and silver stars on the front door, anxious for neighbors to know that someone in their family was fighting or had died for his country. Young girls with boyfriends in the army and navy sold war bonds as part of the war effort" (Macias 2008, 208–9). In this way, all Mexicans were affected by the war, but, in turn, as Mexicans they contributed to the war effort. Moreover, when Mexican Americans *veteranos* returned from the war, many discovered that while they had been fighting to preserve democratic freedoms, they were still denied many of these freedoms at home in the form of continued segregation and discrimination. As such, Mexican American veterans forged an accelerated civil rights movement in the postwar period influenced by their socialization in the war, but also by their commitment to having their ethnicity and culture respected.

Let me conclude by saying that Mary Helen Ponce's *Hoyt Street,* in my opinion, is one of the best autobiographical texts written by a Chicana/o writer. While it lacks the fascinating introspectiveness of Richard Rodriguez's classic *Hunger of Memory,* it compensates for this through its rich ethnographic depiction of Mexican immigrant and Mexican American family and community life. Moreover, as an example of transcultural generational changes among both immigrants and especially U.S.-born Mexican Americans, *Hoyt Street,* from a historical and anthropological perspective, is a most valuable contribution. As such, Ponce's text not only debunks many stereotypes about Mexicans in the United States, but it also reveals the more intricate, nuanced, and creative nature of Chicana/o identity and culture. As a historian who works on such issues, I take much from this text about Mexican everyday life in the United States.

NOTE

1. I borrow the term "reconciliation" from Huffman (2001, 29).

WORKS CITED

García, M. T. *Desert Immigrants: The Mexicans of El Paso, 1880–1920.* New Haven: Yale University Press, 1981.
———. *Mexican-Americans: Leadership, Ideology & Identity, 1930–1960.* New Haven: Yale University Press, 1989.
Huffman, T. "Resistance Theory and the Transculturation Hypothesis as Explanation of College Attrition and Persistence among Culturally Traditional American Indian Students." *Journal of American Indian Education* 40, no. 3 (2001): 1–39.

Ikas, K.R. "Interview with Mary Helen Ponce." In *Chicana Ways: Conversations With Ten Chicana Writers.* Reno: University of Nevada Press, 2002.

Macias, A. *Mexican-American Mojo: Popular Music, Dance, and Urban Culture in Los Angeles, 1935–1968.* Durham, NC: Duke University Press, 2008.

Ortiz, F. *Cuban Counterpoint: Tobacco and Sugar.* Durham, NC: Duke University Press, 1995.

Ponce, M.H. *Hoyt Street—An Autobiography.* Albuquerque: University of New Mexico Press, 1993.

Pratt, M.L. *Imperial Eyes: Travel Writing and Transculturation.* London: Routledge, 1992.

Sánchez, G.J. *Becoming Mexican-American: Ethnicity, Culture, and Identity in Chicano Los Angeles, 1900–1945.* New York: Oxford University Press, 1993.

Part II

From the Regional to the Global

Chicana/o identities developed in a heterogeneous territory complicated by national and individual relations. They grew out of workers' struggles and a need for peoples of multiple allegiances to demand rights and recognition, situated in a precise geographical positioning, where the border defines and decides citizenship, but does not necessarily determine belonging. This border looms large metaphorically and physically, and may have fixity on the map that has real human consequences for the individuals who cross it, live near it, or operate in its interstitial terrain, but it can also be blurred by definitional ambiguities.

In recent years, the border has been associated with the violence of the drug cartels and the Mexican president Felipe Calderón's (2006–12) so-called war on drugs, and as a point of contention for both the United States and Mexico because of the movement of people and goods across it. As María Herrera-Sobek notes in her chapter in this volume on the artistic representation of the border, citing Gloria Anzaldúa's theory, the borderlands are also the site of cultural exchange and diversity that can convert a territory marked by conflict and violence into a uniquely creative and vibrant space. The chapters in this segment look at how the border as idea and reality is engaged with by writers and filmmakers.

Niamh Thornton considers the border through cultural practice. Her chapter examines the *quinceañera* as an evolving tradition that was previously associated only with Mexico and has now travelled across the border north and southwards, dispersing among communities who appropriate it and adapt it to create new traditions and practices. It has become a rite of passage that no longer defines Mexicanness and, instead, is pan-Hispanic. The *quinceañera* is at once a ritual that takes place to celebrate adulthood, a way to welcome a young woman into her community, and an exuberant party that provides an opportunity to display a family's financial status. It can be, variously, laden with preconceived expectations, overdetermined by assumed traditions, filled with anxiety for parents and teenagers, or hampered by accusations of transgressions of taste, while simultaneously, for many, it is lots of fun. The complex matrix of market forces, familial pressures, and the gendering of cultural value and responsibility make it a fascinating focus of study.

Curiously, despite its strong roots in Mexico, the *quinceañera* has seldom been considered by Mexican or Chicana/o novelists or filmmakers. It has received invaluable attention from academics, however, who provide useful frameworks for its analysis. Thornton considers multiple textual and filmic representations of the *quinceañera* and positions their creators culturally and geographically in order to better understand how Hispanic young womanhood is conceived of in the twentieth and twenty-first centuries.

Tatiana Voronchenko takes a careful look at the representation of borders and borderlands through literature. The territories she considers reach far beyond the usual limitations, that is, the areas surrounding the Mexican-U.S. border, and move much further north and east to Siberia. Voronchenko traces the commonalities of experiences between poets and novelists and considers how both Mexico and Russia have been frequently seen as wild locations to be conquered, places on which to project fantasies, and its inhabitants as exotic Others, with all that this implies. She supplies insight into the literatures of, as well as about, the two locations, and gives a detailed survey of the reception of recent Chicana/o fiction in Siberia.

Her chapter serves as a useful historical overview of the political events leading up to the current geopolitical boundaries between Mexico and the United States. She considers the racialization of the tensions between the two countries that resulted in the denigration of non-Whites and the privileging of Whiteness that has determined much of the discourse around Mexicans, Blacks, indigenous peoples and, consequently, Chicana/os in the United States. Starting with the early writers of the nineteenth century, Voronchenko provides an overview of literary production up to the present day. As with many chapters in this collection, Anzaldúa informs this study, which links Siberia to Mexico and the United States in unique and perceptive ways.

Nuala Finnegan considers the real dangers of living in an interstitial city such as Juárez where the specificities of the locale are determined by global trade. Having attracted workers from throughout Mexico by the promise of factory work and other employment opportunities, it has developed an unsavoury reputation. Located just across the border within sight of the United States, it has become a site of considerable cartel warfare, but also a place where thousands of women have been kidnapped, often sexually assaulted, and then brutally murdered. Their bodies are left in the desert, sometimes unfound for years, whilst their families' hope for their safe return fades to despair, sorrow, loss, and anger. These crimes have been partially investigated, but not resolved. Families and nongovernmental organisations have set up campaigns to try and recover the bodies and to seek justice. So far, this has led to much frustration and little success.

Finnegan's chapter looks at two novels, Alicia Gaspar de Alba's *Desert Blood: The Juárez Murders* (2005) and Kama Gutier's *Ciudad final* (2007) [*Final City*], that explore these crimes from the perspective of women from outside of Juárez, one from just across the border in the United States (Gaspar de Alba), the other from Spain (Gutier). Their outsider status provides an opportunity to explore the crimes and seek answers on behalf of the reader, whilst they both have specific relationships and knowledge of the local that allow them to connect to the conditions on the ground. Their protagonists are lesbians, which fits with a growing trend within detective fiction, but is still rare in Chicana/o writing. This move crosses its own border in that it challenges the heteronormativity of many narratives as well as making welcome incursions into the growing number of novels addressing these crimes.

This section concludes with Francisco Lomelí's study of the plastic figurines known as Homies. He considers the transformation of Homies from representations of the barrio to hip countercultural artefacts, as well as the way in which their depiction of characters often stigmatised as undesirable and even criminal by Anglo-Americans provoked criticism and inspired much debate. The mixed reaction to the Homies underlines the constant reinvention of Chicana/o culture, while exposing the tensions related to artistic freedom and responsibility. Lomelí's study synthesizes many of the issues discussed in this section, namely the stereotypical and racist views of Chicanas/os that continue to permeate U.S. society, the ways in which visual art seeks to counter such prejudices, and the continuing evolution and inventiveness of Chicana/o artistic practice. Lomelí's application of the idea of *rasquachismo,* the idea of making much out of nothing, recalls the early visual and literary productions of the Chicano Movement and returns us to the central theme of this volume—the transitions and continuities of contemporary Chicana/o culture in a global world.

Borders are potentially both porous and rigid. The transversal flows happen because of the commonality of human experience, as demonstrated by Thornton, where she discusses how a rite of passage belonging to a specific sociocultural group is shared and reinvented for contemporary needs, or by Voronchenko, where fruitful comparisons are drawn between the experiences of ethnically marked peoples of Siberia and the Chicanas/os in the United States. While this movement and exchange can be lively and expansive, the limits and dangers of border territories are also not to be ignored, as Finnegan explores. Through an examination of the way in which the Homies have become a mass-market phenomenon, Lomelí reveals their power as subversively humorous border crossers who challenge racist stereotypes that extend far beyond the barrio.

All of these chapters show the inequality of relationships across borders. In Voronchenko's it is in the fight for the right to access the public space of theatrical performance and publication, for Thornton it is in the ambivalence of the appropriation of another's cultural practice by non-Chicanas/os, in Finnegan's work it is evident in the variable access to justice on either side of the border, while in Lomelí's it is manifest in the endurance of racist stereotypes that relegate Chicanas/os to the status of subaltern Other. These chapters explore place, location, and identity through a multiplicity of films, popular culture, and literature in order to expand on the ideas around place and space in an increasingly globalised world.

4   My Super Sweet Fifteen
The Internationalisation of *Quinceañeras* in Literature and Film

Niamh Thornton

In episode 6, season 4 of the popular Nickelodeon children's animated TV series, *Dora the Explorer*, Dora is charged with taking "cultural icons" (Cantú 2002, 19), that is, high heels and a crown, to her cousin Daisy's *quinceañera*. Time is marked by the ringing of church bells, implying a religious dimension to the celebration without underscoring it through showing any ceremony in the visuals. The bells are merely indicators of the impending party that Dora is to attend. While on her adventurous journey to get to the *quinceañera*, Dora practices dancing the mambo, which she encourages her young audience to imitate. This episode emphasises both the cultural icons, and the significance of these as integral parts of inherited traditions, yet suggests a loosely transnational approach to the celebrations. Through the foregrounding of the *quinceañera* as a narrative device and the rehearsal of the Cuban mambo, *Dora the Explorer* demonstrates how a Chicana/*Mexicana* tradition has travelled beyond the boundaries of its original community and is now a display of *Latinidad*, which has become popular across the United States and Latin America.

The *quinceañera* is a festivity that has its origins in centuries-old ritual, and is a Chicana "life-cycle marker" (Cantú 2002, 15). While there have been important studies of this significant life event by theorists and there is a growing body of novels and films on the subject, relatively few Chicanas/os or Mexicans have fictionalised this event. Ilan Stavans concisely describes how the *quinceañera* has "acquired a distinct *gringo* taste" (2010, ix) by blending traditional rites and rituals from one locale to become part of the practices of a wider Hispanic community and a marker of Latina, rather than just specifically Chicana or Mexican, identity. This chapter will consider the evolution of these representations. First, it will seek to position the *quinceañera* celebration from its possible origins to its present-day incarnation, and then it will examine some representative texts.

As a ritual that "aims to legitimate and control the sexuality of the pubescent girl" (Marling 2010, 5) it can be read as an inherently conservative practice, which tries, but never succeeds in, resolving the old with the new in the face of the sometimes traumatic change and displacement of migration. For Karal Ann Marling, the *quinceañera* accurately portrays old-country expectations, even as they come under increasing pressure from contemporary culture at large. Quincing is about retaining respect for the old ways, even if they are sometimes honoured in startling new forms. (2010, 6)

The *quinceañera* is a highly symbolic ritual, not just for the family and community involved, but also for filmmakers and writers. It has mutated from what it was originally intended to be, and from the geopolitical space where it originated, to become an international rite of passage that has as much in common (if not more) with MTV's *My Super Sweet Sixteen* than it does to its original source tradition.[1] The *quinceañera* is worthy of consideration because it takes an originary activity and redeploys it for the creation of a transnational Latina identity (both U.S. and Latin American) and, therefore, it is a useful case study in how a Mexican/Chicana cultural practice becomes Latina through travel across borders. This chapter will look at exemplary films and texts that have *quinceañeras* at their centre in order to best understand the evolution of the phenomenon.

The *quinceañera* party is a rite of passage that celebrates a young woman's coming of age. Although it is often unproblematically referred to as an ancient inheritance from Aztec or Mayan traditions, according to theorists such as Karen Mary Dávalos its origins are highly contested, and may be a carryover from French or Spanish courtly practices (2003, 149–50).[2] The day-long celebration usually begins with a religious service and then continues with a large party that has particular ritualised markers. These include the passing over of the "last doll"; a father-daughter dance (usually a waltz); publically changing out of flat shoes into high heels; the *quinceañera*'s parade with her "court"; and so on.[3] All represent the transition from child to adulthood, and some (for example, high heels) are indicators of burgeoning sexuality.

The *quinceañera* party has been described as "a community and family celebration full of tradition and meaning when a young girl is symbolically escorted into womanhood by her family and the event is witnessed by her community" (Alomar and Zwolinski 2002, n.p.). However, amongst the wealthy there is a tradition of going on a trip abroad, either instead of or in addition to the party. That travel is understood as a feasible option is reflected in a blog question on *Quinceañera* website: "Do You Prefer a Party or to Travel?" (*Quinceanera* 2009). Travel is an alternative marker and demonstrates how a community-based activity can take on a different dimension. Through travel the birthday thereby becomes an individual rite of passage rather than one that is defined by tradition and group belonging. On these Web pages and on those of other sites you can also discover how to plan, prepare for, and survive the big day with tips as varied as whom to invite, the party girl's horoscope for the day, recommendations on how to ensure that nobody wears the same outfit as the *quinceañera*, and so on. The economic value of the *quinceañera* party can be seen online.

Internet sites such as *Misquince*: "your source for *quinceañera*" (http://www.misquincemag.com) and *Quinceanera* [sic] *Party*: "How to Have a New Millennium Quinceañera Celebration" (http://www.quinceaneraparty .com/) are packed with advice on how to plan the perfect party, such as lists of possible songs for the father-daughter dance, party rules, and must-haves. Individuality is stressed, while the expectations are that this will be a lavish affair. For example, *Quinceanera Party* advises its readers what to expect:

> Everyone is dressed formally and the scene resembles a wedding complete with bridesmaids and the *Quinceañera* will wear something that stands her above the rest, usually a ball gown and some stunning jewelry. In ancient times, when ball gowns didn't exist, she would still have been attired in a manner that would distinguish her from everyone else. (*Quinceanera Party* 2009)

This is a typical example of the sort of instruction given to the *quince*.[4] The writer here draws parallels with a wedding in terms of the importance of the event as a life marker, and these are evident in some of the rituals, such as the entry into the church on the arms of a male, carrying a bunch of flowers, and the father-daughter dance, which gives an extra significance to the day. "Everyone" places emphasis on conformity, while the passage indicates that the *quinceañera* should stand out. It is her expensive outfit that, purportedly, connects her to her ancestors. The message appears to be that culture can be commoditised: buy the right dress and you will have a direct link to your past. It is such statements and the sentiment within that invite comparisons with MTV's *My Super Sweet Sixteen*. The super sweet sixteen-year-old may not have the heavy hand of history hanging over his/her event; nonetheless, he/she does have all the pressures of consumer culture impelling him/her to have the perfect outfit and to be more than anyone else in the room. For example, in episode 303 of MTV's *My Super Sweet Sixteen,* the cameras follow Alex, a young woman from Bloomfield Hills, Michigan, to Paris in her quest for the perfect dress as part of her attempt to live up to her self-imagining as "heiress-in-waiting." Her excess and later renting of models to act as her escorts are all part of her presentation of a self that is all about money and consumption.

Where MTV's *My Super Sweet Sixteen*'s Alex may have both the means for excess and crass displays of wealth and an unproblematic relationship to these, there is a tension in many of the *quinceañera* narratives between the idealized millenarian ritual and the presentation of the self as consuming subject. This chapter will consider how these tensions are represented, examine how the event has evolved from a Chicana/Mexican celebration into a Latina one, and reflect on the significance of who has chosen to write about and film it. It will trace the trajectory of the *quinceañera* narrative starting with *Quinceañera* (Alfredo B. Crevenna, 1956), the first film to feature the tradition as a key plot device. It reflects the mores of 1950s

Mexico and is a useful establishing text. The other texts are a sampling of more contemporary representations, as the *quinceañera* has become a more widespread phenomenon: Julia Alvarez's *Once Upon a Quinceañera: Coming of Age in the USA* (2007), which is part research project, part memoir; and *Echo Park, L.A.* (Richard Glatzer and Wash Westmoreland, 2005), a film that tackles social issues in a very modern fairy tale narrative. Finally, I briefly consider two *Quinceañera* Club novels by Belinda Acosta, *Damas, Dramas, and Ana Ruiz* (2009) and *Sisters, Strangers, and Starting Over* (2010), which meld personal crisis and political issues with the coming-of-age narrative.[5]

The first film, *Quinceañera* (Alfredo B. Crevenna, 1956), is a conventional melodrama. It opens on the high-school graduation day of three friends, Beatriz (Martha Mijares), Leonor (Tere Velázquez), and Maria Antonia (Maricruz Olivier), from different segments of Mexican society. As they consider their futures, they discuss what they plan to do on their respective fifteenth birthdays, which take place on the same day. Over the course of the narrative, how they celebrate this event is set up as a symbolic marker of their class differences. Beatriz has a no-expense-spared celebration, Leonor's normally honest father is moved to steal to satisfy both his daughter's and wife's social aspirations, and Maria Antonia's working-class father takes on double shifts to pay for a basic party, only for the money to be stolen in the street. Subplots involving Beatriz's unfaithful father, Leonor's spinster aunt, and Maria Antonia's beau, further enhance the sociological scope and implicitly build a complete picture of 1950s Mexico in its aspirations, hypocrisy, and greed.

However, despite the criticisms of the excess that the *quince* ball represents in the film, all three get the party they dreamt of in the end: Beatriz's father realises the error of his ways and returns to the family home, having left his possessive lover; Leonor's father is forgiven for robbing the bank he works for; and Maria Antonia is gifted a party by an admirer. Within the framework of the narrative, Maria Antonia's celebration gets the most attention, as she is the good girl who begs her father not to overwork himself, repeatedly admonishes her mother for spending money on her, and insists, despite her many daydreams, that she is happy not to have a party. The message is clear: self-sacrifice and poverty will be rewarded, not greed.

The music accompanying the traditional final, joyous dance between father and daughter is one that is unfamiliar to the contemporary *quinceañeras*. Johann Strauss II's "Emperor Waltz" is a recurrent musical motif in the film and is played when the young women imagine themselves dancing with their date at their ball as well as returning at the end, when we see all three dance at their respective parties. It is a choice that is likely influenced by director Alfredo Crevenna's German origins. The universalizing (or Europeanizing) effect of this music takes from the local and traditional aspect of the event, and makes it something that invites comparisons to the European debutante ball or the U.S. cotillion. Apart from the shared church service, there is little sense that the party itself is governed by traditional cultural norms. This contrasts with more recent versions, both in literature and film, where there are a number of defined and prescribed moments that are included in the narrative in order to ensure authenticity.

Julia Alvarez enunciates this tension between conformity and individuality in her book, *Once Upon a Quinceañera: Coming of Age in the USA* (2007). This is part memoir and part testimonial account of Alvarez's year travelling around the United States as she "immersed myself in this tradition" (2007, 5). As someone who was born in the Dominican Republic and spent much of her youth in New York, she never had her own *quinceañera* party. She comments throughout her book that only recently has it become a widespread celebration. Transformed from being a Mexican tradition, it has now become part of U.S. Latina identity. Alvarez provides detail of her journey as a representation of a new hybrid Latina identity:

> I traveled to various Latino communities in the United States: Dominican-Americans in Lawrence, Massachusetts, and Queens, New York; Cuban Americans in Miami; Mexican Americans in San Antonio and Los Angeles. Even as I ascribe distinct nationalities to these communities, I have to qualify that these nationalities are mixing with other Hispanic as well as non-Hispanic nationalities. The parents of the *quinceañera* I attended in San Antonio were Panamanian and Mexican American; of the two *quinceañeras* I attended in Lawrence, only one was Dominican, the other was Ecuadorian; Monica's *quinceañera* court in Queens included Colombians, Peruvians, and one Italian-Irish-American (Alvarez 2007, 5).

The detail that she provides gives a sense of the degree to which a once Mexican practice, with its specific tropes, motifs, and rituals, now belongs to a wider community of U.S. Latinas. Alvarez also writes about how the *quinceañera* has travelled back to countries from where the migrants come and where it previously wasn't traditional before, such as her native Dominican Republic. The narrative mixes the results of Alvarez's research on Latina youth and the *quinceañera;* interviews with service providers; Alvarez's account of her struggle to negotiate between two worlds (her parents as recent migrants and her own burgeoning identity as a hyphenated U.S. citizen); and the above-mentioned Monica, whose preparation and party are described by Alvarez as she accompanies her over the course of several months. In sum, she describes the blending of her own story and those of the young Latinas she is writing about as follows:

> And so, as I attended *quinceañeras*, I felt as if I were getting a peek into the future as well as the past. A future that—given the demographics— would have, if not a Spanish accent, a Latino flavor. And a past that was my past, growing up in a USA just beginning to wake up to its own

identity as a multicultural country with women and minorities demanding equal rights. (Alvarez 2007, 7)

This is a look at Latina teens with serious inflections: "our teen Latinas are
topping the charts for all sorts of at-risk behaviors: from teen pregnancy
to substance abuse to dropping out of high school" (Alvarez 2007, 6). By
softening down the politically contentious growing demographics of Latinas and reducing them to mere non-threatening flavor and away from the
danger of language or accent, Alvarez sets the tone for the book that is
to follow. This is a book for non-Latinas/os with Alvarez acting as native
informant or as an intermediary between outsiders and insiders. She also
self-ascribes expertise on the subject, proclaiming to know so much about
the rituals that "in some cases I served as the authority on some detail of the
ceremony" (Alvarez 2007, 8). Thus, she declares her involvement as beyond
mere observer and stakes her claim on the tradition. As a result, Alvarez
both carefully acknowledges the origins and evolution of the *quinceañera*
and collapses it into a trans-Latina identity.

In a breezily written account of the girls, their planning, description of
facts and social context, full of idiosyncratic use of exclamation marks and
upper case font, there is an attempt to critique, from a feminist perspective,
the significance of the *quinceañera*. For example, Alvarez speculates on why
many of the young women become mothers shortly after their *quinceañera*
and surmises that it is related to the fact that the party has many of the trappings of a wedding ceremony: "[I]t sends a clear message to the Latina girl:
we expect you to get married, have children, devote yourself to your family.
It's no wonder that girls end up getting pregnant soon after celebrating their
quinces" (Alvarez 2007, 56). She continues:

> And so, although it gives her a momentary illusion of power (the princess
> rhetoric, the celebration of her sexual power, her youth, her beauty), in
> fact, the ritual enacts an old paradigm of the patriarchy increasingly (in
> the USA) pumped up by a greedy market. (Alvarez 2007, 57)

This tension between the parental and communities' aim to control the
young women's sexuality and its celebration resonates in all of the representations. Alvarez draws on Arnold Van Gennep's theory about rites of
passage, which suggests (in her words) that "[m]ale initiation rites of passage involve the stripping, testing, and reintegration of the young man into
the sociopolitical adult society" (2007, 57), whilst "the girl is decked in
ceremonial finery" (2007, 57).[6]

Alvarez reminds the reader repeatedly of her own discomfort regarding
the sexual politics, the money spent on the *quinceañera,* and its provenance
as ritual. But, there is a kind of resigned inevitability with which she embraces
the event. After talking to a cake maker, identified as Miguelina, who grew
up too poor in the Dominican Republic to afford a party, and talks about the

quinceañera as being an invention, Alvarez concludes that "[t]he apparatus is in place and I am part of it, the writer with one foot in and one foot out of a Pan-Hispanic community America is creating out of our diversity, reporting on a curious tradition that supposedly binds us together" (2007, 148). The logic of her engagement with the process is contradictory. For Alvarez, on the one hand, the *quinceañera* should be critiqued, Latina teens need to be helped along out of a cycle of teen pregnancy and disadvantage, but, on the other, they should get their party and a chance to be a princess for a day. Neither is simple nor unproblematic. However, Cantú sees critiques such as Alvarez's to be indicative of a lack of comprehension of the "patterns of resistance . . . embedded in the performance even within the very sites of the subject's oppression" (2002, 16) that "baffles outsiders who do not understand the contradictions that it underscores in a community with excessively high dropout rates, high teen pregnancy, double-digit unemployment rates, and high levels of poverty" (2002, 16). The *quinceañera,* for Cantú, is an opportunity to negotiate her way through the Mexican-American communities' expectations of what and who she should be and declare this publicly through the careful negotiation and use of the rituals, the spaces they take place in and the cultural icons that are employed in order to express her individuality and own position amongst her peers. For Alvarez, it is a puzzling new development that she grapples with on the (White) readers' behalf.

An important addendum to this is that, for Alvarez, you can have your party as long as you are working class. Rich Dominicans, who celebrate in a fashion that, for her, bears a greater resemblance to MTV's *My Super Sweet Sixteen* because it lacks ritual and is only about demonstrations of wealth, come in for her particular disdain. For Alvarez, the *quinceañera* is a practice that rightfully belongs in the migrant barrios of the United States, not the elite neighborhoods of the Dominican Republic. She says:

> A tradition, of course, can be celebrated only in the context of a community, and though working-class Latin Americans and Caribbeans and Mexicans might emigrate in droves and create barrios and comunidades in this country, let's face it, for the most part the rich and powerful have no reason to leave their home countries and build enclaves in Hialeah or Washington Heights or East Los Angeles (2007, 151).

Alvarez, here, is not recognising the idea of tradition "as an open and sometimes chaotic terrain that is constantly reconfigured in everyday experience" (Dávalos 2003, 143). Alvarez's "of course" is an attempt to normalize her own bias. She problematically associates the maintenance and authenticity of culture purely to the working classes and denies other classes the right to practice the tradition, because, for her, community can only be understood in working-class terms. In addition, her opinions are based on the absence of specific rituals in the party she attended in the Dominican Republic, which suggests that there is a stultified and limited set of practices that determine whether an event is a *quinceañera* or not, rather than there being a more complex set of determinants.[7]

Alvarez pre-empts criticisms of her own contradictory attitude to *quinceañera*s in her conclusion, entitled "Bendición" [blessing], a name that both references a part of the ceremony and suggests little ambivalence. She states that "the swings in my feelings towards the tradition were downright dizzying and baffling. Did I believe in the Q-tradition or not? Yes and no. Sí y no. Back and forth" (Alvarez 2007, 253).[8] The word *baffling,* no doubt, is a deliberate nod to Cantú, who is referenced in Alvarez's bibliography. This apparent bewilderment is based on her uncertainty at the statistical negatives that surround Latina teens, and her own inability to reconcile the patriarchal trappings of the ritual with her own celebration of the passing on and identification with a recent manifestation of a borrowed cultural rite of passage. Her expressed ambivalence is shared by this reader. However, how her discomfort is elucidated is unconvincing in the face of her obvious celebration of the forms and rituals. So too is her decision to imbricate herself into the narrative through the juxtaposition of her own story with those of Monica and others. This method invites comparison and suggests that their story is just a modern version of her own migrant story, and that the critiques of the festivities are but a way of ingratiating herself to her implied White, middle-class reader. Alvarez is comfortable with the elision of Chicana and Mexican tradition into a Latina whole, thereby unproblematising any differences within the various national affiliations. The *quinceañera* thereby is easily decoupled from its origins and assimilated into a set of Latina practices.

Mexican American Belinda Acosta in her two *Quinceañera* Club novels, *Damas, Dramas and Ana Ruiz* (2009) and *Sisters, Strangers and Starting Over* (2010), doesn't concentrate on the *quinceañera* as a ritual. Instead, the surrounding events in the narrative are what define the girls' rite of passage. The *quinceañera* festivity becomes merely incidental or symbolic of other things. Both novels share a struggle to navigate through family and cultural allegiances and the challenges of teenage identity in the face of long-standing tradition. In this sense Acosta's treatment of the *quinceañera* bears comparison with the Glatzer and Westmoreland film to be discussed later, rather than with Alvarez's stories of consumption and excess. In *Damas, Dramas and Ana Ruiz* the story focuses on a university administrator, Ana Ruiz, who has recently been left by her husband, Esteban, for another woman. Her daughter, Carmen, is nearing her fifteenth birthday and is ambivalent about having a party. Ana feels that it might be a way of cementing what has become a difficult relationship, as Carmen, unfairly, blames Ana for the separation. The narrative is concerned with Ana's struggle to regain her confidence after the break-up, her quest to find herself after losing a man who had been her childhood sweetheart, her negotiation with her extended family's judgmental attitude toward the marital problems, and the possibility of a new romantic relationship with Carlos Montalvo, a visiting Mexican artist.

By shifting the emphasis from daughter to mother, and giving the party so little space in the novel (a mere two pages), Acosta is re-signifying the event and exploring the multiple reasons individuals have for celebrating the *quinceañera*. It is a popular novel that easily fits into Emily Hind's "boob lit" (2010, 55) category, which allows for the protagonist to have a (self-) conscious, sense of her sexuality as she enjoys watching Montalvo at work, as well as being concerned with her role in the home. As Hind puts it, she is a protagonist "with problematised breasts and familiar struggles with . . . domestic roles" (2010, 55). There is reassurance for the reader, akin to that found in women's magazines, that "in direct contradiction to the advertising images inevitably featured in and around these texts, that men love women's 'real', imperfect, aging, and overweight bodies" (Hind 2010, 54). This is the *quinceañera* story told from the mother's perspective. It does not celebrate the perfect realization of a traditional ritual but rather captures the buildup to a modest version, compromised by the complications of what is represented as a non-traditional, but contemporary scenario.

As with *Damas, Dramas and Ana Ruiz*, the second *Quinceañera* Club novel, *Sisters, Strangers and Starting Over*, deals with an atypical scenario. It is told from the point of view of Beatriz, who takes in her sister's daughter, Celeste, after her mother is murdered. Again, the focus is on the *quinceañera* as a normalizing practice to facilitate the therapeutic recovery of a teenager who has recently experienced trauma. Beatriz is married to Irish-American Larry Milligan, with the result that their status as a mixed-race couple adds a further complicating factor into the narrative. Again, because the narrative is more concerned with the mother's reconciliation with her past and culture, while the *quinceañera* has considerable meaning for both Celeste and Beatriz, the actual event occupies little space in the novel in favour of bringing the reader's attention to the femicide in Juárez. Acosta's popular novels are attempts at creating a new and more heterogeneous version of the *quinceañera* narrative, with more in common with *Echo Park, L.A.* than with Alvarez's work.

Interestingly, Acosta's decision to write these novels was in reaction to a call for authors on this theme, and it is clear that she is not writing from experience. In an interview she has described her source of inspiration for writing these novels:

> I responded to a call from a book packager—Jacob Packaged Goods. They proposed an idea for a book about *quinceañeras*, but unlike most of the other books out there this one would focus on mothers, not just daughters. I admit I didn't have a lot of personal experience with the ceremonies at the time. In fact I didn't actually attend my first quince until I was researching the book. But I liked the idea, and once I learned a little more about the project, I signed on to write the first two books in the *Quinceañera* Club series. (Calvani 2009, n.p.)

Ostensibly, as a daughter of a Texan mother and a Mexican father, her credentials would appear to be cultural, when, in fact, her knowledge of the ritual is not as deep as Glatzer, Westmoreland, or Alvarez.[9] Acosta cites Alvarez as a source, and Alvarez, in turn, is quoted on the cover praising Acosta's book. With the support of a well-known publishing house, this book is accompanied by many of the meta-textual features that marketing departments employ in order to sell books: a bilingual set of questions for your book club; an extract of the next novel at the back; the author's Facebook and Twitter details; author book readings; and so on. This is a complex interrelationship between market, culture, and author that means that the *quinceañera* phenomenon can be employed by multiple authors and filmmakers that have no obvious cultural ownership over the material and, more curiously except in teen novels, simultaneously is an event barely touched upon by Chicanas/os or Mexicans outside of academia.

Another film, also made by non-Mexicans/Chicanas/os, is *Echo Park, L.A.* (Richard Glatzer and Wash Westmoreland, 2005). On its U.S. release this film was originally entitled *Quinceañera,* but to avoid confusion with the earlier Crevenna film, I am using its European title, which posits the neighbourhood, rather than the less familiar event, as the more marketable option. In this version of the *quinceañera* story, Mexico and the border region loom large, as do class issues of the gentrification of the formerly, predominantly Latino Echo Park neighbourhood. This time the *quince* represents a symbolic connection with Mexico as imagined by two non-Latinos. Unlike Alvarez, Glatzer and Westmoreland see the ritual as belonging to a specific and narrowly defined community, rather than being a pan-Latina practice. The narrative is, therefore, an account of permanent migration and of a need to keep the culture and traditions of the originating country alive.

Echo Park, L.A. tells the story of Magdalena (Emily Rios), a fourteen-year old girl planning her *quinceañera*. In the midst of worries, such as fretting over the possibility of convincing her minister father that, like Eileen (Alicia Sixtos) her older cousin, she should be allowed to rent a Hummer limousine for the day, she discovers that she is pregnant. As a result, she is kicked out of home and goes to live with her great-uncle Tomás (Chalo González) and her cousin Carlos (Jesse García), who has also been forced to leave home because he is gay. The household becomes an alternative family unit, which evolves from one originally connected through blood ties into a family of choice. Carlos is first signaled as a *cholo,* that is, a probable gang member, with the area code 213 tattooed on his neck and *travieso* [bad boy] on his stomach, who evolves from a dope-smoking underemployed young man to a responsible adult.[10] By the end of the narrative he proposes taking on parental roles and responsibilities to young Magdalena's child to ensure that she can continue in education. The film is both a gay coming-of-age story, centering around Carlos' first gay relationship with one of his uncle's new landlords who live upstairs from them, and a teen pregnancy film similar to that of the more recent *Juno* (Jason Reitman, 2007). What is interesting to the representation of the *quinceañera* is the relationship between the characters and Mexico. It is represented as a distant space, tinged with nostalgia, associated with Tomás's sepia photographs and stories, and an inherited cultural weight that determines social practices and family relationships.

The film was co-written and directed by Wash Westmoreland and Richard Glatzer. Westmoreland, who is from Leeds, England, has worked in the United States previously making post-modern adult films. Glatzer is a former producer and consultant on *America's Next Top Model*. In the DVD extra from the LA Film Festival, both explain that the story originated in a personal experience of being invited by neighbours to be photographers at a *quinceañera* party. The exotic otherness of this experience is underlined in a comment: "[W]e were dazzled by everything we saw that day" (LA Film Festival DVD extra). This impelled them to write the story and create the film. The opening sequence of the film, which shows Eileen's *quinceañera,* lays the ground for the uninitiated to the festivities and rituals involved, and is implicitly directed at an audience unfamiliar with the traditions. Eileen's *quince* has both respect for tradition (religious service, dress, chambelán, court, etc.) and her own negotiation of these (Hummer limo with a pole that she and her court dance around, raucous dancing after the waltzes are over, and so on). This sequence both draws attention to the key markers of the event and its cultural specificity as well as inviting comparisons to other similar displays of teenage celebration familiar from *My Super Sweet Sixteen*.

Tomás is a key character, who is pivotal to both of these aspects of cultural understanding. At 83 he has been witness to many changes on both sides of the border and has lived in the same rented apartment for 28 years. He has worked at many different trades and is now well-known in the neighbourhood as a seller of the sweet chocolate-based Mexican drink *champurrado*. He is the carrier of family histories, many of which he tells to Carlos and Magdalena. His house, with its family tree of photographs on the wall, and other niches and spaces laden with trinkets, artifacts, and religious iconography, is a dynamic folk museum that sharply contrasts with others' uncluttered homes. This practice is integral to the sojourner's relationship with the originating country. According to Rubén Hernández-León:

> [B]ecause individuals conduct social interactions through objects and artifacts . . . sending goods (even if they were of little monetary value) allowed persons living and working in one place to assert a symbolic presence in another while claiming participation in the daily lives of distant family members. (2008, 173)

The distance that Tomás experiences is one of time more than geography. Mexico is becoming part of a folkloric past, made plastic in these objects, whose presence in Echo Park is diminishing through the gentrification of the area, evident in both the narrative and the mise en scène. While the objects in Tomás' house may create a visual connection with Mexico, when he dies they are packed away and their power and that tie look likely to be loosened. These objects have a similar connection to Mexico as that of the *quinceañera* party. Both are represented as transient and superficial connections to the past, whose value is dwindling.

Tomás is a figure who has some authority amongst his extended family as an arbiter. This is signaled early in the film when he intervenes between Carlos and bouncers at Carlos' sister's *quinceañera* party, which Carlos had gate-crashed, and is reinforced later when Tomás tries to negotiate with Magdalena's father. That Tomás is not always powerful in this role is more than just a useful plot device. His power is diminished over the course of the film, just as the neighborhood appears to become de-Mexicanised through a process of gentrification.

Through the character of Tomás and his relationship to the younger generation the connection with Mexico is played out. They show more interest in Mexico and the past than their parents, whose relationship with their *patria* is more fraught. For Silvia (Carmen Aguirre), Carlos's mother, Mexico is the old country from which they escaped to come to the land of opportunity. She is shown to be a ruthless and ambitious social climber. In contrast, Magdalena's parents, and in particular her dad, Ernesto (Jesus Castano Chima), are hidebound by the conservative and traditional elements of Mexican culture. As second-generation migrants, Magdalena and Carlos are free of the burden of the conflicted relationship of the new arrivals and can negotiate more freely what aspects of both cultures they want to take on board.

Tomás is the social entrepreneur signaled in Hernández-León's text, which is the source of his authority. He was the first to come over and establish a "kinship network" (2008, 188) between the two countries and facilitated the migration of the extended family. This is an extended family that now has stronger ties to the United States than Mexico. Their legal status is never under question; instead, they are represented as belonging to the melting pot, with a long history in Echo Park and a firmly established relationship with the adopted country. Within this framework, Mexico is the past and the United States is the present and future. Returning to Mexico is not presented as an option. These are not the sojourners described by Hernández-León as typical of recent migrants; they are part of a firmly established migrant community. Even Tomás, who has the strongest ties with Mexico, does not see return as an option. He is the last surviving member of a family of 22; with him the connection dies. In its place is the Hummer limousine, the break with the traditional family unit toward a family of choice, and a brave new future, which even the conservative Ernesto embraces. This is underlined in Ernesto's embrace with Magdalena, and his decision to minister to his pregnant daughter's *quinceañera* celebration at the end of the film. This neat, somewhat resolved fairy-tale ending shows that the forces of progress win over tradition and conservatism, which, in turn, are co-terminous.

Not only do the domestic spaces and the characters play out the relationship with Mexico, so too do the outside spaces. There is a near-anthropological intention to create an authentic vision of Echo Park as a largely Hispanic neighbourhood gradually being gentrified. Wide and tracking shots show that the names of places, trendy cafés located beside Mexican food stands, and Spanish-named shops are gradually being replaced by English-named ones, and so on. There are repeated references by Anglo characters in the film to the area as a "hot property" development location. In addition, there are issues on the production side that denote this as a film lamenting the loss of Mexican-ness among this community and location.

Conscious of their distance from their subjects, the filmmakers were keen to be seen to have been faithful chroniclers of a tradition. The director of photography, Eric Steelberg, aspired to documentary-like authenticity in the mise en scène. He says that he decided to include "nothing that would cover up or take away". In addition, the interviews with cast and crew on the DVD extras underline this attempt at authenticity, and the biographical details given determine the individual's proximity or other-wise to Latina/o culture. The credentials of others are put forward. For example, Mexican-born Chelo González (Tomás) was a fixer and actor on Hollywood films set in Mexico such as Sam Peckinpah's *Wild Bunch* (1969). Jesse García (Carlos) distances himself from the Echo Park loca-tion, describing himself as a Wyoming-born boy of a religious family with no association with gang culture. Emily Rios (Magdalena) is a Los Angeles-born Jehovah Witness whose religion doesn't allow *quinceañera* parties. J. R. Cruz (Herman, Magdalena's boyfriend) was brought up by his grandparents in the projects and had many uncles who were gang mem-bers. These autobiographical details indicate a realisation that part of the marketing and packaging of the film would necessitate some defensive action by the filmmakers, as their own backgrounds and race could come under attack for not having any close tie to the subject of the film. It also has echoes in Alvarez's positioning of herself as having an insider's per-spective on what she emphasises is a Latina celebration.

The directors' relationship to Mexicans and Mexican Americans is underlined as neighbourly (reiterated through mention in the commentary of many extras being from the area), and talk about themselves as benign and bemused spectators of another communities' customs and practices. However, their intention is not to create a study of otherness. For example, certain universality is supplied in the commentary of the funeral oration delivered by Carlos over Tomás' grave. It was inspired by Westmoreland's English great-uncle, Thomas, whose role in his upbringing was similar to that of Tomás in Carlos' life. This suggests that Tomás, while firmly located as a migrant Mexican, has characteristics that shift him to another particu-larity.[11] In this way, attention is drawn to difference and sameness between individuals and cultures.

Another Echo Park film, which came under considerable fire, is a film that dealt with female Mexican American gang members, yet was written and directed by Allison Anders, a White Echo Park resident, like Westmoreland

and Glatzer. According to Susan Dever, Anders as creator of *Mi vida loca* (1993) "is a kind of participant ethnographer . . . trying to figure out how to relate to her 'subjects' and convey their (fictionalized) stories to her various potential audience without losing a lot in the translation" (2003, 126). The DVD commentary for *Echo Park, L.A.* attests to this same desire in Westmoreland and Glatzer. Theirs is an attempt at authenticity that is reinforced through underlining the proximity of neighbourliness and their taking on an issue of insider concern: the gradual erosion of a Latina/o community through the very gentrification that the directors are personally implicated in. This is epitomised through the use of their own home as a set for that of the newly arrived gay couple in the film. Their discomfort at being outsiders to the Mexican American community is an underlining tension that does not need to be resolved, but is interestingly confronted head on in the DVD extras by individuals who are obviously aware of possible criticism and are eager to head them off.

Reconciliation in the film happens at Magdalena's *quinceañera*. A relatively modest affair, with the ceremony conducted by her father, it is the moment when Magdalena and her father publicly display their private truce. In addition, it is the enactment of what could be read as an alternative wedding ceremony as Carlos has declared that he will take responsibility for his cousin's unborn child. This commitment seals their pact and the formation of their family of choice, and provides both a fairy-tale, happy-ever-after ending and a radical reconfiguration of the traditional patriarchal family structure. The *quinceañera* functions to celebrate difference and reconcile the conservative values of Magdalena's father with the young people's decision to re-define the family.

The *quinceañera* narrative has evolved from the conservative melodrama of Crevenna's 1950s film through to the Los Angeles-based exploration of teen sexuality in *Echo Park, L.A.* However, there still is a meta-narrative that has a vested interest in maintaining the status quo, as represented in Alvarez and Acosta. As Dávalos concludes in her study of the *quinceañera* in Chicago:

> The discourse and practice of the *quinceañera* encourages us to examine the paradoxical and ambiguous nature of "tradition." The discourse and practice suggest that what we intend as "cultural" is fluid, slippery, contradictory, spontaneous, and chaotic. (2003, 158)

Unlike the codifying inscription of the *quinceañera* indulged in by Alvarez, the tentative version by Glatzer and Westmoreland, with its questioning of the difficulties implicit in change, and the exploratory and contestatory versions put forward by Acosta are more desirable, acting to challenge the idea of a stultifying singular cultural practice and propose it as flux.

The selection of novels under consideration is not exhaustive. However, much recent fiction has been primarily aimed at children or at teen readers.

These merit future study as they have their own particularities and patterns, which this present chapter doesn't have the space to consider.

Stavans has described the significance of the ritual of the *quinceañera:*

> While it is celebrated in corners of the Spanish-speaking world, it has become an important social occasion in the Latino community in the United States especially among Mexicans, Salvadoreans, Dominicans, Puerto Ricans, and Cubans. It is a rite of passage whereby a girl, when turning fifteen years of age, is acknowledged as a full-fledged member of the community. (2010, ix)

This recalls and turns into a positive Alvarez's critique of wealthy Dominicans' practice of the *quinceañera* as inauthentic. The emphasis on the *quince* as the bearer of the community rituals and traditions, and as representative of the implicit conservatism of these, is a considerable weight on her shoulders. There is this consistent thread throughout all of the narratives that the *quince,* who is celebrating what is a personal milestone, sits uncomfortably between the burden of tradition and the pressures of consumer culture, between the rites and rituals inherited (or borrowed) from the past and the aspirational image of the perfect celebration as shown on MTV's *My Super Sweet Sixteen.* The *quinceañera* may fall primarily under the purview of Chicana/o Studies, yet the literary and filmic representations reveal that it is a compelling event in which to explore Mexican, Latina, Mexican American, and Chicana identity.

NOTES

1. *MTVs My Super Sweet Sixteen* is a reality TV show featuring elaborate birthday celebrations, and has become shorthand for parental indulgence and teenage excess. The children on display are greedy, wealthy, and spoilt. This nightmare vision of contemporary coming of age has some parallels with how the *quinceañera* celebrations are portrayed in literature and film.
2. Cantú also refutes claims that it has its origins in indigenous or pre-Colombian traditions (2002, 21). The suggestion that it is an ancient Aztec tradition appears in Lankford (1994, 12) as well as several of the cited websites; many of these sources also detail the protocol and rituals of the festivity.
3. Cantú (2002) discusses the significance of the cultural icons and rituals.
4. I shall refer to the girl celebrating her *quinceañera* as a *quince.* There are others, such as Cantú, who refer to her as an "honoree" (2002, 18).
5. Whilst this is not an exhaustive look at the representation of the *quinceañera,* relatively little has been written or made about the ritual. There is a Mexican/Cuban soap opera *Quinceañera* (1987) remade as *Primer amor . . . a mil por hora* (2000), as well as a rumoured further remake planned by Televisa in 2010, *Mis X . . . sueña princesa.* There are also teen books, such as *Estrella's Quinceañera* by Malin Alegría (Simon and Schuster, 2006); and books and television programmes for children, such as the aforementioned *Dora the Explorer* episode.

6. For more on Van Gennep and the significance of the "wedding without a husband", see Napolitano (2010, 67–69).
7. For more on the diversity of practices and its significance, see Dávalos (2003, 153–56).
8. Throughout the book Alvarez shortens *quinceañera* to 'Q'.
9. She was born in Lincoln, Nebraska and, in an interview has said, "I get my *Tejana* creds from my mother, who was raised in deep South Texas. My father is Mexicano (San Luis Potosi—ajua! That's Mexican for 'Woo-Hoo!'). I've been living in Austin, Texas, since 1985 or so" (Calvani 2009, n.p.).
10. Music has a further role in introducing characters and establishing them in the narrative. McNelis discusses how particular musical choices are associated with individual characters in this film and "creates and re-enforces ethnically coded ideas of tradition and change" (2010, 174).
11. The film is dedicated to this uncle, Thomas Patterson.

WORKS CITED

Acosta, B. *Damas, Dramas, and Ana Ruiz.* New York: Grand Central, 2009.
———. *Sisters, Strangers, and Starting Over.* New York: Grand Central, 2010.
"Alex." Episode 306 MTV. *My Super Sweet Sixteen,* aired April 30, 2010. http://www.mtv.co.uk/shows/my-super-sweet-16/episode/episode-306-alex. Accessed March 3, 2013.
Alomar, L., and M. Zwolinski. "*Quinceañera*: A Celebration of Latina Womanhood." In *Voices: The Journal of New York Folklore* 28 (Fall-Winter, 2002). http://www.nyfolklore.org/pubs/voic28–3-4/onair.html. Accessed March 16, 2009.
Alvarez, J. *Once Upon a Quinceañera: Coming of Age in the USA.* New York: Plume Book/Penguin, 2007.
Calvani, M. "Interview with Belinda Acosta, author of Damas, Dramas, and Ana Ruiz". *Examiner,* July 28, 2009. http://www.examiner.com/latino-books-in-national/interview-with-belinda-acosta-author-of-damas-dramas-and-ana-ruiz. Accessed October 4, 2010.
Cantú, N.E. "Chicana Life-Cycle Rituals." In *Chicana Traditions: Continuity and Change,* edited by Norma E. Cantú and Olga Nájera-Ramírez. Urbana: University of Illinois, 2002.
Daisy. La Quinceañera, It's a Party, Dora the Explorer. Nick Jr. 2007. DVD.
Dávalos, K.M. "*La Quinceañera*: Making Gender and Ethnic Identities." In *Velvet Barrios: Popular Cultures and Chicana/o Sexualities* (141–162), edited by Alicia Gaspar de Alba. New York: Palgrave Macmillan, 2003.
Dever, S. *Celluloid Nationalism and Other Melodramas: From Post-Revolutionary Mexico to fin de siglo Mexamérica.* New York: State University of New York Press, 2003.
Echo Park, L.A./Quinceañera. Directed by Richard Glatzer and Wash Westmoreland. Cinetic Media & Kitchen Sink Entertainment LLC. 2005. DVD.
Hernández-León, R. *Metropolitan Migrants: The Migration of Urban Mexicans to the United States.* Berkeley: University of California Press, 2008.
Hind, E. "Six Authors on the Conservative Side of the *Boom Femenino,* 1985–2003: Boullosa, Esquivel, Loaeza, Mastretta, Nissán, Sefchovich." In *The Boom Femenino in Mexico: Reading Contemporary Women's Writing* (48–72), edited by N. Finnegan and J.E. Lavery. Newcastle: Cambridge Scholars, 2010.
Juno. Directed by Jason Reitman. Fox Searchlight Pictures & Mandate Pictures, 2007. DVD.

Lankford, M. D. *Quinceañera: A Latina's Journey to Womanhood*. Brookfield, CT: Millbrook Press, 1994.

Marling, K. A. "*Quinceañera* Debutante: Rites and Regalia of American Debdom." In *Quinceañera*, edited by Ilan Stavans. Santa Barbara: Greenwood, 2010.

McNelis, T. R. *Popmusic, Identity, and Musical Agency in U.S. Youth Films*. PhD dissertation, University of Liverpool, 2010.

Misquince. http://www.misquincemag.com. Accessed October 7, 2010.

Mi vida loca. Directed by Allison Anders. Channel Four Films & Cineville, 1993. VHS.

Napolitano, V. "Becoming a *Mujercita*: Rituals, Fiestas, and Religious Discourses." In *Quinceañera*, edited by Ilan Stavans. Santa Barbara: Greenwood, 2010.

Quinceañera. Directed by Alfredo B. Crevenna. Cinematografía Latinoamericana, 1956. DVD.

Quinceanera. "Do you Prefer a Party or to Travel?" http://www.quinceanera .com/index.php/lang-es/quinceanera-blog/Do-you-prefer-Party-or-Travel-.html. Accessed March 9, 2009.

Quinceanera Party. "How to Have a New Millennium Quinceañera Celebration." http://www.quinceaneraparty.com/. Accessed October 7, 2010.

Stavans, I. *Quinceañera*. Santa Barbara: Greenwood, 2010.

The Wild Bunch. Directed by Sam Peckinpah. Warner Brothers/Seven Arts, 1969. DVD.

5   American Studies in Russia
Learning Chicana/o Literature in Chita (Siberia)

Tatiana Voronchenko

The frontier character of U.S. culture and the multicultural discourse of recent years mean that the field of American Studies should no longer be looked at purely from within, but from a global context. Russian interest in the United States is not a recent phenomenon. During the Cold War, institutes of American Studies existed in Soviet Russia, among them the prominent Institute of America and Canada in Moscow headed by Professor George Arbatov. As is to be expected, at this time the teaching of North American literature and culture was influenced to a great extent by political imperatives and depended on the character of mutual relationships between East and West. Improvements in political relations after the fall of the Iron Curtain coincided with the foundation of the Centers for American Studies in Siberian universities in such cities as Tomsk, Novosibirsk, and Chita.

I shall consider just one of these, Chita, and the School for Multiculturalism (which I head at Zabaikalsky State University), whose aim is to establish literary and sociological parallels between Siberia and the United States. My book *На перекрестке миров: мексикано-американский феномен в литературе США* [*On the Crossroads of the World: The Mexican-American Phenomenon in American Literature*, 1998], which focused on the origin(s) and main tendencies of Chicana/o literature, was the first book on Chicana/o literature in Russia. It appeared in Trans-Baikal Siberia about ten years after the renowned book by Marcienne Rocard, *The Children of the Sun* (1989), was published in France, indicating that interest in Chicana/o Studies in Russia has been later than elsewhere in Europe, but is no less enthusiastic for that.

This chapter will present a Russian-Siberian view of Chicana/o literature, which is a constituent part of U.S. literature but has its own trajectory, presents its own perspective, and provides access to the creative production of a significant group. This chapter compares Chicana/o literature to similar cultural phenomena in Russia, particularly identifying those aspects that are of special interest for Russian students because of these commonalities. Being a Russian-Siberian, I have always felt that Russia has special reasons to feel close to the American continent and its cultures. In his forward to the

Russian edition of the famous book of poems *Leaves of Grass—A Letter to Russia* (1881), the great poet Walt Whitman wrote:

> You Russians and we Americans! Our countries so distant, so unlike at first glance, such a difference in social and political conditions, and our respective methods of moral and practical development the last hundred years;—and yet in certain features, and vastest ones, so resembling each other. (Whitman 1982, 1049)

The recognition of this commonality was to continue in the writings of Peterim Sorokin, then professor of sociology at Harvard University, in his book *Russia and America* (1944), which pointed out that some supposedly basic differences between Russia and the United States have been exaggerated. It was his contention that both countries have similar geographical and geopolitical conditions that greatly influence their citizens, and that they are characterized by *unity in diversity* and multiculturalism (Sorokin 1944, 33). This is particularly evident in the cultural production of the southern border region of the United States and is a salient feature of the cultural life of Russia, especially in Siberia.

The concept of multiculturalism helps us considerably to change the traditional understanding of the historical and literary process in the United States. It seems symbolic that Whitman not only acknowledged what Russia and the United States shared, but also paid attention to the role of what he called "The Spanish Element of our Nationality" in the eponymous letter that was sent to citizens of Santa Fe on the 333rd anniversary of its founding. He wrote:

> As to the Spanish stock of our Southwest, it is certain to me that we do not begin to appreciate the splendor and sterling value of its race elements. Who knows but that element, like the course of some subterranean river, dipping invisibly for a hundred or two years, is now to emerge in broadest flow and permanent action? (Whitman 1968, 403).

For the contemporary reader, Whitman's message greatly stimulates the interest of international audiences in Chicana/o literature, as does Mexican philosopher José Vasconcelos's *La raza cósmica* [*The Cosmic Race*] (1925), where the author articulated the idea of *mestizaje* and proposed the conceptualization of a new race. He stressed that it would result in "the creation of a new race fashioned out of the treasures of all the previous ones: the final race, the cosmic race" (1997, 40).

The demographic and cultural situation in Trans-Baikal Siberia is not too different from that of the American Southwest in terms of *mestizaje*. Geographically, there is the Russian border with Mongolia and China, which exists as a space of multiple instances of ethnic and cultural exchange.

Thus, Chicana/o literature and search for identity both speak to the Siberian population of a situation that they know, as, like Chicana/os, many Siberians are of mixed blood. The Caucasoid and Mongoloid races meet at Siberia's borders. There is a special term in Trans-Baikal Siberia, Guran, which means a fourth-generation person of mixed blood. Guran people are a mixture of Russians, who came to this area in the seventeenth century, and native Siberians (Evenks), Buryat-Mongol, and Chinese. Gurans can be figuratively called the Chicana/os of Siberia. Russian and Asian people met at the Siberian borderland to begin a process of *mestizaje*.

Gloria Anzaldúa writes in her book *Borderlands/La Frontera: The New Mestiza* (1987): "Our Spanish, Indian and *mestizo* ancestors explored and settled parts of the American Southwest as early as the 16th century" (1999, 27), thus establishing the historical entitlement to these territories. To paraphrase Anzaldúa, we can say that our Russian, Evenk, Mongolian, and *mestizo* ancestors explored and settled parts of the Siberian Southeast as early as the seventeenth century. There are evident similarities between both cultures. The folklore of our cultures also includes some similar figures, such as the Chicano bogeyman El Kookooee, whom Russians know as Babayka.

Like Chicana/os, Siberian ethnic minority writers are bicultural and bilingual. Their creativity is marked by the influence of the Russian environment and an ancestral consciousness. Border cultures, like Mexican American culture, are hybrid. To describe this, I could take an amusing but precise metaphor from Anzaldúa, which holds that the cultural encounter is like putting "chili into borscht" (borscht is a vegetable soup made with beetroot), an apparent incongruity that nonetheless has a lively flavor. Chicana/o literature, thus, in some senses, speaks to the Siberian population about concepts and ideas that they are already familiar with.

There are further possible historic links between the two areas. There is a widespread hypothesis that Native Americans came first to the American Continent from Siberia through Alaska. On the map showing the migration route as revealed in verses from the "Wallam Olum: The Oldest Native North American History," translated and annotated by McCutchen (1995), the initial point of migration is the area of North China and Trans-Baikal Siberia. There are potentially foundational connections between the two territories and peoples. For this reason, Russian students react very emotionally to some passages from Rudolfo Anaya's *Chicano in China* (1986), which seeks to establish ties between Chicana/o and Asian cultures. Anaya positions his identities among their ethnic and geographic origins:

> First I am a native son of the Mexican community of the U.S., and I proudly identify myself with that community, and, second, as a Chicano, I also take pride in that part of me that is a Native American. . . . I go there to find understanding of that other half of my nature. . . . I seek the history and thought of Americas because by understanding that past I understand better my present. That was an ancient Asian who settled

in North China and then, thousands of years ago, wandered over the Bering Strait into Americas. What does he communicate to us across the millennium time? (1986, 202)

Anaya, like many Chicana/o and Siberian writers, seems to present the landscape as alive, as speaking and exerting a special influence upon the people. He also recognizes the plurality of his background, which fosters connections with others, including my students in Russia.

This chapter aims to illuminate the main approaches and trends of Chicana/o literature, focusing on the Chicano Literary Renaissance, which are of special interest to Russian readers. I concentrate on the creativity of some renowned Chicana/o writers, such as Anaya, Richard Rodriguez, Sandra Cisneros, and Anzaldúa, who belong to different time periods and literary trends and whose creativity is always thought-provoking. Consequently, they help Russian Siberian people to better understand the multicultural reality of the modern world.

After the annexation of a considerable part of Mexican border territory from Brownsville, Texas, along the Gulf of Mexico up to Tijuana on the Pacific, the Spanish-speaking citizens of the United States were incorporated into the country as a result of the Mexican-American War (1846–1848). Many of these Mexican Americans traced their origins to the Spanish conquistadors. Gradually, as Chicana/o identity evolved into a political and cultural movement, others, happy to identify with an indigenous past, saw their roots in Aztec and Mayan culture. According to Rocard: "To Chicanos the Southwest forever remained 'Chicanolandia,' where their ancestors had once lived in peace" (1989, 219). Chicana/os often call themselves Aztecas del Norte [Aztecs of the North], referring to an ancient legend, which holds that their maternal ancestors emerged on the Earth at this place in the north and started their way to the south, to Mexico.

As a consequence of this idea of a border that moved over the population and led to their integration into a new political geography, there are particularities to the Mexican American experience that were not studied until the 1970s, when Luis Valdez, the first Chicano playwright and founder of El Teatro Campesino, initiated significant research into the issues concerning the U.S. Spanish-speaking population. Writing in 1970, he declared that:

There are years and years of discoveries we have to make of our people. . . . There is no textbook of the history of *La Raza*. Yet the history of the Mexican in this country is four hundred years old. We know we pre-date the landing of the Pilgrims and the American Revolution. But beyond that? What really happened? (Steiner 1970, 218)

This was to prove to be a powerful and influential call to others to begin to write and talk about what it means to be a Mexican American.

The recovery of a past took place in the United States against a difficult backdrop. As Russian scholar Alexander Vaschenko notes: "Anglo-Americans' general contemptuous attitude to any 'non-white' ethnic culture led to the emergence and development of isolating stereotypes" (1983, 223). For example, U.S. theaters of the nineteenth century commonly employed negative stereotypes of Native Americans and Black people. Likewise, the Mexican American has long been encumbered with facile and dubious stereotypes. When Chicana/o literature was first established in the 1960s, its authors had to work hard to counter these racist stereotypes.

THE IMAGE OF MEXICAN AMERICAN DEVELOPMENT

Up to the second half of the twentieth century, the North American novel scarcely acknowledged Mexican American writers. Some names are noted in literary criticism: Manuel M. Salazar, Eusebio Chakon, Felipe Maximiliano Chakon, Miguel Otero, and Andrew Garcia, whose *Tough Trip through Paradise, 1878–1879* was published in 1967. Otero, the governor of New Mexico (1897–1906), and his memoirs *My Life on the Frontier 1865–1882* achieved some fame. In the two-volume novel, Otero narrates his childhood and youth in Kansas, Colorado, and New Mexico. As Charles Tatum remarks, Otero's account of his years in boarding school under the tutelage of a stern schoolmaster reminds us of *Oliver Twist* (1838) by Charles Dickens (1982, 31). It is necessary to note, nevertheless, that *My Life on the Frontier 1865–1882* is interesting not so much from the point of view of the evolution of Chicana/o prose but because of its image of Mexican American development. The literary image of the Mexican American originates in narratives by Anglo-American authors of the second half of the nineteenth century and, together with the writings of these authors, begins to actively resist the stereotypes prevalent in mass consciousness. Works by Mexican American authors in the late nineteenth century anticipate the appearance of Chicana/o literature in the period from 1950 to the1960s and can be defined as Chicana/o pre-literature.

The evolution of the image of the Mexican American in U.S. literature up to the 1950s is caused by changes in the political life of the country, as authors such as George Emery, Francis Bret Harte, Jack London, Hamlin Harland, Stephen Crane, Henry Miller, John Steinbeck, and Ray Bradbury express their understanding of the Mexican American's nature. The most significant author among this selection of Anglo-American writers who creates a bright multi-featured image of the Mexican American is Steinbeck, who depicts Mexican American characters in *Tortilla Flat* (1935), *Flight* (1938), *The Wayward Bus* (1947), and in his book of travel sketches *Travels with Charley: In Search of America* (1962). Steinbeck shows the unity of the North American, the native of the Southwest, with Mexican Americans, who see him as a brother and describe him as one of their own (2007, 900 and 994).

Unlike any other group of immigrants, Mexican Americans have been in the United States for 450 years or longer when one considers their indigenous origins. Emerging at the crossroads of Mexican and Anglo-American cultural traditions, Chicana/o literature has proved that it has its own system of key themes, images, symbols, and its own trajectory of development, while belonging, academically, to U.S. literature. Postwar Chicana/o literature became visible at the end of the 1950s with the publication of the novel *Pocho* by José Antonio Villarreal (1959) and of Richard Vasquez's *Chicano* (1971). Chicana/o writers of that period paid more attention to content than to artistic form. Rodolfo "Corky" González's epic poem "*Yo soy Joaquín*" ("I am Joaquin," 1967) was a popular manifesto of the first stage of the Chicano Movement, declaring the cultural awakening of Mexican Americans (Orleck and Hazirjian 2011, 341).

The Chicana/o Literary Renaissance, which started in 1965 and flourished in the 1970s, marks the achievement of harmony between the reflection on social problems and the perfection of the literary form, through fiction by Anaya, Tomás Rivera, Rolando Hinojosa, and Miguel Méndez; poetry by Alurista, Ricardo Sánchez, and Omar Salinas; "mitos" ["myths"] by Valdez; and drama by Carlos Morton, Estella Portillo Trambley, and others.

The Chicana/o authors of this period raise the problem of identity and call for a return to their roots. One of the most remarkable features of the Chicana/o Literary Renaissance is the theme of la Raza and *La raza cósmica*, which is explored frequently in the poetry of Ricardo Sánchez, Alurista, and others. Many Chicana/o authors try to emphasize the philosophical aspect of the problem of the movement of civilizations; their characters feel they are at the crossroads of Western and Eastern civilizations. In the search for their roots, they often refer to the myth of Aztlán, which contains the image of the ancestral motherland. They focus on the many-sided notion of Aztlán as a historical, geographical, and spiritual entity in works such as *The Heart of Aztlán* (1988) by Anaya, *Peregrinos de Aztlán* (1991) by Méndez, and *Floricanto en Aztlán* (1971) by Alurista. The most essential traits of the Chicana/o Literary Renaissance resemble the Mexican Renaissance of the 1920s and 1930s. The Mexican Renaissance is characterized by Indian motifs, which are reflected in works of art such as the murals and paintings by David Alfaro Siqueiros, Diego Rivera, and José Clemente Orozco, and in literature, such as Alfonso Reyes's poetry.

Parallels can be found between Mexico and Russia when Leopoldo Zea states that it is difficult to understand the origin of both Mexican and Russian national identity (Zea and Oliver 1992, 117). We can find this idea in the verse by famous Russian poet Feodor Tyutchev, which was written in 1866, and in the novel by Carlos Fuentes, *La región más transparente* [*Where the Air is Clear*] (1958), where the authors were trying to decipher the historic riddles of their respective countries:

> Умом Россию не понять,
> Аршином общим не измерить:
> У ней особенная стать, –
> В Россию можно только верить. (Тютчев 1913, 468)

[Russia is understood not by the mind,
Nor by a common rule.
She has a special stature of her own:
In Russia one can only believe.]

This resonates with an intelligent reflection on Mexican identity by Fuentes' hero Zamakona, who says: "To explain Mexico! Oh, no! he said to himself . . . Mexico cannot be explained, you can just believe in Mexico, and your belief should be passionate, hopeless and outrageous" (1958, 61–2). Octavio Paz, in his much-cited work *El laberinto de la soledad* [*The Labyrinth of Solitude*] (1950) and later in his essay "Posdata" [*Postdate*] (1956), states that Mexico cannot be understood by the rational mind. He considers that the root of this phenomenon is the indigenous tradition, which is present in all the spheres of Mexican life. This notion of a nebulous, complex place of origin is, therefore, common to both Russian and Mexican writers and was carried forward into the imaginings of the Chicana/o writers.

For the investigation into the most essential renaissance symbols in Mexican American literature and their linguistic representation in literary texts, Russian scholar Yuri Lotman's theories provide a useful framework. He emphasizes that "the symbol never belongs to any synchronic layer of culture; it always permeates culture vertically, coming from the past and going to the future" (Lotman 1992, 191–9). The fact is that the condensation of essential symbols is most conspicuous in Chicana/o Renaissance literature. During such periods of artistic development the correlation of symbols with the cultural context gets enhanced and such symbols are more active in being transformed and transforming the cultural context. The discovery of new human dimensions, the aspiration to synthesize thoughts and feelings, enforces the development of some new literary symbols. So, the key figures and imagery found in different works of Chicana/o writers are those of *la Raza* and *mestizaje,* the sun, and the Virgin of Guadalupe.

The central theme of Chicana/o creative works, their search for identity (self-awareness, identity formation, self-determination), originates in Latin American writers' meditation on the unique character of the historic and ethnic experience of the Continent. This peculiarity was emphasized by Alejo Carpentier, the Cuban writer with Russian roots:

From its very start our history is totally different, as the land of America has become a stage for one of the most sensational encounters of different ethnicities: that was the encounter of the Indian, the Negro and the European . . . All of them were destined to blend with each other. . . . We had been original much earlier than the moment when we recognized originality as our goal. (cited in Kuteyschikova and Ospovat 1976, 234)

Carpentier's comments find echoes in Chicana/o writers' search for identity, where they emphasize the Mexican American's natural pluralism considering that, as Guillermo Fuenfrios states, "[W]ith the possible exception of the Hawaiian, there are no people on earth with a more legitimate claim to universality"(1972, 234). Such ideas inevitably lead their authors to the conclusion that Chicana/os were given a special role: to be a linking element between the South and the North. The philosophic grounds for these ideas are found in Armando B. Rendon's *The Chicano Manifesto* (1972). In the chapter "Americas' Chicano" he speaks of their unifying role and greets them as the citizens of the twenty-first-century Americas. Similarly, the leading poet of the Chicana/o Literary Renaissance, Alurista, compares the unusual ethnic blending to his sarape, "which comes in fantastic colors" (1971, 10).

Literary and journalistic works created during the Chicano Renaissance are marked by a certain degree of the fantastic in Chicanas'/os' self-perception. The key figure found in different works of this period is that of *la Raza*, a special mestizo race, Bronze or Brown. As Chicanas/os see it, literature is the soul of the race, while the term "Bronze" was coined by the writers to characterize the race as a unique fusion. It is noteworthy that several prose writers use the attribute "Brown," among them Oscar Zeta Acosta. The hero of his novel *The Autobiography of a Brown Buffalo* (1972) defines his identity in the following way: "I am neither a Mexican nor an American. I am neither a Catholic nor a Protestant. I am Chicano by ancestry and a Brown Buffalo by choice" (1972, 199).

The theme of *la Raza* is all-permeating. It is generally revealed as a sort of ethnic and cultural brotherhood and a symbol of Latinas'/os' union: "Today I marry La Raza," as Alurista writes in his *Floricanto en Aztlán* (1971, 70). The native land is very often associated with the Mother, a key concept in Russian poetry, or with a beloved woman, such as a wife in Alexander Block's "Oh, my Rus! My wife" (1991, 243).

In Sánchez's poem, "It Is Urgent" (1971), *la Raza* is a cup where a new ethnic amalgam is born. This cup seems much more powerful than the all-American or Soviet so-called melting pots:

WE ARE LA RAZA
The cradle of humanity. (Sedano 1980, 47)

In this poem, Sánchez explores a new "cosmic" layer of the given theme. This follows Rendon's *The Chicano Manifesto* where the emergence of the "Bronze race" heralds the blending of all the races into the "cosmic" race. In his poetry Sánchez presents the image of a Chicano as a new man who will unite all the people of the world. Here, we can trace Whitman's tradition of self-identity, which is closely connected with the person's feeling of solidarity with mankind and with the universe.

To explore the symbol of race, Alurista uses the scope of the universe and suggests an all-embracing symbolic image in his "Poem 10" from *Floricanto en Aztlán*: a "colorful wheel of humanity," which reflects a Chicano spiritual quest: "*la esencia de mi Raza es fundamental basic* / to the chromatic wheel of humanity" (1971, 10). The image of the wheel is quite traditional for many philosophical systems. Following Alurista, Carlos Morton successfully reveals the theme of the race using the same image in his allegorical play "El Jardín" (1974), turning it into the "wheel of racial harmony" (Morton 1974, 37).

It is interesting that in the Russian literature of the first half of the twentieth century, the motifs of the new *mestizo* race are especially seen in the science-fiction genre. One example is the classic communist utopia by Ivan Efremov "Andromeda: A Space-Age Tale" (Иван Ефремов «Туманность Андромеды», 1957), where the cosmonauts flying to a new star represent the traits of all races and different nationalities.

The theme of the sun in the literature of the Chicana/o literary renaissance of the 1970s to 1980s is closely connected with the process of self-revelation and interest in Indian mythology. Originally, the sun motif came from the myths of the Aztecs and the Maya. Worship of the sun personifies the sun in the zenith, which conquers the night with its burning force. This image is ambivalent, however, as Huitzilopochtli possesses power over life and death and is the Father-God of the people, the "spiritual force of the state . . . Huitzilopochtli came to embody the sun" (Boone 1989, 2).

This use of the symbol of the sun is very close to that seen in Russian culture, where there was a strong belief in the power of the sun among ancient Russians before Christianity. In Russian folklore we encounter Dazhbog, the sun god and a kind of chief god, who is somewhat similar to Zeus or the Dagda. Dazhbog travels in a chariot across the sky every day like Helios, bringing justice, prosperity, and sunshine to the world. He is known as the grandfather of the Russian people. Actually, the symbol of the sun (the circle of the sun) is seen on all ancient Russian vessels, temporal rings, ornaments, and spinning wheels. In the Russian epic poem of twelfth century, *The Tale of Igor's Campaign,* Russians are called Dazhbog's (the sun's) grandchildren. More recently, the famous Russian scientist and poet Mikhail Lomonosov wrote:

> Уже прекрасное светило
> Простерло блеск свой по земли,
> И Божия дела открыло:
> Мой дух, с веселием внемли;
> Чудяся ясным толь лучам,
> Представь, каков Зиждитель сам! (Lomonosov 1897, 350).
> [The splendid star of day stretched the blaze
> over the earth
> and revealed God's ongoings.
> We hark to the spirit,
> worship those shining rays,
> Imagine! How great The Creator is!]

In Russian literature, the symbol of the sun is also ambivalent. The sun symbolizes life, truth, and good. It is not only "the symbol of God, heavenly height, true light" (Уткина 2003, n.p.), but at the same time can represent death.

The indigenous idea of the interaction between death and rebirth personified in the image of the sun becomes widespread in literature, especially in poetry. Taking into account the main ideas of the Aztec and Mayan philosophical aesthetic system, Chicana/o Renaissance writers focus on the image of the sun as the chief cosmic symbol.

The image of the Virgin of Guadalupe functions in Chicana/o Renaissance literature as the most significant archetype. As the Virgin appeared as a dark-skinned woman and spoke Nahuatl, she was proclaimed forever the patroness of the indigenous and Mexico. In Alurista's poem "Fruto de bronce" ["Bronze Fruit"] (1971), the appearance of a "Bronze" race is similar to the bearing of Christ to the dark-skinned Virgin. As discussed elsewhere in this volume, many Chicana/o authors, poets, and visual artists make reference to the Virgin of Guadalupe in their work.

The same tendencies are found in prose. In Anaya's *Bless Me, Ultima* (1972), her image is central to the thoughts of young Antonio Marez. Here, the Virgin of Guadalupe symbolizes forgiveness, understanding, and the resolution of cultural conflict. Antonio turns to the Virgin repeatedly when he is frustrated by his failure to find a forgiving god. He proclaims an idea of special trust and intimacy in people's addresses to the Virgin of Guadalupe, their protector and defender: "My mother said the Virgin was the saint of our land, and although there were many other good saints, I loved none as dearly as the Virgin. . . . The Virgin always was full of a quiet, peaceful love" (Anaya 1972, 42).

The Chicana/o Renaissance's image of the Virgin of Guadalupe is interesting in the light of the Mexican-Russian cultural dialogue, because Russia's reverence for the Virgin Mary is second only to Mexico's. In Russia she is referred to as God's Mother. The miracle-working icon is a monument of spiritual greatness in Russia. Russian Orthodox believers have always considered that Russia is a home for God's Mother and the symbol of God's Mother is identified as the symbol of Russia. For instance, the image of God's Mother is one central to women's poetry. According to the Russian poet Zinaida Gippius, the ideal implementation of "womanness" is in the image of God's Mother (Савкина 1995, 155–68). The Russian modernist poet Anna Akhmatova presents the image of a protecting, guarding mother's force, the image of salutary intercession of God's Mother, watching over Russia (Savkina 1995, 155–68). Similarly, male poets have used her as a significant image. The famous Russian poet Mikhail Lermontov sees God's Mother as a protector of a young girl whom we can identify with Russia, and according to the Russian poet Maximilian Voloshin, God's Mother "led Rus through dirt, blood and shame" (Kochneva 2008, 33). Therefore the image of God's Mother employed in Russian literature and the Chicana/o reimagining of the Virgin of Guadalupe are in many ways alike.

In the books written by the authors of the Chicana/o literary renaissance, a mythological perception of the world interacts with modern social and cultural thinking. During this period, Chicana/o works marked by realism can be found alongside fantastic literature using devices common to Latin American magical realist authors. In the 1970s, what Francisco Lomelí called the "Isolated Generation" advances the idea of "a vertical conceptualization" of marginalized social sectors, which is evident in the writings of Alejandro Morales, Ron Arias, and Isabella Ríos (1993, 97). The Chicana voice now becomes distinguishable. Chicana creativity reveals sociological and psychological aspects of the Chicana world in the work of Estella Portillo Trambley, Denise Chávez, Lorna Dee Cervantes, and others.

At the same time a corpus of works called Chicanesca Literature was introduced by Lomelí and Donaldo W. Urioste in 1976 in the work *Chicano Perspectives in Literature: A Critical and Annotated Bibliography* (12) to refer to authors who are not Mexican Americans who become an integral part of Chicana/o literature. The author Natalie Petesch sums up the feelings of Chicanesca writers in a manner that helps to explain their role in communicating the Mexican American experience:

> I have always felt a deep communication of spirit with the Mexican people, not only because historically they were defeated by cunning Cortes, nor because they were enslaved by the Spaniards, but also because their Indian past recalls for me some Jungian memory, and, perhaps, of the Russian steppes where my own roots began. (Simmen 1992, 2)

Recent Chicana/o writers take into consideration a new philosophy: "Being Mexican is a state of soul" (Anzaldúa 1987, 62). The key points of contemporary Chicana/o creativity are a *"mestiza/o voice"* and "border consciousness" in the context of U.S. postcolonial cultural discourse. As Lomelí noted in his talk given at the international conference "The Open World: Multicultural Discourse and Intercultural Communications," held in Chita in 2006:

> [B]orders have their external dimensions, but women affirm that understanding internal factors that have shaped and conditioned their being is of greater importance. Chicanas indeed allude to border conflict and tension, except that they explain it in terms of the inner workings of what makes it unique. In this way, "borders," "borderness" and "borderlessness" take on new meanings. (2006, 187)

Although he is foregrounding how this ties into women's experience, it can be expanded to consider a wider Chicana/o writers' consciousness of the border and locatedness. Contemporary Chicana/o literature develops a specific creative psychology, based on a nonstandard and non-Eurocentric understanding of history; an appeal to a specific spiritual and cultural cosmos;

concern about the community, family, and *carnalismo* (brotherhood); and elements of magical realism in a postmodern paradigm.

The Aztlán myth and its modifications would still tend to characterize Chicana/o literature. At the same time, the rationalist and feminist trends of the 1980s changed the notion of Aztlán as a sacred space. In order to displace the older cultural models, a new vision of Aztlán is created to serve a paradigm of modern Chicana/o literature, transforming it from homeland to borderland as observed in the Chicana/o creative works of the 1980s. Rafael Pérez-Torres calls this phenomenon an opening within the Chicana/o cultural discourse of the present-day period:

> It marks a significant transformation away from the dream of origin towards an engagement with the construction of cultural identity. . . . The geographic Aztlán as a site of origins and nation has been rejected. But Aztlán as a realm of historical convergence and discontinuous positionalities becomes another configuration embraced and employed in the borderlands that is Chicano culture. (1995, 96)

In recent writing, some folk images like the *bruja* (witch) and *curandera/o* (healer) continue to be a rich source for writers. At the same time, contemporary Chicana/o writers, such as Anaya, Sandra Cisneros, and Ana Castillo, rethink the emblematic figures of their indigenous heritage: La Llorona, La Malinche, and La Virgen de Guadalupe. It is especially characteristic of the works by Chicana writers, whose literary debut was in the 1970s to 1980s, to rewrite these icons of history and female identity.

Chicana/o literary space was definitely undergoing a profound transformation in the 1980s. As Juan Bruce-Novoa remarks, "The most significant change was not generic, thematic nor stylistic, but much more fundamental and radical: it was sexual" (1990, 86). The 1980s is oftentimes called the Decade of Chicanas. This is to some extent true, as the 1980s saw the flourishing of Chicana literature of different genres through the work of talented Chicana authors of the period: Trambley and Chávez (representing the older generation), Bernice Zamora, Lucha Corpi, Cervantes, Anzaldúa, Cherríe Moraga, Cisneros, Helena María Viramontes, Castillo, Alicia Gaspar de Alba, Pat Mora, Norma Cantú, Erlinda Gonzales-Berry, and others.

Gaspar de Alba compares Chicana writers to *curanderas* and *brujas* because "they are keepers of the culture, the memories, the rituals, the stories, the superstitions, the language and the imagery of the Mexican heritage" (Rebolledo and Rivero 1993, 291). Moreover, as Ada Savin has suggested, a new Chicana poetic discourse addresses the interrelated issues of ethnicity, gender, and class from a depolarized perspective.

Chicana literary criticism is just as remarkable. A group of critics made their appearance on the literary scene and began to carve a female space in critical discourse before and during the 1980s. Among these notable critics are Rosaura Sanchez, María Herrera-Sobek, Norma Alarcón, Tey Diana

Rebolledo, Cordelia Candelaria, Yolanda Broyles-González, Alvina Quin-
tana, Gaspar de Alba, Cantú, and Clara Lomas. Women academics in U.S.
universities produced publications on Chicana/o literature and culture as
well as their literary output, thus expanding the field.

Taking into account the fact that Chicana/o literature is only beginning
to attract readers in the Russian-speaking world, it is useful to give some
sketches of different well-known representatives of Chicano/a literature.

One of the most remarkable figures of the latest period is Anzaldúa with
her book *Borderlands/La Frontera: The New Mestiza* (1987). She was a
Chicana, *tejana* lesbian-feminist poet and fiction writer, literary critic, and
a winner of the Before Columbus Foundation American Book Award. As a
vanguard Chicana writer she is "beyond stereotypes" (using Herrera-Sobek's
metaphorical title of her book of 1983) in her "new *mestiza*" consciousness
and in her style of writing. Anzaldúa shows that her "new *mestiza* consciousness" means constant collisions between different cultural traditions.
Like others living in more than one culture, as a mestiza she perceives her
own vision of reality and negotiates different, often controversial messages.
As Lamia Khalil Hammad observes, border consciousness "emerged from
subjectivity structured by multiple determinants—gender, class, sexuality
and contradictory membership in competing cultures and racial identities"
(2010, 303). Anzaldúa's character is in constant search for a definition of
who and what she wants to be.

According to Anzaldúa, *mestiza* consciousness has to be created and
presented as a new culture and practice. The future depends on this new
consciousness. Like those writers of the Chicana/o literary renaissance of the
1970s who have been influenced by the idea of *la raza cósmica* articulated
by Vasconcelos, Anzaldúa supports the idea of the "fifth" or "cosmic" Race,
which would combine the features of all existing cultures.

At the same time, Rosaura Sanchez has noted that "works like those of
Anzaldúa . . . need to be seen in the context of other . . . texts written by Chicanos, like those of Richard Rodriguez or Ruben Navarette, for example"
(1997, 362). While these Chicano writers strive to make a place for themselves in mainstream U.S. society, Anzaldúa, Moraga, and Castillo express
a profound dissatisfaction with the status and condition of the Chicana/o
community and, more specifically, with the place of women in it.

Another figure of note is the controversial Richard Rodriguez, who has
received enthusiastic reviews over the last two decades of the twentieth century in the mainstream press for his first two books, *Hunger of Memory: The
Education of Richard Rodriguez* (1982) and *Days of Obligation: An Argument with My Mexican Father* (1992). The novel *Hunger of Memory* deals
with the problem of cultural assimilation. It aroused heated debates among
both supporters and opponents of cultural assimilation and was much criticized by radical Chicanas/os. In many regards, the novel can be read as a
description of the universal experience of growing up in any culture. Its title
recalls the famous novel *The Education of Henry Adams* (1918), written by

Henry Adams. Adams is one of the first advocates of the American Dream as a national ideal. In *Hunger of Memory,* the parents dream about their son's success in the United States and are greatly influenced by F. Scott Fitzgerald's admiration for the rich.

As the hero grows into a representative of the middle class, Rodriguez shows the connection of assimilation with the problem of class. He is against bilingual education and leans toward Protestant values, thus denying his Catholicism. Despite the position of the author, the reader feels his nostalgia, his hunger of memory, first of all, for the Spanish language, the language of a "joyful return," his family language, and the language of his ancestors. In his adult years Rodriguez acknowledges a sense of guilt about having difficulty in pronouncing some Spanish words. Nevertheless, he strives to distance himself from his parents and their culture. He is different. The sense of difference is intensified by his being a queer Catholic. In his next book, *Days of Obligation: An Argument with My Mexican Father* (1992), Rodriguez tries to renew the dialogue with his Mexican parents. Rodriguez seeks to conceptualize the ambivalence of his personality. In his creativity he tries to extend the point of Noel Ignatiev's *How the Irish Became White* (1995) to European and non-European immigrants to the United States to understand better what the country and its people are.

Cisneros is a poet, fiction writer, and essayist who is similarly concerned with autobiography and memory. Cisneros says of her writing:

> [W]hen I was eleven years old in Chicago, teachers thought if you were poor and Mexican you didn't have anything to say. Now I think that what I was put on the planet for was to tell these stories. Use what you know to help heal the pain in your community. We've got to tell our own history. I am very conscious that I want to write about us so that there is communication happening between the cultures. (Cited in López, 1993, 155)

Her first novel *The House on Mango Street* comprises 44 vignettes. The main heroine's name *Esperanza* [hope] recalls those heroines in Western patriarchal literature based on fairy tales that have hopeful and happy endings, but Cisneros offers an example of an "anti-fairy tale." Cisneros shows that in real life there are usually neither princesses nor happy endings. She exposes social, cultural, and economic conditions in which poverty, domestic abuse, and sexism take place. In her second book, *Woman Hollering Creek* (1992), Cisneros continues the theme of the social and personal consequences for Chicanas who believe in TV-fairy tales, and shows another type of modern woman.

The final figure I want to consider is Anaya, who is known as the godfather of Chicana/o literature in English. He is purportedly the most widely read Chicano author in the United States and abroad. His bestseller *Bless Me, Ultima* (1972) has become a modern classic. The sales of the novel have surpassed 360,000 and it has been translated into many languages. Anaya is still the only Mexican American writer who is translated into Russian (there are three translations by Kirichenko (2000), Vaschenko (1989), and Voronchenko (2001)).

Chicana/o critics have paid a great deal of attention to his work. Luis Leal compares Anaya's interpretation of historical reality to its vision in works by the most famous Latin American writers, such as Miguel Ángel Asturias, Carpentier, Juan Rulfo, and Gabriel García Márquez. With the publication of *Albuquerque* (1992), *Newsweek* proclaimed the writer a front-runner in "what is better called not new multicultural writing, but the new American writing" (Dunaway 1995, 17).

Anaya has revitalized the popular mystery tradition as well. He explores the "cultural mystery" formula that such modern writers as Tony Hillerman employ. Samuel Coale correctly points out that: "Hillerman uses both Navajo and Hopi myth and ceremonies . . . as a way of creating a new sense of order and harmony. . . . In effect the 'white' mystery has been purified by Native American traditions" (2000, 34). Similarly, Anaya introduces new perspectives and opens up "the genre to newer visions of restoration, order and harmony" (Coale 2000, 34). In *Zia Summer* (1995) Anaya incorporates his realistic view of New Mexican reality, provides a romantic vision of history, and includes bright descriptions of Aztec ceremonies and rituals into a detective story. Nevertheless, critics see this novel as very realistic and brutally raw when he comes to describing characters.

Anaya's novel *Shaman Winter* (1999) blends magic realism with elements of crime fiction. As well as being a mystery novel, it contains elements of magical realism, and images and motifs typical of Native American literature and folklore. In 1994, Anaya signed a five-book contract with Warner Books, including murder-mysteries *Zia Summer, Rio Grande Fair* (1996), *Shaman Winter, Hemes Springs,* and *Bless Me, Ultima,* thus defining a new genre in Chicana/o literature.

CONCLUSION

The early twenty-first century saw a flowering in the study of Chicana/o literature in Russia, which has led to the development of master's and PhD programs under the rubric of American literary studies open to a multicultural discourse focused on Chicano/a literature. These have included four PhD dissertations and five MA theses that are already defended, and there are four PhD dissertations and four MA theses in process now. Zabaikalsky State University in Chita is still the only place in Russia where Chicana/o literature is studied in the PhD and MA programs.

During the past decade, works by Anaya, Luis A. Urrea, Maria Amparo Ruiz de Burton, Anzaldúa, Dagoberto Gilb, Viramontes, Morales, and Castillo were studied in the PhD program in Zabaikalsky State University under the supervision of this author. The master's program coordinated and established by this author in 2009 with the support of University of California, Santa Barbara, focuses on contemporary Chicana/o literature.

Contacts with U.S. academics have helped to promote Chicana/o literature in Siberia. In 2003, Professor Collette Morrow from Purdue University, a Fulbright Fellow, was a visiting scholar in Zabaikalsky State University to promote gender studies and Chicana literature; then in 2006, the renowned Chicana/o scholars Sobek and Lomelí (UC, Santa Barbara) and the librarian and critic María Teresa Márquez of the University of New Mexico participated in the first conference on "Contemporary American Multicultural Discourse and Intercultural Communications" focused on Chicana/o literature, in Chita.

At the beginning of the twenty-first century, a new page in the development of Chicana/o literature was opened. As Roberto Fernández stresses: "As the general American culture has changed at the turn of the new millennium, so have U.S. Latinos" (cited in Knippling 1996, 230). What does Chicana/o Literature communicate to those of us outside the United States in the new millennium? Would it play its role in remapping the North American multicultural literary cosmos? Today the study of Chicana/o literature is recognized in different countries in the world and one proof of this phenomenon is the editing of this book in Ireland. Here, in Trans-Baikal Siberia, we understand that the study of Chicana/o literary history is significant in itself, but it also helps to better understand contemporary U.S. literary discourse better. This is especially important in view of taking stock of the changes and challenges in a globalizing world and confronting similar problems in different parts of the world.

WORKS CITED

Alurista. *Floricanto en Aztlán*. Los Angeles: Chicano Studies Center, UCLA, 1971.

Anaya, R. A. "Aztlan: A Homeland without Boundaries." Translated by T. Voronchenko. 2001. *Translator* 3 (2001): 47–60. / Анайя Р. Ацтлан: Отечество без границ (перевод Т. Воронченко) 2001. Университетский периодический журнал «Переводчик», выпуск 3. Чита: Изд-во ЗабГПУ. 160 с., с. 47–60.

———. *Bless Me, Ultima*. Tonatiuh: Quinto Sol International Publishers, 1972. Translated by O. Kirichenko. / « *Bless Me, Ultima*». Moscow: Gudial-Press (translation from English by O. Krichenko), 2000.

———. *Chicano in China*. Albuquerque: University of New Mexico Press, 1986.

———. *Shaman Winter*. New York: Warner Books, 1999.

———. "The Village Which the Gods Painted Yellow." Translated by A. Vaschenko. *"Literary Study"* (1989): 175–184. / Анайя Р. Деревня, которую боги выкрасили в жёлтый цвет (перевод А. Ващенко) 1989. Литературная учёба. – М., № 4, (1989): 175–184.

———. "The Writer's Landscape: Epiphany in Landscape." Translated by T. Voronchenko. *Translator* 1 (2001): 46–52. / Анайя Р. Писательский пейзаж: Эпифания в пейзаже (перевод Т. Воронченко) 2001. Университетский периодический журнал «Переводчик», выпуск 1. Чита: Изд-во ЗабГПУ. 121 с., с. 46–52.

———. *Zia Summer*. New York: Warner Books, 1995.

Anzaldúa, G. *Borderlands/La Frontera* (2nd ed.). Iowa City: Aunt Lute Books, 1999.

Ващенко, А. В. *Проблемы этнических литератур*, в *Литература США в 70-е годы XX века* под ред. Я.Н. Засурского и др. (Наука, 1983), 223. / Vaschenko, A. V. *The Problems of the Ethnic Literatures in the USA in 1970s.* Edited by Y.N. Zasursky et al. Moscow: Nauka, 1983.

Блок, А. *На поле Куликовом* // *Избранные сочинения.* Москва: Художественная литература, 1991. / Block, A. *On the Kulikovo Field: Selected Works.* Moscow: Artistic Literature, 1991.

Boone, E.H. *Incarnations of the Aztec Supernatural: The Image of Huitzilopochtli in Mexico and Europe.* Darby, Pennsylvania: Diane, 1989.

Bruce-Novoa, J. *Retrospace.* Houston: Arte Publico Press, 1990.

———. "An interview with Rudolfo Anaya." Translated by T. Voronchenko. *Translator* 2 (2001): 20–30. / Анайя Р. Писатель и литература (интервью Рудольфо Анайи, данное Брюсу-Новоа) (перевод Т. Воронченко) 2001. Университетский периодический журнал «Переводчик», выпуск 2. Чита: Изд-во ЗабГПУ. 84 с., с. 20–30.

Савкина, И.Л. 1995. *Образ Богоматери и проблема идеально женского в русской женской поэзии XX века* // *Преображение* № 3. С. 155-168. – Savkina, I.L. "The Image of God's Mother and the Problem of the Ideal Woman in Russian Women Poetry of XX Century." *Transformation* 3 (1995): 155–68.

Cisneros, S. *Woman Hollering Creek: And Other Stories.* New York: Vintage Books, 1992.

Coale, S. *The Mystery of Mysteries. Cultural Differences and Designs.* Bowling Green, OH: Bowling Green State University Press, 2000.

Fuenfrios, Guillermo. "The Emergence of the New Chicano." In *Aztlán: An Anthology of Mexican American Literature.* Edited by L. Valdez and St. Steiner. New York: Random House, 1972.

Fuentes, C. *La región más transparente.* Edición conmemorativa, Santillana, 2009.

Hammad, L.K. "Border Identity Politics: The New Mestiza in Borderlands." *Rupkatha Journal* 2, no. 3 (2010): 303–8.

Ignatiev, N. *How the Irish Became White.* New York: Routledge, 1995.

Knippling, A.S. *New Immigrant Literatures in the United States: A Sourcebook to Our Multicultural Literary Heritage.* Westport, CT: Greenwood, 1996.

Кочнева Т. А. *Образ Богоматери в русской художественной литературе* Курск: Курская областная научная библиотека, 2008 / T.A. Kochneva. *The Image of God's Mother in Russian Literature.* Kursk: Kursk Regional Scientific Library, 2008.

Kuteyschikova, V., and L. Ospovat, eds. *New Latin American Novel.* Moscow: Soviet Writer, 1976.

Lomelí, F. *Handbook of Hispanic Cultures in the United States: Literature and Art.* Houston: Arte Publico Press, 1993.

———. "The Border as a Moving Tortilla Curtain: Media and Chicana/o Literary Representations." In *The Open World: Multicultural Discourse and Intercultural Communication* (76–82), edited by T. Voronchenko. Chita: Zabaikalsky State University Press, 2006.

———, and D.W. Urioste. *Chicano Perspective in Literature: A Critical and Annotated Bibliography.* Albuquerque: Pajarito,1976.

Ломоносов М. В. 1897. *Сочинения в стихах.* Санкт-Петербург: Издание А.Ф. Маркса, 350 с. – Lomonosov, M.V. *The poetic works.* St. Petersburg: A.F. Marks, 1897.

Lopez, Tiffany Ana, ed. *Growing Up Chicana/o. An Anthology.* Foreword by R. Anaya. New York: William Morrow, 1993.

Лотман Ю. М. Символ в системе культуры. Избранные статьи. Т. 1. – Таллинн: Александра, 1992. - С. 191-199. С. 192 / Lotman, Y.M. *The Symbol in the System of Culture. Selected Articles.* Vol. 1. Tallinn: Alexandra, 1992.

McCutchen, D. *The Red Record: Wallam Olum: The Oldest Native North American History.* New York: Avery Pub. Group, 1993.

Morton, C. "*El Jardín.*" *El Grito* 7, June-August (1974): 37.

Orleck, A., and Hazirjian, L. G. *The War on Poverty: A New Grassroots History, 1964–1980.* Athens: University of Georgia Press, 2011.

Perez-Torrez, R. *Chicano Poetry: Against Myths, Against Margins.* Cambridge: Cambridge University Press, 1995.

Rebolledo, Tey D., and E. S. Rivero, eds. *Infinite Divisions: An Anthology of Chicano Literature.* Tucson: Arizona University Press, 1993.

Rocard, M. *The Children of the Sun: Mexican-Americans of the United States.* Tucson: University of Arizona Press, 1989.

Rodriguez, R. *Days of Obligation: An Argument with My Mexican Father.* New York: Penguin Books, 1992.

———. *The Hunger of Memory: The Education of Richard Rodriguez.* New York: Bantam Books, 1982.

Sanchez, R. "Reconstructing Chicana Gender Identity." *American Literary History* 9, no. 2, Summer (1997): 350–63.

Sedano, M. V. *Chicanismo in Selected Poetry from the Chicano Movement, 1969–1972: A Rhetorical Study.* Santa Barbara: University of Southern California, 1980.

Simmen, E., ed. *North of Rio Grande: The Mexican-American Experience in Short Fiction.* New York: A Mentor Book, 1992.

Steinbeck, J. *Travel with Charley and Later Novels 1947–1962.* New York: Library of America, 2007.

Steiner, S. *La Raza: The Mexican-Americans.* New York: Harper, 1970.

Tatum, C. M. *Chicano Literature.* Boston: Twayne, 1982.

Тютчев Ф. И. 1913. *Полное собрание сочинений.* Санкт-Петербург: Издание А. Ф. Маркса, 468 с. / Tyutchev, F. I. *The Complete Set of Works.* St. Petersburg: A. F. Marks, 1913.

Уткина Ж. Глобальные природные символы в романе М. Булгакова «Мастер и Маргарита». Журнал «Филолог», 2003, выпуск 2. http://philolog.pspu.ru/module/magazine/do/mpub_1_23.

Utkina, Zh. "The Global Symbols of the Nature in the Novel by M. Bulgakov 'The Master and Margarita.'" *Philologist* 2 (2003). http://philolog.pspu.ru/module/magazine/do/mpub_1_23. Accessed February 28, 2013.

Vasconcelos, J. *The Cosmic Race/La raza cósmica: A Bilingual Edition.* Translated by D. T. Jaén. Baltimore: Johns Hopkins University Press, 1997.

Voronchenko, T., ed. Materials of the International Symposium "The Open World: Multicultural Discourse and Intercultural Communication as Part of the International Conference on Transborderland in the Changing World." Chita: Zabaikalsky State Pedagogical University Press, 2002.

Whitman, W. *Complete Poetry and Collected Prose.* New York: Penguin, 1982.

Zea, L., and A. A. Oliver. *The Role of the Americas in History.* Lanham: Rowman & Littlefield, 1992.

Zeta Acosta, O. *The Autobiography of a Brown Buffalo.* San Francisco: Straight Arrow Books, 1972.

6 Moving Subjects
The Politics of Death in Narratives of the Juárez Murders

Nuala Finnegan

Since 1993, when the murders of young girls on the streets of Ciudad Juárez first began to capture headlines in both Mexico and further afield, a set of dynamic cultural responses has been generated.[1] Literature, feature films, songs, art, documentaries, theatrical works, photography, and digital materials from around the world have sought to encapsulate the horrors of the crimes and to question the systems of power that sustain and nurture their continuance.[2] Such is the extent of the cultural explorations of the murders that it has been argued that the "'fictional' narratives have become both the site where victims are mourned and the means by which justice can be restored" (Volk and Schlotterbeck 2010, 122). Such assertions, while highly questionable, do register the central role played by the Juárez cultural narratives in the way that they serve as vehicles for transnational communication about the murders, inviting patterns of identification and inciting outrage and activism.

This chapter seeks to examine two works of detective fiction in relation to the femicides, Alicia Gaspar de Alba's *Desert Blood: The Juárez Murders* (2005) and Kama Gutier's *Ciudad final* (2007) [*Final City*]. In particular, I wish to focus on the central protagonists of each novel—both lesbian, Chicana academics employed at U.S. universities, in precarious contractual situations—who take on the investigations into the murders prompted by a sense of horror at the cruelty of the crimes and incredulity at the official responses elicited by them. My focus in the chapter is to seek to understand how the construction of the protagonists as quintessential *mestiza* figures, as explored by Gloria Anzaldúa (1987), offers a way of unsettling the polarised discourses that inflect debates about the murders. Second, I examine the pivotal importance of other voices in the detection of the crimes and explore the ways in which this rich confluence of voices forms part of a polyvocal community that destabilises ideas about knowledge as rooted in the individual. The final area of enquiry concerns genre and the use of detective fiction as a model through which to explore real-life crimes. Located in a rich history of crime fiction by Chicano writers, the narrative grammar of both texts engages with the very limits of conventional detective fiction formulae. I consider how the narrative frames of detective fiction work to construct metafictional narratives that seek to integrate the acts of writing and activism that go beyond the textual boundaries posed by the conventions of the genre.

LITERATURE, AUTOBIOGRAPHY, ACTIVISM

In many ways, both books function as relatively conventional tales of detective fiction in which a series of murders is investigated by a detective-like figure. Both also constitute exemplary metanarratives in the sense that the interweaving of fact, fiction, and autobiography within the detective plots leads to an "other" story in which the solutions are not so clear-cut and the murders remain unsolved. The texts negotiate the complex movement between these two sets of narratives and indeed the notion of movement and mobility are of paramount importance in the narratives themselves. Gaspar de Alba is a well-known academic and writer, who currently works as professor of Chicana/o Studies, English, and Women's Studies at UCLA. *Desert Blood: The Juárez Murders* is by no means her only foray into fiction: she is the successful author of three novels, two books of poetry and a collection of short stories. The novel has been a commercial success and has been translated into Italian (2007), Spanish (2008) and, most recently, French (2012).[3] The book forms part of an academic and personal interest in the murders on the part of Gaspar de Alba, who is a native of the El Paso/ Juárez border. She has been involved in research on the crimes since 1998, organizing an international conference of major importance on the murders that was held UCLA in 2003.[4] Furthermore, she is heavily involved as an activist in terms of raising awareness about the murders in Juárez and continues to raise funds for various organizations, including Amigos de las Mujeres de Juárez, to which a portion of the royalties for the book is donated (Gaspar de Alba 2005, 345).[5] *Desert Blood* tells the story of Ivon Villa, an academic, married to a woman named Brigit and living in Los Angeles, who returns to El Paso, her place of birth, to formalize the adoption of a baby in Ciudad Juárez organized by her cousin, Ximena. While there, the mother of their soon-to-be-adopted baby is brutally murdered and this event precipitates Ivon's participation in the murder narrative in ways that she had hitherto not imagined. When her younger sister, Irene, disappears, the horror becomes personal as Ivon tries to track down the perpetrators. After a painstaking search, a snuff movie network, led by a corrupt INS agent, is discovered in a smelter plant and Ivon manages to find Irene alive though suffering from horrific injuries, the result of repeated violent sexual assault. A series of dead bodies are also discovered at the site, though the entire episode is blatantly covered up by the authorities. The novel ends as Ivon and Brigit plan their return to Los Angeles with their newly adopted son, Jorgito, the son of a *maquila* worker who is soon to die from cancer contracted through her work conditions.

Kama Gutier is a pseudonym for Josebe Martínez, a writer and academic with a similar profile to Gaspar de Alba as an author of both fiction about the border and a scholarly interest in border issues. A native of Navarra, Spain, Gutier graduated with a doctorate in Hispanic literatures from the University of California and has worked at the University of Miami, Colegio de México, and the University of El País Vasco, where she is currently on the Faculty of Hispanic literature. Based for more than 14 years on the Mexican-U.S. border, she has been involved in a number of projects including experimental film on or about the region (Montero 2010). The novel is the result of painstaking research into the femicides; and the decision to use a pseudonym was a precautionary measure adopted by the author and the publishing house, given the nature of the research undertaken.

Ciudad final was published in Spanish in Barcelona in 2007 by the publishing house Montesinos, and thus, while *Ciudad final* is not a Chicana novel because its author is from Spain, it is its use of a Chicana protagonist that is of such interest in this study. Gutier presented the book in Spain most recently in Pamplona, at the *VI Muestra de Cine: El mundo y los derechos humanos,* organized by Amnesty International and the Navarra-based, Instituto Promoción Estudios Sociales (IPES). There she spoke forcefully in terms of the social fabric underpinning the crimes as well as the culture of impunity embedded within the justice systems:

> "En un mundo global la denuncia tiene que ser global. Cuanta más gente se conciencie, sepa, vea, escuche y lea lo que hay, mayor es la presión internacional." [In a global world, condemnation must also be global. The more people that become aware, know, see, listen and read about what's going on, the greater the international pressure.] (Montero 2010, n.p.)[6]

Ciudad final narrates the story of the eponymous protagonist, Kama Gutier, who, in common with Ivon Villa, is a native of the border region and travels to Ciudad Juárez at the invitation of the Corte del Estado (de Chihuahua) [Chihuahua State Court] to cover the investigation into the Juárez femicides. While there, she is plunged into an investigative maelstrom marred by errors at the level of policing, forensic examination, autopsies, and legal processing. Piecing together the puzzle with help from a wide network of informants, Kama is finally able to unravel the mysteries behind the deaths of a number of the girls, and the book ends as she joins a number of protests against the apathy and corruption she has unveiled at the heart of the investigations. In defiance of the judge who has invited her to Juárez, she withholds some of the evidence she has collected and the novel ends on a rather open-ended note, with the final, *"teníamos mucho que contar"* [we had much to tell] (Gutier 2007, 206) resonating clearly as a pledge to seek justice beyond the pages of the book.

The connections between both authors and their protagonists in terms of origins (*Desert Blood*), occupation, and name (*Ciudad final*), mean that readers are explicitly invited to draw autobiographical inferences and thus to read the books as part fact, part fiction. Both the main characters are U.S.-based Chicana academics who are at the centre of novels about the Juárez cases in which both authors have been involved professionally. This is not in any way to start the relatively pointless quest of trying to establish autobiographical linkages[7] but rather to focus on the fact that both novels are unequivocally set up as texts that interweave fact, fiction, and indeed, activism into their folds from the outset in intriguing and innovative ways. The appeals to the readers to become part of a global "*denuncia*" in *Desert Blood,* the convergence between fact and fiction at the end of *Ciudad final,* Gaspar de Alba's contribution to fund-raising for justice in Juárez, and Gutier's involvement in human rights events, all point to a marked ethical dimension present in the texts in which ideas about activism, protest, and the search for justice are embedded both within the plots (where you might expect to find them) but also beyond the narrative frames in terms of how the books are presented, marketed, and distributed.[8] Furthermore, the activist roles played by both authors and their other academic activities, such as publishing about the border (both authors have written extensively on the topic), point to the ways in which the "literary apparatus" (Moreiras 2001, 2), incorporating the relationship between author-text-context, is imbricated within real discourses of human rights, activism, and protest.

BORDER VOICES: MOBILITY AND *MESTIZAJE*

The protagonists of both detective narratives under study are of interest in the ways in which their construction as moving subjects serves to restage the settled dynamics of the femicide narratives. Both protagonists are "of" the border: Ivon in *Desert Blood* is from El Paso and in *Ciudad final,* the in-betweenness of the principal protagonist, Kama, is established as a geographical fact of birth: "*Nací en un carro robado (o prestado, como decía mi padre) en un puente sobre el Río Bravo, cruzando la frontera de México, de Juárez a El Paso, Estado Unidos. Esa noche crucé la frontera por primera vez.*" [I was born in a stolen car (or borrowed, as my father used to say) on a bridge over the Rio Bravo, crossing the Mexican border from Juárez to El Paso, United States. That night, I crossed the border for the first time] (Gutier 2007, 7).

In establishing the narrator's links with movement from the very moment of childbirth, the novel establishes the travelling perspective as an epistemological standpoint that affords insight and knowledge. Aside from the links with the two central protagonists, references to travel permeate both books and cars, in particular, and their ability to move protagonists around and out of trouble, function as key signifiers in a textual space that is marked by frenetic movement. Movement is also central to the primary protagonist of *Desert Blood*, whose opening lines see her travel from Los Angeles where she is resident, to her city of birth, El Paso. In the novel, Ivon traverses the border countless times while remaining an outsider in both spaces, a depiction that is illuminated in a series of dialogues with the local informants, her cousin Ximena and Father Francis, a priest working for a local nonprofit organization, *Contra el Silencio* [Against Silence]: "Look [. . .] I'm sorry I'm asking really dumb questions, okay? And I'm really sorry that I haven't lived here since 1989, and that I haven't been back since 1996, and that I don't know shit. Okay, that's been established" (Gaspar de Alba 2005, 39–40). Many of these exchanges encompass Ivon's incredulity about life on the border and are framed through a series of questions posed in relation to the inhumane conditions in the *maquilas* about which she is becoming informed: "She'll get fired if she's pregnant?" (Gaspar de Alba 2005, 12). When Ximena explains that this is routine ("Take your birth control if you want to keep your job"), Ivon replies, "Are you shitting me?" (Gaspar de Alba 2005, 12). These exchanges posit Ivon as the dubious outsider, a classification she resists, certainly initially, as exemplified in the following conversation with Ximena when her insistence on being "native" is showcased:

-Five minutes in Juárez and you're already pissing off the natives, huh?
-*I am a native,* said Ivon.
-You don't look like no native to me, homegirl, wearing shorts and leaning against the car looking all sexy in your California tan. *Te miras muy* Hollywood. (Gaspar de Alba 2005, 22, emphasis added)

These exchanges confirm Ivon's position as ambivalent witness to the reality of life in both El Paso and Juárez and inscribe the context of the murders as definitively binational, an idea that is underscored through the textual demarcation of "here" and "there" throughout the text: "Look, that's the way things work over *there*. I don't make the *pinche* rules" (Gaspar de Alba 2005, 16, emphasis added). It is only when her little sister disappears that Ivon becomes an integral part of the unfolding mystery, and it is after this point that she immerses herself in trying to seriously solve the crimes from the inside out.

The narrator in *Ciudad final* navigates a similarly ambiguous terrain to Ivon and references to her "origins" are dispersed throughout the text. From her first dialogues with Sabina, the employee at the motel *El Fronterizo* with whom she strikes up an immediate friendship, she is marked ethnically and socially as a *gringa*. Responding to Kama's revelations about the recent demise of her relationship with a woman suffering from anorexia, Sabina states:

-*Pues a mí no me gustó que me lo dijera. ¿Por qué los gringos tienen la manía de soltarlo todo el primer día?*

-*Pues es la identidad de una* . . . (Gutier 2007, 41)
-[I didn't like you telling me that. Why do gringos let everything out on the first day?
-Well, it's one's identity . . .]

Later, however, in her first encounter with the Judge, Catita Lombardi, she is accused of being a "compatriot" in surprised and somewhat betrayed tones: "*Ah, pero no es norteamericana?—no aprobó mi aspecto no tan blanco, ni mi lengua no tan inglesa—por su nombre me engañó usted, creí que sería una güerita anglo.* . . . *Y es una compatriota*" (Gutier 2007, 21). [Ah, but aren't you North American? She didn't approve of my not-so-white appearance or my not so English language.—Your name deceived me, I thought you were an American blondie and instead you're a compatriot.] Gutier's lack of direct response to this assertion cements this ambiguous notion of herself where, on one occasion, she refers to herself as one of "*los medio gringos*" [half Americans] (Gutier 2007, 84), again underscoring the binational context of the murder environment in which she operates.

The sense of instability that surrounds the protagonists' origins and ethnicity is anchored in this here/there structuring trope that is further underlined by their insecure personal and professional positions in the United States. The narrator at the start of *Desert Blood* states that, "For the locals on each side of the river, the border is nothing more than a way to get home" (7). For both protagonists, however, the very notion of "home" is problematic from the outset. This is shown in their yearning for a certain kind of U.S. dream of prosperity that resonates throughout their lives. In addition, they are presented as alienated from their supposed origins in Mexico, and yet, at more than first remove from attaining the goal of stability in the United States. This is exemplified through their badly paid, untenured academic jobs in universities, where their employers are either sceptical about their research (in the case of Saint Ignatius College's attitude toward Ivon's doctorate) or where they have been hired purely on the basis of tokenistic gestures of adherence to affirmative-action programmes (in the case of the University of Texas El Paso's hiring of Gutier): *Y así llegué a ser profesora de la Universidad de El Paso, por la buena razón de que no soy blanca y necesitaban cubrir la cuota racial de contratos* (Gutier 2007, 17). [And that's how I came to be a professor at the University of El Paso, for the good reason that I wasn't white and they needed to reach their racial quota]. Ivon recalls her father's words, "Dissertation, tenure, real estate—that was the order of things" (Gaspar de Alba 2005, 18), and the pressure to finish her dissertation in order to secure tenure forms a core part of the narrative. So, while the protagonists are seen as frequently hankering toward the United States as a topos of stability, it nevertheless remains elusive. This double-edged alienation, then, cements their positions as outsiders and locates them as subjects in constant flux, suspended somewhere between "here" and "there" in a space that is marked by intense movements back and forth.

The idea of subjects in flux is further explored through the sexual relationships highlighted in the novels and forged with women they meet (Kama) or reconnect with (Ivon) as the result of their attempts to untangle the mysteries of the Juárez femicides. The novels' frank exploration of lesbian desire is pronounced throughout and the importance of their sexual identity is casually introduced from the beginning as in one of the first conversations between Sabina and Kama in *Ciudad final:*

> *-O sea que tú también andas con mujeres.*
> *-Pues eso se ve. ¿A poco no lo notó?*
> *-Sí, y me gustó, por eso te conté lo de mi novia.* (Gutier 2007, 40–41)
> [– So you also go with women.
> -Well, that's obvious. Surely you noticed that?
> -Yes, and I liked it. That's why I told you about my girlfriend].

In *Desert Blood,* Ivon mentions her marriage to Brigit in the opening pages and the references to her as *marimacha* [butch], *manflora* [queer], and *sin vergüenza* [shameless] (her mother's words), are interspersed throughout the narrative at frequent intervals. In *Ciudad final,* Kama divulges intimate details of her romantic life and engages in sex with a stranger during an unexpected meeting in the bathroom of a local bar:

> *La muchacha siguió sonriendo y* [. . .] *me metió con ella en uno de los excusados y cerró la puerta.* [. . .] *Me acerqué a su cuello y a su cabello por olerle a ella, y olvidar el resto. Olía suave y envolvente. Sonreía y me besaban, tan perdida como yo. Se quitó el vestido. Puro deleite. Al cabo de un rato volví a la barra.* (Gutier 2007, 52–53, emphasis added).
>
> [The girl continued to smile and [. . .] led me to one of the cubicles and closed the door. [. . .] I moved closer to her neck and hair to smell her and to forget the rest. She smelled soft and overpowering. She smiled and kissed me, as lost in the act as I was. She took off her dress. Pure pleasure. After a while I returned to the bar].

Similarly, Ivon, in a state of extreme anxiety over Irene's disappearance, finally gives in to her desire for Raquel Montenegro, her first love from whom she has never recovered:

> She stroked the back of Ivon's neck. Ivon closed her eyes, absorbing the cool softness of Raquel's hand, the light scratch of her nails, the perfumed scent of her wrist. She turned her face toward Raquel's and kissed her, gently at first, then roughly, pulling her close, gnawing at her mouth with a hunger she didn't even realize she felt. Raquel did not resist. (Gaspar de Alba 2005, 264)

As is seen in this passage, Ivon's long-buried love for Raquel is reignited and it is later revealed that Raquel is having an affair with Ximena, Ivon's cousin and chief confidante. In *Ciudad final*, all the primary characters are lesbian—Kama, Sabina (who becomes her closest friend throughout the investigations), as well as her cousin Bea. It would seem therefore, that the integration of lesbian desire and sexual activity into the fabric of both plots draws attention to sexuality as a normative part of human experience and brings it into the mainstream in ways that are still very uncommon in conventional detective fiction, which from its inception was overwhelmingly dominated by central detective figures frequently characterised as aggressive and domineering.[9]

This notion of in-betweenness, then—accentuated by both protagonists' links to the border and their sexuality—is centrally connected to the characters' mobility and their seamless movements between the United States (Los Angeles and El Paso) and Mexico. Furthermore, as frequent border crossers, the protagonists are posited as nomadic subjects, so eloquently theorised by Rosa Braidotti and Caren Kaplan, who signal the nomadic subject as one of hybridity, mobility, and flux (Braidotti 1994; Kaplan 1996, 92). Both texts are characterized by constant border crossing between El Paso and Juárez, as the subjects go back and forth to collect evidence and talk to students (Kama) or to connect with family and conduct further investigations (Ivon). Indeed, movement and travel become keys to the actual process of detection of the crimes. In *Ciudad final*, Kama decides to hide out on the *maquila* bus to travel the same route with El Chófer, the suspected killer, a risky strategy that finally pays dividends and sees him being apprehended. Similarly, it is while trying to cross the border in her sister's car that Ivon is detained by the corrupt border guard, Wilcox. This, in turn, leads to her discovery of the snuff-film network that is sadistically torturing and murdering girls in acts that are filmed and streamed live. In this way, the ritualistic crossings over and back form part of the rhythms of detection as though the movement itself might contribute to the uncovering of the crimes. Furthermore, these mysteries remain inaccessible to other characters, including the El Paso-based investigating officer, Pete McCuts, in *Desert Blood,* and Escobar, the Juárez-based lawyer in *Ciudad final*, both subjects who remain static on either side of the border, unable to effect change.

This construction of female subjectivity in flux would seem to invite a reading of the characters as fluid, hybrid, quintessential borderlands subjects as invoked by Anzaldúa's still pivotal work, *Borderlands/La Frontera: The New Mestiza* (1987). Indeed *Desert Blood* seems to suggest this critical interpretation explicitly, as Ivon—musing on her dissertation in the latter stages of the book—says: "she was thinking about Anzaldúa's theories on border identity" (Gaspar de Alba 2005, 321). Furthermore, Anzaldúa's famous definition of the border (where "the Third World grates against the first and bleeds" (1987, 335) features in the penultimate chapter of the book, which includes Ivon's reflections on the wider theoretical parameters framing the context of the murders in Juárez. *Ciudad final,* while not as obvious in its invocation of border theory around subjectivity, nevertheless weaves a sustained commentary about border life into the narrative thread through the frequent interventions of Sabina:

> *Es cabrón, Kama, los gringos vienen a sacar lo que pueden y luego parece que todo lo malo les llega de aquí, no? ¿De dónde les viene el Sida? De la frontera. ¿Las enfermedades, y la contaminación, y los males, y la pobreza? De la frontera.* (Gutier 2007, 84) [It's fucked up, Kama, the gringos come to take what they can and later they think that everything bad has come from here. Where does AIDS come from? The border. Disease, pollution, evil, poverty? From the border.]

According to Anzaldúa, the *mestiza* subject occupies multiple migratory speaking positions and, certainly, Kama and Ivon's freedom of movement enables them to enunciate from multiple positions, in both cases allowing them to solve the murder cases but also propelling them on emancipatory journeys of sexual self-discovery. Furthermore, Anzaldúa insists that the *mestiza* figure "not only sustains contradictions, she turns the ambivalence into something else" (1987, 79). This vital component of Anzaldúa's philosophy reads the *mestiza*'s fluid relationship with the spaces she inhabits as a creative act, one in this case that results in resolution (of the crime) and also rupture (with current ways of configuring the murders in cultural and political terms). It is to this notion of rupture that I will turn next to tease out the differing ways in which the murders have been focalised and represented.

Rosa Linda Fregoso maintains that two discourses dominate current debates around and about the murders: on the one hand that which posits the women as *maqui-locas* or "sluts," in which the victims are blamed for their own demise (2000, 138). This forms part of what she denominates a "moralizing discourse," which has found expression in media reportage and official pronouncements among other interventions. On the other hand, Fregoso points to the "globalization" discourse, in which all the problems of Juárez, including the savage murders of the girls from the *maquilas,* are based on the impact of late capitalism.[10] The first discourse has seen myriad pronouncements by the authorities as well as questionable promotional campaigns, which detect moral differences between women who are safely ensconced at home (where they should be) and women (the "working girls") who are out roaming the streets at night, by definition transgressing patriarchal norms and therefore punishable by society. Indeed, as María Socorro Tabuenca Córdoba points out, the *maquila* worker came to "transgress different spaces in the city's (and the nation's) *usos y costumbres,* defying a social construction of gender" (2010, 97). On the opposite end of the spectrum, scholars have identified the aggressive model of globalization in operation in this part of the world and the misogynistic culture it nurtures as a major element in designating women as corporate garbage—disposable (in labour terms at any rate) and easily replaceable. In this conceptualisation, Juárez became a prototype of unapologetic globalization that, in the words of its critics, is devouring its children (Hu-Dehart, 2007). As Chandra Talpade Mohanty reminds us, "It is especially on the bodies and lives of women and girls from the third World/South . . . that global capitalism writes its script" (2003, 514), a notion further underscored by Melissa Wright's work on *maquila* culture (2006). Small wonder, then, that in viewing these women as the primary victims of a crime spree that sees the disposability of women's bodies on the global assembly line and the mutilation of women's bodies as part of the same singular process, the need to memorialise and commemorate is aligned with the desperate desire to foreground ideas around innocence and childhood. Both discourses are referred to in the novels' structural frameworks. The detectives make repeated reference to the role of globalization and the social impact of the *maquilas* on gender roles in Juárez. In *Ciudad final*, Sabina is introduced as a former *maquila* worker and *Desert Blood* features the story of (among others) Elsa, the victim of scientific testing of contraceptives as part of routine pregnancy testing in the plants. Voices from the other end of the spectrum include the Judge (*Ciudad final*) and Wilcox (*Desert Blood*), who articulate the widely accepted societal views about the women as "bad girls." In both of these polarised sets of imaging of the victims, neither is attributed agency and both are somehow frozen in a grotesque pastiche.

The characterization of Ivon and Kama as migrating, desiring, questioning subjects, therefore, undermines those static freeze-frames of the femicide victims and unsettles the very dynamics surrounding how the murders are narrativised. The textual constructions of Kama and Ivon that foreground female sexuality, and indeed sexual pleasure, as central to feminine identity interrogate these very divergent viewpoints that continue to define the conceptualisation and memorialisation of the victims. One of the most evocative passages from Anzaldúa's work concerns the ways in which the mestiza subject can be a force for healing. In this sense, she becomes a vital source of restorative energy:

> *Soy un amasamiento,* I am an act of kneading, of uniting, and joining that not only has produced both a creature of darkness and a creature of light, but also a creature that questions the definitions of light and dark and gives them new meanings. (1987, 182)

By uniting information and intervening in the investigations, both Ivon and Kama participate as creatures who interrogate the definitions of light and dark in Juárez and help to move the focalisation of the murders (and the murder victims) away from these polarised sets of extremes. When the image of the *"maqui-loca"* is thrust on to Ivon's radar in the form of a Barbie doll for sale by a young boy in a *colonia* (Gaspar de Alba 2005, 43), the reader is forced to contemplate the media-generated image of the "bad" factory girls, drunk on their new-found disposable income. In a similar fashion, the powerful commemorations of the victims through images erected on crosses throughout Juárez, and of which there are numerous examples in both novels, seek to remind the community of the children who have been so brutally erased. It is in this context, then, that the images of the border-crossing women who drink to excess, have sex with women, and constantly get into trouble, challenge those fossilised perceptions and remind readers that identity is a complex, multifaceted process.

This vision of the empowered, knowing, borderlands subject, therefore, serves to underscore notions of difference. Indeed, the subjects' movement *per se* is conceptualised as a privilege or condition of the protagonists' in-betweenness and also their U.S. citizenship. The books are careful to map the connections between movement and questions of class and ethnicity, staging the radically different consequences of border crossing for different subjects. In fact, the freedom to border cross enjoyed by the principal protagonists in both novels stands in marked contrast to the experiences of the non-U.S. citizens. The most obvious example of this is played out in *Ciudad final* in the scene where Sabina and Kama—both drunk after a night socializing—are apprehended at the border. While Kama is subject to arrest, as a U.S. citizen the consequences are of little import and are not mentioned again. Sabina, on the other hand, is denied, indefinitely, the chance of attaining the *papeles* needed to cross over to the other side. The novels are punctuated by continuous references to the freedom of movement enjoyed by the Chicana characters vis-à-vis the serious curtailment of movement of the Mexican characters. The Mexican characters in both texts appear as either murder victims (and therefore immobilized forever); paralysed by fear in their *colonias* (Marta and her mother after the attack in *Ciudad final*); dying from the ill effects of *maquila* life (Elsa, who has contracted cancer in *Desert Blood*); or fleeing inland from fear (Rubí Reyna, the media reporter, in *Desert Blood*). The pleasures of "interstitial subjectivity" (Kaplan 1996, 89) enjoyed by Ivon and Kama, therefore, are by no means available to all and here the glaring differences serve to illustrate the ethnic and class dimensions that are so fundamental in understanding the murders. This dimension is marked in the texts and references to race and ethnicity that abound in both novels. Ivon ponders at length and throughout the novel about the significance of the disappearing brown bodies: "What to do with all these fertile brown female bodies on the border?" (Gaspar de Alba 2005, 332); and Kama's musings about the dolls left in her motel room, "*Yo nunca había visto por aquí carnes tan blancas*" (Gutier 2007, 11) [I had never seen such white flesh around here] point to the ways in which the nation-state serves as the limit to this mobility in obvious and very brutal ways.

Qué familia—Community, Polyvocality, Agency

Further questions emerge from this probing into the construction of agency and subjectivity in both novels. We have already seen how the dynamic, fluid nature of the main protagonists serves to deconstruct the existing understanding of the murders through an unsettling of the dominant frames used to focalise the crimes and their victims. It is also clear that these protagonists, through their ability to narrate from and through different speaking positions, embody the very essence of *mestizaje* theorized at length by Anzaldúa. Central to Anzaldúa's imagining of the borderlands is the notion of polyvocality: a space of plurality and ambiguity in which multiple speaking voices can perforate established modes of behaviour and categorization. Anzaldúa's insistence on polyvocality as a cornerstone of borderlands subjectivity receives explicit treatment in both novels through the productive personal relationships forged between the protagonists and members of the local community, and that would seem to point to the marked importance of *comunidad* as a way of confronting and understanding the unfolding realities. We have seen how the nuanced complexity of the books' central protagonists offers new ways of framing the murder narratives. The novels also suggest, however, that they form part of a confluence of voices, a community of knowledge, which functions as a circuit of knowledge transfer leading ultimately to wisdom and resolution. Indeed, the novels posit the notion of "community" as absolutely critical to the detection of the crimes through the establishment of a panorama of characters who serve to assist, explain, translate, and help the "outsiders" to piece together the complex puzzle of the murders under investigation.

In the case of *Ciudad final,* this involves multiple peripheral characters including, most importantly, Sabina, the local cipher of knowledge, and the Judge, Catita Lombardi, who, while frequently hostile, provides vital clues into the authorities' attitudes toward the perpetrators of the crimes and their victims. There are also Kama's students from El Paso, who intervene in specific ways to assist the investigation; her cousin, Bea; the mother of the victim, Ana Amalia; the survivor, Marta, whom she interviews; the lawyer, Escóbar (who is gunned down in the latter stages); and her uncle Segundo. Forming a diverse *vox populi,* it is through her interaction with these characters that Kama ultimately makes sense of the framework of mystery surrounding the femicides. Similarly, in *Desert Blood,* Ivon utilizes a wide network of cross-border knowledge bases including her cousin, Ximena; the policeman, McCuts; the priest, Father Francis; as well as her former lover, Raquel. It is through the painstaking collation of data from this broad range of sources that the puzzle is finally solved for Ivon. Many of the voices function to explain and translate the murders for their disbelieving detectives: "They're called *muchachas del sur* because so many of them come from small towns and villages in the south. Their families never even find out they're missing. Or worse: dead" (Gaspar de Alba 2005, 24). Similarly, Sabina informs Kama about the circulating theories on the femicides and indeed drug trafficking more generally, as well as sharing her own personal views at length and in detail: "*Si todo el mundo lo sabe, eso son los juniors, los niños ricos, que tienen dinero y pueden hacer lo que les antoje*" (Gutier 2007, 14). [Sure everybody knows, it's the juniors. Little rich kids that have money and can do what they like.]

This emphasis on community view is located within a rich tradition of Chicano detective fiction in which a *Raza* perspective frequently pervades. Departing from classical models of hard-boiled detectives who represent "solitary, existential perspectives," according to Francisco Lomelí, Teresa Márquez, and María Herrera-Sobek, *Raza* detectives represent "a community view" (2000, 301). According to their formulation, many Chicano detectives have a communal viewpoint, and Chicano detective novels generally are inflected by a political commitment and awareness of social injustice.[11] They go so far as to suggest that "the Raza detective promises to become a vigorous agent for social and cultural change" (2000, 302). The idea of community-based resistance finds its strongest echo in the final lines of *Ciudad final,* when the community comes together to mourn but also to protest. It is perhaps at this moment that the potential for the *Raza* detective to become an agent of cultural change, as imagined by Lomelí, Márquez, and Herrera-Sobek, is most clearly realized. Critics have noted the didactic element present in Chicano crime fiction with its history of mixing fact and fiction, elements of Mexico's past and present. The subgenre of lesbian detective fiction has further emphasised this dimension with its emphasis on transgression on a sexual level, an aspect that is explored in both of the novels under study here. The trilogy of novels by Lucha Corpi (1992; 1995; 1999), for example, which features detective Gloria Damasco, is steeped in the context of the Chicano Movement, and her novel *Crimson Moon* (2004) incorporates reference to the Zapatista movement in Mexico.[12] This didactic element, then, is of paramount importance and may be detected in the closing lines of *Ciudad final,* which ends with an image of a community united in solidarity: "*Pasamos la noche encadenados, frente a unas montañas enormes. Mis estudiantes, muchas madres, gentes de la comunidad, de las asociaciones, de las maquilas . . . nos acompañaron en la vigilia*" (Gutier 2007, 205). [We spent the night entwined with each other, facing these enormous mountains. My students, many mothers, people from the community, the associations, the maquilas . . . accompanied us in the vigil.]

The singular voice of Kama becomes sutured into a united voice of community and into the realization that it is only through this mode of resistance that any justice can be envisaged. *Desert Blood* ends on a similarly optimistic note as Ivon's family unite to support Ivon's sister, Irene, to come to terms with the devastating impact of her rape and enforced imprisonment. The words "*qué familia*" (Gaspar de Alba 2005, 341) [what a family] bear testimony to the ideological import of the trope of "family" and reveal a process of healing, which, while not quite complete, points to a quiet note of redemption and hope. This powerful image of a committed force against impunity resonates insistently at the end of the novel where the fictional and the metafictional narrative modes begin to converge. It is on this complex interweaving of fact and fiction that the final section will centre, examining the effectiveness of the generic conventions of detective fiction to focalise these particular explorations of "real" gender violence being perpetrated in Northern Mexico.

Narrative Frames: *Welcome to the Real World of the Border, Baby Girl*

It goes without saying that the use of a detective-fiction structure places a frame on the narratives that is frustratingly and tragically absent from the real murder stories. On one level, the novels function as relatively conventional detective tales, employing a classic whodunit narrative mode that features a resolution, albeit partial, in the closing pages. In *Desert Blood,* the resolution comes from the discovery of the snuff movie network (www .extremelylucky.com) led by Jeremy Wilcox, a corrupt border guard in collaboration with the so-called narco juniors, that is, the obscenely spoilt rich offspring of drug lords. A series of clues is placed early in the narrative from the moment in Chapter 2 when the border guard is presented as Ivon's airplane companion through a long chain of other evidence that finally leads Ivon to the grim discovery in the ASARCO smelter plant. Reader satisfaction is gleaned from Ivon's ability to crack the clues placed during this early conversation, including the roll of pennies produced by Wilcox during their conversation and which haunts her throughout the text. In a similar fashion, *Ciudad final* tracks a series of clues that finally leads Kama to reveal the complicity of Juárez's most powerful narco families in the murders of the *maquila* girls. It leads specifically to the exposure of the Judge's close family, whose recently constructed mansion we later learn is the graveyard of countless young victims who have been chosen from an online beauty catalogue.

Notwithstanding this conventional approach to cracking the crimes, the novels utilize this narrative framework as a way of asking bigger questions about the structures that uphold the abuses of power committed in Juárez. In this way, the protagonists don't function as normal detectives in the sense that they try and apprehend the guilty. Indeed, when that happens it can feel somewhat artificial, given that the readers of both novels are aware, through the disclaimers and the extra-textual information provided, of the real story with its history of impunity and incompetence. Instead the novels' force comes from the questions they pose in relation to the networks of power that conspire to conceal and that the texts attempt to overcome. In *Desert Blood,* Ivon devotes considerable time to trying to understand the wider configurations of knowledge that support the culture of impunity surrounding the crimes: "This wasn't a case of 'whodunit,' but rather of who was allowing these crimes to happen? Whose interests were being served? Who was covering it up? Who was profiting from the deaths of all these women?" (Gaspar de Alba 2005, 333).

Similarly, *Ciudad final* uses the detective template as a way to critique the very fabric of border life that enables the crimes to occur: "*Desgraciadamente hay que culpabilizar a la descomposición social de la frontera*" (Gutier 2007, 98). [Unfortunately, the social decomposition of the border was to blame.] Furthermore, both texts employ the diverse range of voices that make up the detective community as a way of explaining and critiquing the social environment that perpetuates the crimes.

Gutier and Gaspar de Alba are by no means the first, of course, to use detective fiction as a means by which to critique real societal and state corruption. The search for justice implicit in the very act of detection means that issues pertaining to social justice and the moral order *per se* are frequently embedded within detective narratives. Indeed, writers have traditionally used crime fiction—particularly that sub-genre referred to as hard-boiled or *novela negra*—as a vehicle for sociopolitical critique, and politicized detective and crime fiction are commonplace in both the Anglophone and Hispanophone detective crime traditions. As Lee Horsley asserts in the introduction to her comprehensive study (2005), crime fiction has frequently deployed oppositional strategies:

> from Depression-era protests against economic injustice to more recent decades during which the genre has been adapted for a wide variety of purposes, with writers launching protests, for example, against a complacent conformist ethos, commodification and commercialism, ecological crimes, racism, and sexism. (2005, vi)

The political dimension of much Chicano crime narrative has already been noted, and in the Mexican context, Paco Ignacio Taibo II's Belascoarán Shayne series (1976–1993) perfectly exemplifies the potential of detective fiction to destabilise perceived notions about law, order, and the state.[13] Kama Gutier notes the attractiveness of the *novela negra* form for the examination of such real-life crimes:

> *El libro también ha requerido dificultad para "adaptar un tema tan espantoso, real y de denuncia de una forma que literariamente fuese atractiva", aunque ha señalado que "para esto creo que sirve el género de la novela negra". Para ella, este género debe "levantar estos cadáveres sociales y dar luz e investigar lo que realmente está oculto en estas tramas sociales".* (Montero 2010, n.p.) [The book too has presented difficulties in terms of "adapting such a disturbing real theme of condemnation to a form that would be attractive in a literary kind of way", even though she has also pointed out that, "I believe this is one function of the hard-boiled detective novel genre". To achieve this aim, this genre should examine those social corpses and show them up to the light, investigating what is really hidden behind the social fabric.]

In this way, both authors employ the conventions of detective fiction as a way of framing the real stories behind the crimes and their perpetrators. When Ximena says, "Welcome to the real world of the border, baby girl" (Gaspar de Alba 2005, 16), she invites Ivon—and by extension, the reader—not only to enter the real world of the crimes but also to confront the metafictional nature of the text with its complex interweaving of facts with the fictionalised elements. Both novels engage explicitly with established facts about the murders in numerous ways with the use of a former FBI expert in profiling (mentioned in both novels)[14] and the inclusion of an Egyptian male character deemed responsible for some of the crimes, featuring in distinct subplots in both novels. The metafictional process is exploited to great effect in *Ciudad final* whereby the "fictional" plot—who is killing the girls of Juárez?—is explained using one of the frequently cited "real" theories. This involves Marcela Lagarde de los Ríos's contention that the girls' photographs form part of an online catalogue created by the *maquilas* and given to juniors to use and dispose of them as they will. In this way, the fictional and factual elements are seamlessly fused in the text (cited in López-Lozano 2010, 139). Indeed, in *Ciudad final,* the gaps between the fictional plot of the novel and the factual framework begin to collapse at the end where the personal network of fictional characters (Sabina et al.) is aligned with an established list of real participants, including family associations. It is here, for example, that the novel makes reference to real reportage on the murders in the form of the groundbreaking work of journalists Sergio González and Diana Washington, and thus a forceful dissolution between the novelistic and real communities is enacted.

Similarly, *Desert Blood,* while staging a resolution of its plot, is at its most powerful in Chapter 45, when Ivon poses a series of blistering questions about the murders, the perpetrators, and the frameworks of corruption that result in the slaughter of innocent brown women in the desert:

> Why were the bodies of one-hundred-thirty-nine *hijas de Juárez* rotting somewhere in the desert or the morgue? (331)

> > What's the price of "free trade"? (332)
> > Serial Killers or judiciales?
> > Gangs or Border Patrol?
> > All of the above?
> > A factory of Killers? (333)

In the early stage of this chapter, the way in which activism forms part of the textual fabric of the texts was noted. It emerges again at the end of *Ciudad final* in the image of the enchained protestors—Kama among them—determined to continue investigating with the promise of telling more (*"teníamos mucho que contar"* [we had much to tell]), echoing long after the protests have abated. The narrator says: *Y pensé que no importaba que me sacaran del país, que al día siguiente volvería a estar* allí, *porque todos debíamos estar* allí. [I thought that it didn't matter if they took me out of the country, because the next day I would return to be *there* because all of us should be *there*] (Gutier 2007, 206, emphasis added).

In this passage, she establishes the need to be in Juárez as an ethical act, to turn away from an indifferent United States and to actively take up the cause *for* Juárez, *in* Juárez. *Desert Blood* ends on a similarly resolute note, with a definitive affirmation of the power of *familia* immediately followed by a long section of acknowledgements that culminates in an appeal for readers to sign an online petition to end the violence against girls and women in Juárez (www.petitiononline.com/NiUnaMas). Gaspar de Alba writes:

> I hope this book inspires its readers to join the friends and families of the dead and the disappeared women of Juárez. Only in solidarity can we help bring an end to this pandemic of femicides on the border. Ni una más! (Gaspar de Alba 2005, 346)

What is perhaps more interesting in these cases, then, is not that the novels are employed in time-honoured fashion to provide a thinly veiled critique of the murders and the structures of power that sustain them. Rather, it is in the interstices between fact, fiction, and (crucially) the link to activism through their use of borderlands subjects, that their political charge might ultimately be located.

Returning to the issues raised in the opening section of the chapter, it is timely to reaffirm the significance of the use of nomadic, lesbian Chicana subjects as lenses through which to reconfigure the existing frameworks about the murders. Much of the work produced in response to the Juárez killings would seem to be an attempt to uncover the cultural logic that informs the gendered intersections of economics, culture, and politics and that has resulted in the systematic obliteration of women in the town since the early 1990s. The suggestion that the cultural narratives of and about Juárez become a site whereby justice might be restored receives innovative consideration in these novels, in which the lines between fact, fiction, and activism are so inextricably linked. Indeed, the elliptical ending of *Ciudad final*—evidence of Anzaldúa's polyvocality—suggests that a *Borderlands* approach might pave the way for an activist response to injustice and impunity. In this sense, both texts seek to tell a coherent fictional story about the murders, one that is not possible in real life where the murders are mired in chaotic, fragmented disputes about globalization and the role of women located on a borderline writ large as a space of violent death. While these fictional narratives may not solve any of these disputes (nor indeed the mystery of the murders), they do offer another way of looking that goes beyond the static frameworks that currently circumscribe the debate—and more importantly the victims—in an endless cycle of impunity and despair.

NOTES

1. The precise date from which the femicides are counted is disputed amongst scholars, but 1993 is the most commonly employed date (Monárrez Fragoso 2009; Staudt 2005).
2. See Alicia Gaspar de Alba and Georgina Guzmán's introduction, "Feminicidio: The 'Black Legend' of the Border" in *Making a Killing: Femicide, Free*

Trade and La Frontera (2010, 1–21) for a useful overview of some of these cultural responses.

3. The book was published in Italian by La Nuovo Frontiera Press, entitled *Il deserto delle morti silenziose: Femincidi di Juarez,* and has just been published in French, *Le sang du desert,* translated by Santiago Artozqui (http:// www.desertblood.net/ Accessed November 15, 2012).

4. *The Maquiladora Murders or, Who is Killing the Women of Juárez?* was organized by the Chicano Studies Research Center at UCLA in cosponsorship with Amnesty International (http://www.sscnet.ucla.edu/chavez/maqui_ murders/). In early discussion about the murders, the connection between globalization and its concrete expression in Juárez—the *maquila*—was paramount in discussion and debates about them.

5. In her blog on the book tour, Gaspar de Alba also states that she donated 50% of all honoraria to the same organization. The blog makes several references to the fund-raising initiatives undertaken in relation to the book tour generally. See http://www.desertblood.net/8.html and the conference featured multiple fund-raising opportunities including a silent auction of artwork and a donations section on the website.

6. For more information on Gutier's engagement with the public during these events, please see Unzué (2010).

7. These linkages are in some ways very explicit as in Ivon's discovery of the murders in the opening pages through an article in *Ms* magazine written by a male author (not named) entitled, "The Maquiladora Murders" (Gaspar de Alba 2005, 3). In the introduction to the edited collection of essays, *Making a Killing,* Gaspar de Alba writes that she first came across the murders (like Ivon) through reading Sam Quiñones's article "The Maquiladora Murders" in *Ms.* magazine in 1998. These and other obvious details make it difficult to read against the grain of the "reality" or "facts" and in any event, contribute to the enjoyment of the work. In the disclaimer to *Desert Blood,* Gaspar de Alba states that some of the suspects and public figures that appear in this book are taken from periodical and television reports (Gaspar de Alba 2005, v–vi).

8. Helena María Viramontes, in her review of the book, crystallises this link explicitly: "Let me say something loud and clear: *Desert Blood: The Juárez Murders* deserves the widest readership possible. In fact, copies of the novel should be delivered to the El Paso Police Department, La Migra, and the FBI with a post-it saying: 'mandatory reading'" (Gaspar de Alba, 2010). The idea of the literary text as a mode of bearing witness, of course, recalls the debates about *testimonio* in Latin America and the wider tradition of literary interventions in human rights debates. In this sense, it forms part of a critical continuum ongoing since the 1960s (Gugelberger 1996).

9. While the feminization of detective fiction is widely acknowledged, the inclusion of lesbian perspectives is still not commonplace (Gregory Klein 1995; Walton et al. 1999). Moreover, there is a relatively established catalogue of lesbian crime fiction authors but still remarkably few from a Chicana perspective (Sotelo 2005).

10. See Miguel López-Lozano's excellent discussion of Juárez detective fiction, "Women in the Global Machine: Patrick Bar's *La frontera,* Carmen Galán Benítez's *Tierra marchita,* and Alicia Gaspar de Alba's *Desert Blood: The Juárez Murders*" (2010, 128–153), in which he makes reference to Fregoso's analysis (134). Fregoso has returned to the subject in subsequent publications (2003; 2006). See also Irene Mata, "Writing on the Walls: Deciphering Violence and Industrialization in Alicia Gaspar de Alba's *Desert Blood*" (2010, 15–40).

11. As has been noted, however, there has recently been a boom of Chicano/a writers publishing detective fiction. Rudolfo Anaya and Rolando Hinojosa are two of the best known Chicano authors who have written detective novels. Hinojosa's novel, *Partners in Crime* (1985,) is characterized by murders and crimes in the Valley of Southern Texas. Other Chicano writers exploring this genre are Michael Nava, a prolific writer of seven detective novels, Max Martínez, Rudy Apodaca, Ricardo Means-Ybarra, Manuel Ramos, Benjamin Alire Sáenz, and Martín Limón. All of these Chicano detective novelists are male and their private investigators are also Chicano males (Lomelí, Márquez, and Herrera-Sobek 2000).

12. The trilogy involves the novels *Eulogy for a Brown Angel* (1992), *Cactus Blood* (1996), and *Black Widow's Wardrobe* (1999). See Tim Libretti, "Lucha Corpi and the Politics of Detective Fiction" (1999, 61–82) and Judy Maloof (2013).

13. Translated into multiple languages and hugely popular in Mexico, the Belascoarán Shayne detective stories weave counter-culture and anarchy into compelling narratives of power and greed (Ignacio Taibo 1976–1993).

14. As is well established, Rob Ressler of the FBI was drafted to Juárez to evaluate the investigative processes and his official report generally exonerated the investigation amid a storm of protest (Washington Valdez 2005). This character appears as Bob Russell in *Desert Blood* and in other fictional explorations of the phenomenon, most notably Albert Kessler in Roberto Bolaño's *2666*.

WORKS CITED

Anzaldúa, Gloria. *Borderlands/La Frontera: The New Mestiza*. San Francisco: Aunt Lute Books, 1987.

Bolaño, R. *2666*. Barcelona: Anagrama, 2004.

Braidotti, R. *Nomadic Subjects: Embodiment and Sexual Difference in Contemporary Feminist Theory*. New York: Columbia University Press, 1994.

Corpi, L. *Cactus Blood*. Houston: Arte Público, 1995.

——. *Eulogy for a Brown Angel*. Houston: Arte Público, 1992.

——. *Black Widow's Wardrobe*. Houston: Arte Público, 1999.

——. *Crimson Moon*. Houston: Arte Público, 2004.

Fregoso, Rosa Linda. "Voices without Echo: The Global Gendered Apartheid." *Emergence Journal for the Study of Media and Composite Cultures* 10, no. 1 (2000): 137–155.

——. *MeXicana Encounters: The Making of Social Identities on the Borderlands*. Berkeley: University of California Press, 2003.

——. "'We Want Them Alive!': The Politics and Culture of Human Rights." *Social Identities* 12, no. 2 (2006): 109–138.

Gaspar de Alba, A. *Desert Blood: The Juárez Murders*. Houston, TX: Arte Público Press, 2005.

——. "Desert Blood: The Juárez Murders by Alicia Gaspar de Alba," 2010. http://www.desertblood.net/2.html. Accessed February 20, 2013.

Gaspar de Alba, A., and Guzmán, G. *Making a Killing: Femicide, Free Trade, and La Frontera*. Austin: University of Texas Press, 2010.

Gregory Klein, K. *The Woman Detective: Gender and Genre*. Urbana: University of Illinois Press, 1995.

Gugelberger, G.M., ed. *The Real Thing: Testimonial Discourse in Latin America*. Durham, NC: Duke University Press, 1996.

Gutier, K. *Ciudad final*. Barcelona: Montesinos, 2007.

Hinojosa, R. *Partners in Crime*. Houston: Arte Público Press, 1985.

Horsley, L. *Twentieth Century Crime Fiction*. Oxford: Oxford University Press, 2005.

Hu-Dehart, E. "Globalization and Its Discontents: Exposing the Underside." In *Gender on the Borderlands: The Frontiers Reader* (244–260), edited by A. Castañeda, S.H. Armitage, P. Hart, and K. Weathermon. Lincoln: University of Nebraska Press, 2007.

Ignacio Taibo II, P. *Todo Belascoarán. La serie completa de Héctor Belascoarán Shayne*. Mexico: Planeta, 2010.

Kaplan, C. *Questions of Travel: Postmodern Discourses of Displacement*. Durham, NC: Duke University Press, 1996.

Libretti, T. "Lucha Corpi and the Politics of Detective Fiction." In *Multicultural Detective Fiction: Murder from the Other Side* (61–82), edited by J. Gosselin. New York: Garland, 1999.

Lomelí, F., Márquez, T., and Herrera-Sobek, M. "Trends and Themes in Chicana/o Writings in Postmodern Times." In *Chicano Renaissance: Contemporary Cultural Trends* (285–305), edited by D.R. Maciel, I.D. Ortiz, and M. Herrera Sobek. Tucson: University of Arizona Press, 2000.

López-Lozano, M. "Women in the Global Machine: Patrick Bard's *La frontera*, Carmen Galán Benítez's *Tierra marchita*, and Alicia Gaspar de Alba's *Desert Blood: The Juárez Murders*." In *Gender Violence at the U.S.-Mexico Border: Media Representation and Public Response* (128–153), edited by H. Domínguez-Ruvalcaba and I. Corona. Tucson: University of Arizona Press, 2010.

Maloof, J. "The Chicana Detective as Clairvoyant in Lucha Corpi's *Eulogy for a Brown Angel* (1992), *Cactus Blood* (1996), and *Black Widow's Wardrobe* (1999)." http://www.lehman.cuny.edu/ciberletras/v15/maloof.html. Accessed January 18, 2013.

Mata, I. "Writing on the Walls: Deciphering Violence and Industrialization in Alicia Gaspar de Alba's *Desert Blood*." *Melus* 35, no. 3 (2010): 15–40.

Monárrez Fragoso, J. *Trama de una injusticia: Feminicidio sexual sistémico en Ciudad Juárez*. Tijuana: El Colegio de la Frontera Norte, 2009.

Montero, O. "La escritora Kama Gutier insta a la 'presión global' para evitar el feminicidio de Ciudad Juárez," 2010. http://www.noticiasdenavarra.com/2010/04/29/ocio-y-cultura/cultura/la-escritora-kama-gutier-insta-a-la-presion-global-para-el-feminicidio-de-ciudad-juarez. Accessed February 20, 2013.

Moreiras, A. *The Exhaustion of Difference: The Politics of Latin American Cultural Studies*. Durham, NC: Duke University Press, 2001.

Socorro Tabuenca Córdoba, M. "Representations of Femicide in Border Cinema." In *Gender Violence at the U.S.-Mexico Border: Media Representation and Public Response* (79–101), edited by H. Domínguez-Ruvalcaba and I. Corona. Tucson: University of Arizona Press, 2010.

Sotelo, S. Baker. *Chicano Crime Fiction: A Critical Study of Five Novelists*. Jefferson, NC: McFarland and Company, 2005.

Staudt, K. *Violence and Activism at the Border: Gender, Fear and Everyday Life in Ciudad Juárez*. Austin: University of Texas Press, 2005.

Talpade Mohanty, C. "'Under Western Eyes' Revisited: Feminist Solidarity through Anticapitalist Struggles." *Signs: A Journal of Women in Culture and Society* 28, no. 2 (2003): 499–535.

Unzué, M. "Ciudad Juárez, 'ciudad final' para miles de mujeres, 2010." April 30, 2010, http://www.diariodenavarra.es/20100430/culturaysociedad/ciudad-juarez-ciudad-final-miles-mujeres.html?not=2010043001445740&idnot=2010043001445740&dia= 20100430&seccion=culturaysociedad&seccion2=culturaysociedad&chnl=40. Accessed February 20, 2013.

Volk, S., and Schlotterbeck, M. E. "Gender, Order, and Femicide: Reading the Popular Culture of Murder in Ciudad Juárez." In *Gender Violence at the U.S.-Mexico Border: Media Representation and Public Response* (128–153), edited by H. Domínguez-Ruvalcaba and I. Corona. Tucson: University of Arizona Press, 2007.

Walton, P. L., and Jones, M. *Detective Agency: Women Rewriting the Hard-Boiled Tradition*. Berkeley: University of California Press, 1999.

Washington Valdez, D. *La cosecha de mujeres: Safari en el desierto mexicano*. Mexico City: Océano, 2005.

Wright, M. *Disposable Women and Other Myths of Global Capitalism*. New York: Routledge, 2006.

7 Origins and Evolution of Homies as Hip *Rasquache* Cultural Artifacts

Taking the Homies Out of the Barrio or the Barrio Out of the Homies

Francisco A. Lomelí

[The pachuco's] clothing spotlights and isolates him, but at the same time, it pays homage to the society he is attempting to den.

Octavio Paz, The Labyrinth of Solitude (1961)

I think that I shall never see
any Chicanos on tv.
It seems as though we don't exist
and we're not even missed
and yet we buy and buy their wares
but no Chicanos anywhere.

No Chicanos on TV
Music and lyrics by Lalo Guerrero (1988)
courtesy of Barrio Libre Music, BMI

The issue of representation and resignification of Mexicans or Chicanas/os in U.S. mass media, and cultural venues for that matter, has been troublesome, thorny, and frequently problematic. More often than not, the gaze tends to return to the prefabricated concoctions of the nineteenth century where "greasers," "spics," *bandidos,* and peons leaning on cacti were first portrayed, inevitably recycling anachronistic or incongruous images that have a life of their own, thus embodying vicious stereotypes difficult to eradicate. At the heart of the problem is a fundamental misunderstanding of Mexicans as a racially and/or culturally mixed people with the Native American, which for Anglo America was hard to fathom. This often provoked descriptions of Mexicans as mongrels, primitive, bloodthirsty, instinct-driven descendants of the Aztecs—as if the latter were the only indigenous group—and culturally backward, or intrinsically flawed because they are supposedly unable to assimilate. In other words, their defects are so many that one can only wonder if they possess any virtues. Commonly viewed as ahistorical villains with a fuzzy background and devoid of a legitimate culture, persons of Mexican descent have been depicted in terms of a cultural deficit model as background characters instead of protagonists, workers and not decision makers, anonymous masses instead of humanized bodies, silenced women in lieu of females with multiple dimensions, superstitious people, recent illegal immigrant interlopers, or suspicious second-class citizens. In other words, Mexicans in the United States have historically had to work against an upward treadmill of disadvantage as invalidated beings because they supposedly do not match the norm.

The formulaic images as well as the impressions of Mexicans in the United States are bountiful, be they overt or sublime, usually recycling notions disproven as antiquated misrepresentations, but the central issue is not their reappearance per se but how these notions inexplicably gain traction over and over again. As Francisco Ríos notes in "The Mexican in Fact, Fiction and Folklore," North Americans have generally viewed Mexicans in Mexico as slow, sleepy, sometimes romantic and quaint, but once they enter the United States they suffer a radical transformation or perverse metamorphosis:

> He loses his picturesque and harmless ways and becomes sinister: he is now proud and hot-blooded, easily offended, intensely jealous, a drinker, a brawler, a knifer, cruel, promiscuous, a flashy dresser, a good dancer, and depending on the judge, a "Latin lover" or a "lousy lover." (Ríos 1969, 16)

An excellent example of such a perception appeared in the 1870s when Hanging Judge Parker, a representative of the judicial system in Texas, declares his final verdict on the following legal case with his notably colorful language:

> And then, José Manuel Xavier Gonzales, I command further that such officer or officers retire quietly from your swinging, dangling corpse, that the vultures may descend from the heaven upon your filthy body and pick the putrid flesh therefrom till nothing remain but the bare, bleached bones of a cold-blooded, copper-colored, blood-thirsty, chili-eating, guilty, sheep-herding, Mexican son-of-a-bitch. (Botkin 1994, 148)

Such disparaging words may seem far-fetched in recent times, but it has not been that long since dancer/actor-turned-senator George Murphy of California stated in 1968 that Mexicans were "genetically suited to farm labor . . . because they were 'built lower to the ground'" since it was supposedly "'easier for them to stoop'" ("George Murphy" 2012, 1–4). Nor has it been that far back that signs appeared in front of restaurants and public places declaring "No Mexicans, No Dogs Allowed." Many more colorful examples could be provided ad nauseam. It is indeed curious how a large number of North Americans assume that such depictions are widely true and they become surprised when these are questioned or challenged. The temporary conclusion is that someone has been fooled, but they figure it can't possibly be them. The typical reaction that emerges is: Why didn't someone tell me before? Or, how can we justify such depictions in modern times? After all, don't we all eat Taco Bell tacos or nachos or chipotle? And, finally, isn't Mexican food as American as apple pie? Try living without it.

Such representations, then, sometimes produce a self-fulfilling prophesy in our community by swallowing the untruths and distortions of who we are, sometimes changing our names (both first and/or last) or faking our background or simply distancing ourselves from what may seem mainstream Chicana/o, such as by using other more acceptable or safe identifiers as "Mexican American," "Hispanic," and even "Latina/o." What we can readily recognize is that such portrayals have had a long, durable life in virtually all areas of North American life (education, labor, media, politics, literature, folklore, history), thus impacting Chicanas'/os' self-perception and self-esteem while prompting an internalized inferiority or a colonized mentality. This David-versus-Goliath syndrome of cultural politics, power relations, disenfranchisement, and deterritorialization brings us to consider how the Homies, a collection of plastic figurines of barely 1-3/8 inches to 2 inches, which originated as comically stylized portraits of barrio or ghetto dwellers, react to and challenge such depictions with an unusual flair and strategic resignification by deconstructing, or at least playing with, past figurative misdeeds. In a real sense, they have created their own iconography in an attempt to fill a void of representation parallel to the way salsas (*verde, roja, pico de gallo*) have tried to authenticate burritos, tacos, and other Mexican foods made in the United States. Homies, however, go beyond a simple plastic figurine because they contradict a sanitized and homogenous version of a "safe" physical creation. For that reason, everyone tends to smile or laugh when they hear the word "Homies": not because they will liberate you of your private belongings or intimidate with violence, but because Homies playfully, or partly subversively, interrogate current as well as common depictions from the past. As a social phenomenon, Homies break various borders of commodification by challenging the very system from which they originate. As subalterns, they have invaded unsuspecting markets with accusatory smiles or body language unlike any previous toys. Yes, they do transgress the production of images and iconography while in fact creating their own iconography. The central question can lead us to a paradoxical Chicana/o aphorism by considering if we end up taking the Homie out of the barrio or the barrio out of the Homie. In a real way, Homies accomplish both objectives and more.

First of all, let us examine their origins from a *rasquache* background, or what Tomás Ybarra-Frausto has called a uniquely Chicano sensibility.[1] Homies share a close affinity with *rasquachismo* through their unconventional appearance while spoofing pretentious forms of art, thanks in part to the strategy of using funky, even tacky and banal characteristics to highlight a "good taste of bad taste." As Ybarra-Frausto suggests, "To be rasquache is to posit a bawdy, spunky consciousness, to seek to subvert and turn ruling paradigms upside down. It is a witty, irreverent, and impertinent posture that recodes and moves outside the established boundaries" (1991, 155). While the term connotes something negative in Mexico for its lower-class or impoverished backdrop, Chicanas/os have managed to reverse its meaning into something kitsch but at the same time resourceful, comprised of whatever is available. Creativity, although funky, even ghetto and busy, is its ultimate motivation. That is, a worldview emerges from a Chicana/o sensibility that recognizes its working-class perspective, drawing from those who are disheveled, vulgar, course, or from the margins, but which somehow attempts an artistic expression. *Rasquache,* then, definitely encompasses a funky, underdog, or outcast attitude toward those who deny Chicana/o existence. *Rasquachismo* is an affirmation and a search for an alternative aesthetics by making the most with the least.[2]

Rasquachismo stands out as an assertive attitude, a fashion statement, sometimes gaudiness and an indifference to conformity. This can be seen among some of the titles or theater groups in Chicana/o literature: Teatro del Piojo [Theater of Louse], *The Revolt of the Cockroach People, Anti-Bicycle Haikus, Hay Plesha Lichans Tu Di Flac* [play on words: "I pledge allegiance to the flag"], *A Taco Testimony, Las aventuras de Don Chipote o cuando los pericos mamen* [The Adventures of Don Chipote or When the Parrots Suckle their Young], *El Malcriado* [The Brat], *Rebozos of Love/ We Have Woven/ Sudor de Pueblos/ On Our Back* [Shawls of Love/ We Have Woven/ A People's Sweat/ On our Backs], *Hechizospells* [play on words: "spell" in Spanish and English combined], *Perros y anti-perros* [Dogs and Anti-Dogs]. We could also propose a tentative list of comparisons in order to show the degree of *Rasquachismos* according to popular practices:

Low Rasquache	Muy Rasquache[3]
Microwaving tamales	Frozen capirotada
Shopping at J.C. Penney	Shopping at K-Mart
Tattoos of la Virgen de Guadalupe	Plastering la Virgen everywhere
Little portrait of Frida Kahlo	Big portraits of Frida Kahlo
Exhibiting a "Chile Addict" bumper sticker	Exhibiting a "Honk if you've seen la Llorona" bumper sticker
Buying Taco Bell tacos or buying Jack in the Box tacos (take your choice)	Buying Jack in the Box tacos or buying Taco Bell tacos (either one)

Let us return to our main topic as an extension of *Rasquachismo.* To utter the word "Homie" in today's American society has many ramifications depending on the context, time, and place. No doubt the term has become more a part of the public sphere where until recently it was encoded as something private and highly subjective as an in-group word with tribalized connotations within the barrio and ghetto. Its trajectory is not much different from the term "dude" except that "Homie" is part of a more recent social and linguistic phenomenon. "Dude," for example, dates back to the middle nineteenth century to refer to an Easterner who served as a vacationing ranch hand and by the late 1930s with the zoot suit phenomenon, it metamorphosed into an identifier of a barrio or ghetto inhabitant. Curiously, "dude" then became part of the vernacular of surfers, and then it was transformed, thanks to popular music and film, into a youthful argot or slang that now applies to both men and women, very much like *güey* is used in Mexican and Chicana/o Spanish. "Homie" emerged in the late 1960s as an abbreviated form of "homeboy" and became popularized in the 1970s when barrio and ghetto culture came out of its social domain to penetrate, influence, and inflect mainstream culture through its language, dress, rhythm, and customs. In the process, it has become appropriated by North American youth as an informal way of addressing each other in order to indicate a casual relationship or denote trust or even suggest equality and reciprocity. Homie, then, is someone from your hometown, a form of endearment, a best friend, a confidant or someone with whom you share immediate camaraderie, affinity, or regional—more urban than rural—origins, including, of course, but not exclusive to gang affiliation. If it was originally part of a particular underclass, it has now transcended that usage to imply a willful act of claiming interpersonal commonalities among, but not limited to, students, recent professionals, and other youth who generally relate to a clear or vague notion of "hip" culture.

Nonetheless, Homie continues to rattle the senses for many as a countercultural label while provoking or conjuring up a series of images that not all prefer or identify with. It is more than a mere word of informal interaction because it originates in hard-core barrios or ghettos with trapped dwellers who find themselves living in vicious cycles of violence, drugs, and destruction. But its semantic anchor reverts back to a blurred notion of home or hometown, nation, homeland, homeboy,[4] brotherhood, or neighborhood, including a reclaimed identity and a refashioned citizenship within a society that has denied them status and a sense of belonging. Whereas Homies started in the "'hood" of African American and Latina/o street cultures of turf warfare, the term also suggests among Latinas/os a reinvention of themselves beyond *pachuco*, zoot suiter, *cholo*, *vato loco*, gangbanger, gangster, and other terms that boxed them into negative stereotypes. The term embodies a new genealogy of modernity that deviates from the old molds while challenging a discourse of subjugation; it is also a synthesis of past fragmentations while becoming a badge of honor of coolness for the youth in affirming difference, somewhat similar and parallel to what Chicano youth experienced with the *pachuco* phenomenon in the early 1940s. When considered part of gangs, they gravitate toward issues of mutual protection and strict loyalty as part of a voluntary association for survival and self-affirmation. But, it must be made clear: not all Homies are gang members or part of a hoodlum culture of delinquents whose pathologies have been inflated, perpetuated, and/or demonized and criminalized, thanks in great part to mass media. The question still remains: How to overcome such perceptions when recycled images of lawless and degenerate lifestyles of barrio and ghetto dwellers are constantly represented as static projections of such minorities, who appear to live in a constant self-fulfilling prophesy of dead-end aspirations and hopelessness. The answer can be found in locating an exit from such a mire of conditions.

Another part of the answer to such concerns might reside, at least in part, in the underground monthly tongue-in-cheek comic strip introduced by David Gonzales for *Lowrider Magazine* around 1985, which he called "Hollywood" after his nickname, a hyperbolic, glamorized self-portrait of style and masculine coolness with definite *rasquache* overtones. The Homie characters in the comic strip resembled friends and acquaintances from his own tough urban neighborhood and their popularity spread to where some schoolmates volunteered as models. The urge to be portrayed by someone who knew them intimately seemed too inviting, thereby exercising their brand of agency, while establishing a Pirandellian relationship of real persons seeking out the portraitist of their "character." A self-taught cartoonist and entrepreneur, David Gonzales from Richmond, California, was fully aware of the limited representations available to the Chicana/o community and he felt compelled to portray them with both authoritative sympathy and empathy, that is, as persons and social types who typically do not inhabit the pages of art and official folklore, thus offering a jovial, picaresque, and sometimes humorous look at folks from an imaginary barrio called V.Q.S. or *Varrio Quién Sabe* (Barrio Whatever).[5] Coincidentally or not, an artistic movement was mushrooming in the mid-1980s that eventually evolved into the *CARA (Chicano Art: Resistance and Affirmation)* exhibit at UCLA in 1995. Their mission statement claims the following:

> Chicano art is the modern, ongoing expression of the long-term cultural, economic and political struggle of the Mexicano people within the United States. It is an affirmation of the complex identity and vitality of the Chicano People. Chicano art arises from and is shaped by our experiences in the Americas. (See Griswold del Castillo, McKenna, and Yarbro-Bejarano 1991, 27.)

Gonzales seemed to share a similar inspiration or sensibility, but he went a step further due to his distinctively hard-core barrio background. The response to his unidimensional cartoonish characters in *Lowrider Magazine* was immediate and favorable from a broad range of readers, and by 1998 he unabashedly accepted an offer to convert the images into a series of diminutive, plastic, made-in-China figurines for general consumption in gumball vending machines sold at retail stores and supermarkets targeting mostly Latina/o neighborhoods. The figurines as packaged commodities in soft plastic bags inside a hard plastic bubble became hot collectors' items; and

Figure 7.1 *Lowrider Magazine* © David Gonzales.

some children likened them to toys or even dolls, in that they could make them act out certain voyeuristic roles. More often than not, holding these unconventional figurines denoted embarking on an implicitly prohibited act, because who would want to possess what society generally scorns? Some Chicanas/os affectionately collected them as members of an extended family, or at least a semblance of one. They ultimately attracted much attention for their peculiarly unconformable and anomalous aura and incongruous presence as fun objects of entertainment—a major departure from the way most

real-life Homies are perceived. In a certain way, the figurines filled and fulfilled a void of a past North American fascination with collections of Army
men, cowboys, and Indians, GI Joe figurines, and Barbie and Ken dolls from
the 1950s through the 1970s that satisfied subliminal desires of conquest, cultural domination, military might, and idealized Anglo beauty, respectively.
Homies, in a real sense, counteract such motives because their resignification
is understood more as a playful reinscription and re-creation of marginal
figures who had been forgotten by an indifferent society insatiably seeking
heroes with prescribed imagistic formulas. After all, our heroes are purportedly true projections of our own image. Homies' raison d'etre, on the other
hand, is not to overthrow, replace, or inflate anyone, nor to establish a new
generic standard of elegance and beauty, but rather, as Gonzales originally
proposed, to reappropriate a controversial body type and create new democratic representations by breaking out of shields of glass ceilings and glass
walls that propagated their invisibility as relegated undesirables and dangerous predators of vice, crime, and depravity. Clearly, his Homie productions
contradict the long tradition of films from the 'hood that have codified and
boxed in Latina/o archetypes as unidimensional people who seem to have
predictable roles and destinies: drugs, prostitution, incarceration, poverty,
social dysfunctionalities, educational dropouts, and many more. In part,
their creator strategized a way to get the Homies out of the barrio so they
would become better known and understood as a full-fledged community—
not by romanticizing them but, rather, by letting them speak for themselves.
To Felisa Cardona, they portray the "real barrio" (2010, 1–4). Gonzales,
moreover, recognizes that Homies represent a wide spectrum of peoples and
racial groups who have lived as victims of stereotyping, oftentimes scarred
by mainstream society's projections of their best qualities as transgressively
infamous. They have countered, for example, the Speedy González syndrome of cartoonish portraits by making these figures funny, except that the
humor is not at the expense of what they represent. The screaming mouse
on steroids has been used as an object to mock and denigrate Mexicans
through the innocent medium of children's cartoons. The butt of the joke
suggests that Mexicans are not expected to be that fast or clever, plus their
accent confirms with every shrill declamation that their limited vocabulary
indicates a low IQ. Instead of laughing *at* the "inherent" goofiness and unexpected speed of a heavily accented Mexican mouse, we can laugh *with* these
contextualized Homies because they possess qualities of personal frailties
without dehumanizing them. Gonzales' objective entailed acknowledging
representations of real people who have generally lived in the shadows of
U.S. society and who have not received their due, first, as regular people and,
second, as cultural and folkloric artifacts. For that reason Sara Bir observes
that "Gonzales has been able to give the Homies a redemptive voice, crafting
a complete mythology" (2003, 1), in this case emerging as a subculture prepared to remind whoever wishes to indulge that they are an integral enclave
of society's contradictions, including its worst and best attributes. In other

Figure 7.2 Mr Raza © David Gonzales.

words, Homies are becoming as North American as any other purchased and sold commodity, or part of what Joe Piasecki calls a "New Americana" in the form of the Barbie Doll, Star Trek, and Shrek figurines, except that Homies are a Chicana/o invention and an alternative insisting on projecting or representing themselves in their own terms (2008, n.p.).

The Homie figurine craze began with a bang, or what Jeremy Loudenback has called "Miniature mayhem" (2004, n.p.) or what Aurelio Sánchez termed a "Tiny sensation" (2003, n.p.). However, the reaction was not all positive at first, but rather, quite mixed, even rancorous and acrimonious. Initially, Gonzales faced considerable resistance in publicly peddling his product, particularly because some community members and police departments in such cities as Los Angeles and San José accused him of glorifying and promoting gang life. The facile assumption was that he was re-creating and appropriating the least desirable Latinas/os within American society—in particular a sector many preferred to capture as objects of criminalization—by turning them into products of mass consumption. The suggestion is that these Homie folks should not receive further acknowledgement or recognition because purchasing their smallish representations meant they were being legitimated and made available to unsuspecting consumers. Instead, some in the Latina/o community wished for them to disappear entirely or simply go away while criticizing the figurines/toys as "reinforcing negative stereotypes" (Sánchez 2004, n.p.). The backlash was such that many stores stopped selling the Homies and the controversy brewed, consequently producing an unprecedented boom in sales. Why were these *rasquache* Lilliputian figurines with bandannas, dark shades, baggy clothes, knit caps, tough-guy attitudes, and tattooed bodies threatening or evoking such ire? What kind of responsibility is shared in representing a certain kind of social type that does not grace a traditional concept of art or measure up to a "regular" doll, toy, or fetish, or simply an object of gratification? Or, are functionality, relevance, and innocence in the eye of the beholder? The Homies spurred considerable debate while polarizing people within the same community, even provoking a furor on "authentic representability." And, of course, the common denominator of *Rasquachism* can be a polarizing quality that some simply abhor. Whose standards or perspective should their creator respect: the characters being portrayed or those who look and gaze at them from afar? How should artistic freedom be handled or should the hegemonic viewers be given a role in their creation? But Gonzales defended his creations by insisting that he was offering a viable way of, and tribute to, combating stereotypes while humanizing a community accustomed to assaults and being snubbed or discounted altogether. Then, again, the ever-present *pachuco* as a social-historical factor returns us to a dichotomy some in our community wish not to face: it is part of our past that we thought we had overcome

Both the Homies and their creator attracted unsuspecting attention by being in the media spotlight and despite the efforts to ban the figurines, the

Figure 7.3 Eightball © David Gonzales.

sales skyrocketed by selling one million Homies in the first four months (Bir 2003, 1). Bir continues to point out:

> Homies . . . have drawn criticism for their decidedly urban, inner-city Latino look. What parent, after all, would want his or her child playing with Payday, who wears a gold dollar-sign medallion, smokes a cigar, and has cash sticking out of his pockets? Or Wino, a rumpled Homie in a stocking cap who clutches a bottle of cheap wine in a paper bag? (2003, 1)

Confronted with a new challenge, Gonzales returned to the drawing board after taking a reprieve with his first series of Homies, consisting of a modest group of six with their distinctly unforgettable folkloric nicknames: Eight Ball, Smiley, Big Loco, Droopy, Sapo, and Mr. Raza. While he recognized that creating 3-D images alone was viewed as potentially subversive and antiestablishment, he answered his critics by demonstrating that his creations did not correspond to an alleged Homie invasion of righteousness, nor did it correspond to an exploitation plot. At the same time, he was not willing to make blanket concessions by sanitizing or diluting his creations simply for the sake of greater acceptability, because he would have to ridicule the characters as objects of mockery as if they were real-life cartoons. The Homies phenomenon exploded to meet the need for self-expression in the Chicano community, something not always readily available, but most of all, Gonzales pushed the boundaries of cultural production. As an alternative commodity and representation, he cleverly concocted the idea of producing short, witty, and sometimes affectionate biographies unlike any other, plus he greatly expanded the characterizations beyond the initial hard-core personifications. One example among many is Topo:

> Topo is a real stupid Homie. He is constantly on some other planet. He rarely speaks, and when he does he leaves the Homies wondering, what the hell he is talking about. Topo is happy though just floating around in his own little world. He is a math genius. The Homies love to give him ridiculously hard math problems so he can work them out instantly in his head, and blow their minds. While he's awesome in math he forgets simple shit, like his name, where he lives, his phone number and stuff like that (Homies, n.d., n.p.).

Another sample is Big Dopey, through whom we can best ascertain the creative process of converting a real person into an affectionate *rasquache* representation:

> Meet my Homie Big Dopey. He may look Dopey . . . but he ain't. He kinda observes things and then speaks up. He don't say much . . . but what he says makes a lot of sense. It's kinda like. . . . tú sabes . . . after I

Figure 7.4 Wino © David Gonzales.

Figure 7.5 Topo © David Gonzales.

think about it . . . that's right! The Vato makes senses! Big Dopey don't trip cuz the Homies call him that . . . he figures it's "con cariño . . . tú sabes . . . with Luv". Besides . . . if someone wants some . . . they can come get some! Big Dopey reminds me of my primo Zack de Burque . . . you veteranos de Albuquerque probably know him. He drives that show winning 64 Impala. But, if I told him I made him a Homie toy, and called it Big Dopey . . . he might come to Cali lookin for me . . . and that could be dangerous. Definately [sic]one of my favorites, with a special place in my heart . . . show Your luv for Big Dopey. (Homies n.d., n.p.)

Suddenly, these Homies gained a personality with individual traits, thus undermining the lampooning generally expected of misunderstood Homies seen as a homogenous group of thugs. Gonzales, in a real way, uncovered a little-known social pocket of humanity that did not figure in the North American imaginary as regular people, and so he set out to highlight certain features and qualities that produce an indelible mark in the viewer. He focused on their uniqueness instead of their predetermined stereotypes, suggesting they are people too. The Homies, thus, gained an original face and body in addition to a personal history of human depth with psychological dimensions. They were decoupled from the mold of stereotypes to acquire features that mirror real people through a filtered realism or, thanks to some exaggerated or cartoonish features, to emphasize playful representations and differential lifestyles.

The result of Gonzales' efforts is that he reappropriated both the real and imaginary Homies: what they are, what they do, and what they may represent in their own terms instead of mainstream society's gaze. In the process, this gallery of characters has expanded in diversity and variety multifold, which explains in part the creation of some 250 Homie characters and sales of over 150 million figurines worldwide. Gonzales has cleverly turned stereotypes on their ears by flaunting their resemblance to real characters, while producing a line of prototypical representations who coexist with personages who might populate a wide spectrum of social spheres. Consequently, Homies can be a grandmother, a religious person, a priest, a break-dancer, a teacher, a nun, or a nurse who form part of the same community with Perico (an ex-con), Vato-Loco (a hip zoot suiter), Tennishoe Pimp (a ripoff artist), La Negra (a female hip-hop rapper), La Chicana, Papi Chulo (a narcissistic Cuban model), P-Rico (an underground Puerto Rican rapper), Gangsta Hoopa (a basketball thug), La Flaca (a barrio pinup girl), and Home Lee (a Korean corner store owner). The representations form part of a tribute to celebrate the quotidian life of a large contingent of people who are generally overlooked as social types of difference. Gonzales, then, does not only concentrate on a subculture but also on a supraculture of mixed folks to show that the barrio and ghetto are now everywhere. His creations have continued to expand recently to now encompass "Mijos," a collection of, ironically, mini-figures, such as Mamón, Chorilo, and Perrodo, who are kids

Figure 7.6   Big Dopey © David Gonzales.

Figure 7.7 Hollywood © David Gonzales.

Figure 7.8 La Chicana © David Gonzales.

as kids with some identifiable hard-core qualities but whose representations go beyond their place of origin to show them in cute, mischievous activities or poses. But Gonzales does not stop there because he has also advanced his multimillion-dollar enterprise of entertainment to include Homie Rollerz, a video car-racing game, Hoodrats, Palermos, Homie t-shirts, model kits, stickers, and even a line of girls' panties. The artist might not be the most polished, but he has managed to shake the foundation of stereotyping, thanks to what Piasecki suggests is a Chicana/o Norman Rockwell prism that redefines barrio folk art and barrio communities for greater consumption, so we can enjoy their humor and laugh all over again, devoid of victimizations (2008, n.p.). The *rasquache* lens allows us to not take them too seriously while retaining a fascination for all they can suggest and represent. What we know is that they are not a false sameness or sanitized homogeneity, nor should we be embarrassed enough to deny their existence. Homies are a way of Chicanas/os spoofing themselves with some respect and even humor, two ingredients that allow us to appreciate their splendor, thanks to their flashiness and coolness. Consequently, their big ears, droopy eyes, dark sunglasses, funny hairdos, and eccentric features all indicate personality, vitality, and a unique expression. Another lesson is that they are not as threatening as they are made out to be, precisely because they are regular people. Their subversiveness entails a cry out for acknowledgement while demanding to be known as common folk instead of stereotypes: they may be small but they pack a lot of meaning into their miniature size, *chiquitos pero picosos* (miniature but with a punch). David Gonzales, their creator, proves once again that self-representation and self-reappropriation can be a powerful tool of agency. So, maybe there is something about Homies: a revenge and vindication to come out of the shadows of North American society.

NOTES

1. One of the best sources that examines this concept with considerable detail is Tomás Ybarra-Frausto's article "Rasquachismo: A Chicano Sensibility" (1991). Although standard Spanish would dictate that *rasquachismo* be written as *rascuachismo,* the former Chicano form is symptomatic of what it represents through its own particular spelling.
2. Both Ybarra-Frausto and Amalia Mesa-Bains discuss some of these points in Barnet-Sanchez (2005).
3. This first line of examples also appears in Ybarra-Frausto's (1991) article on *Rasquachismo,* but the others are my own.
4. Anecdotally, friends and colleagues have reaffirmed that "homeboy" is a term that more than likely originated in the 1930s or 1940s, which is contrary to popular belief. It appears to be the original term from which "Homie" derives years later due to its explicit etymological affinity.
5. There is something poetically coincidental with the characters in the TV program *The Lone Ranger* from the 1940s and 1950s, when the Native American named Tonto called the white man "Kimesabe" (what do you know about me). Somehow an echo of marginality plays dialectically in different directions.

WORKS CITED

Barnet-Sanchez, H. "Tomás Ybarra-Frausto and Amalia Mesa-Bains: A Critical Discourse from Within." *Art Journal* 64, no. 4 (2005): 91–3.

Bir, S. "With Homies, Gangsta Is in the Eye of the Beholder." *Metroactive*, April 10–16, 2003. http://www.metroactive.com/papers/sonoma/04.10.03/homies-0315.html. Accessed February 27, 2013.

Botkin, B. A., ed. *A Treasury of American Folklore*. New York: Crown, 1944.

Cardona, F. "Homies: Portraying a 'Real Barrio.'" *The Denver Post,* May 2, 2010, pp. 1–4. http://www.denverpost.com/commented/ci_8219519?source=commented-news. Accessed February 28, 2013.

Escalante, Vi. "The Politics of Chicano Representation in the Media." In *Chicano Renaissance: Contemporary Cultural Trends* (131–68), edited by D. R. Maciel, I. D. Ortiz, and M. Herrera-Sobek. Tucson: University of Arizona Press, 2000.

"George Murphy." *Wikipedia,* 1–4. http://en.wikipedia.org/wiki/George_Murphy. Accessed February 28, 2013.

Griswold del Castillo, R., T. McKenna, and Y. Yarbro-Bejarano, eds. *Chicano Art: Resistance and Affirmation, 1965–1985.* Los Angeles: Wight Art Gallery, UCLA, 1991.

Guerrero, L. *Lalo Guerrero's Greatest Parodies: Featuring Tacos for Two.* Pasadena, CA: SOS Records, 1998.

Loudenback, J. "Miniature Mayhem: An Interview with David Gonzales, Creator of the Homies." *TD Monthly* 2, no. 9 (September 2003): n.p.

Paz, O. *The Labyrinth of Solitude: Life and Thought in Mexico.* Translated by Lysander Kemp. New York: Grove Press, 1961.

Piasecki, J. "The New Americana: David Gonzales and His Homies Pay a Visit to the Pasadena Museum of California Art." January 3, 2008. http://www.pasadenaweekly.com/cms/story/detail/?id=5510&IssueNum=105. Accessed March 25, 2013.

Ríos, F. A. "The Mexican in Fact, Fiction, and Folklore." *El Grito: Journal of Contemporary Mexican-American Thought* 2, no. 4 (1969): 14–28.

Sánchez, A. "David Gonzales' Barrio Figurines Cause Tiny Sensation." *Albuquerque Journal,* July 6, 2004. http://www.abqjournal.com/venue/personalities/personalities07–06–03.htm. Accessed February 28, 2013.

The Lone Ranger (1949–1957). Television series created by George W. Trendle.

Ybarra-Frausto, T. "Rasquachismo: A Chicano Sensibility." In *Chicano Art: Resistance and Affirmation, 1965–1985* (155–62), edited by R. Griswold del Castillo, T. McKenna, and Y. Yarbro-Bejarano. Los Angeles: Wight Art Gallery, UCLA, 1991.

Part III

Visual Culture

Producing Resistance

Aztec warriors, the *Virgen de Guadalupe,* low riders, borderlands, families, urban barrios, elaborate tattoos, and *pachucos* are just some of the powerful visual images that Chicana/o culture evokes. The murals of East L.A., the Mission District of San Francisco, or Chicano Park in San Diego vividly communicate a message of a shared heritage and celebrate the richness of the pre-Columbian past. In the early days of the Chicano Movement, the United Farm Workers adopted as their flag the symbol of the Aztec and Mexican eagle to communicate a message of resistance and solidarity, while later images such as Ester Hernández's famous *Sun Mad Raisins* (1981) vehemently denounced the dangerous conditions endured by workers in the fields. In the urban area of East Los Angeles in 1973, Sr Karen Boccalero founded Self-Help Graphics & Art, a nonprofit arts centre, which continues to support emerging Latina/o artists by granting them a space to create and exhibit their work. Chicana/o art has developed a rich vocabulary that reimagines long-established motifs and symbols, such as the *Virgen de Guadalupe* or Mexican artist José Guadalupe Posada's signature skeletons, while moving from traditional media such as mural art, paintings, sculptures, and prints to conceptual art and installations. Although undoubtedly a socially and politically engaged means of expression, Chicana/o art is not limited to a message, nor can its diverse styles and techniques be neatly summarised.

Chicana/o artists have long represented the complexity and uniqueness of their experience through their artworks, but, as the writers in this section acknowledge, their recognition by the mainstream art world has until recently been limited, whether because of the persistence of racist stereotypes of the Chicana/o or as a consequence of Anglo-American or Eurocentric prejudices that define art in very restrictive and exclusive ways. In recent decades, however, major exhibitions have gradually led to a greater awareness of their work. The first major exhibition of Chicana/o art, which is mentioned in a number of the chapters in this section, was *CARA: Chicano Art Resistance and Affirmation, 1965–1985,* which toured the United States after opening at the Wight Gallery, Los Angeles, in 1990 and was distinguished not only by the sheer number and breadth of its exhibits but, as Eva Sperling Cockcroft observes, by "a unique curatorial process that tried to replicate the grass roots character of the Chicano movement" (1994, 194). This watershed exhibition led to the 1991 publication of the catalogue of the same name, which was authored by notable scholars including Shifra Goldman, and an in-depth study by Alicia Gaspar de Alba, who notes in her introduction that she was moved to write the work because, despite being an academic and a Chicana, she had not been aware of the richness of Chicana/o art before viewing the exhibition. This realisation led her to reflect on the association between the idea of home and the marginal status of Chicana/o art: "The connection underscored my own invisibility as a Chicana. Not only was I seeing Chicano/a art for the first time in the master's house, I was seeing myself reflected in that art as well" (1998, xv). Other major exhibitions have been curated by the rather unlikely patron of the arts Cheech Marin, the actor and entertainer best known for his portrayal of a happy-go-lucky stoner in the film *Up in Smoke* (1978) with his comedy partner Thomas Chong. Marin has used his considerable fortune to amass a substantial collection of Chicana/o art and has mounted several exhibitions, most recently *Los Angelenos/Chicano Painters of L.A.: Selections from the Cheech Marin Collection* at LACMA in 2008 (http://cheechmarin.com/chicano-art). While these major exhibitions had their detractors and were not, of course, the first to showcase Chicana/o art, their scale and success in terms of attendance numbers and in the exposure they brought to the art of this community were notable.

Although Chicana/o art has its own unique history and vocabulary, it is also an art that engages with international art, and as such, should not be regarded, as it has been, as an art that only speaks to its own community. As Thomas Wilson asserts:

> Chicano artists do not work in a vacuum; they are aware of the great traditions of art history. Looking at these works of art, one recognizes references to Goya, Sargent, Monet, Matisse, Gauguin, Picasso, Duchamp, and even Vermeer, to movements such as surrealism and German expressionism, and to pre-Hispanic, Spanish, Spanish colonial, and Mexican art. In Chicano art one sees references to the European pantheon from the Renaissance to impressionism and beyond. (Keller 2004: xii)

The broad frame of reference of Chicana/o art is suggested in the chapters that follow. Cristina Elgue-Martini deals with the enduring concern of Chicana/o art with justice through the decades since the Chicano Movement. María Herrera-Sobek reflects on how several Chicana/o artists use barbed wire as a motif for oppression and activism, and Catherine Leen compares religious imagery in Chicana and Irish art. Aesthetics aside, art undoubtedly continues to be a catalyst for change in the Chicana/o community. Consequently, some of the changes in Chicana/o art from the days of the Movement to the representation of this work in, to use Gaspar de Alba's evocative term, the "master's house" represented by mainstream galleries and museums, are also examined in this section.

Cristina Elgue-Martini traces the evolution of Chicana/o art from the era of the Chicano Movement to the present. Like García in Part I, she brings an international theoretical perspective to her study, using the works of Jürgen Habermas, Richard Rorty, Jacques Derrida, and others as a framework for her investigation into the ways in which Chicana/o art represents and demands justice. She begins by examining the politically motivated art of the Chicano Movement from the 1960s to the late twentieth century. The second part of her study considers the changes evident in a new generation of Chicana/o artists, such as Adrián Esparza and Juan Capistrán, whose work reflects on their hybrid identities. She also considers the work of artists including Margarita Cabrera, who denounce the exploitation of Chicana/os in the United States while also engaging with issues such as the pollution of the borderlands and the human relation to the natural world. Returning to the problem of the exclusion of Chicana/o art from the mainstream galleries and museums of the United States, Elgue-Martini concludes by commenting on LACMA's latest show of Chicana/o art entitled *Apariciones fantasmales. Arte después del movimiento chicano/Phantom Sightings: Art after the Chicano Movement* as a reflection of the position of Chicana/o art in twenty-first-century U.S. culture.

María Herrera-Sobek also reflects on the ways in which Chicana/o artists have evolved a distinct vocabulary to denounce injustice. She coins the term "aesthetic activism" to describe the work of a number of artists, including the works of such visual artists as Rupert García, Malaquías Montoya, Manuel Unzueta, Consuelo Jiménez Underwood, Adriana Yadira Gallego, and Daniel Márquez, who employ the motif of barbed wire to create a contestatory art practice that deals with the subject of immigration. Combining an overview of the history of barbed wire and its connection to pain and suffering with an analysis of the changing fortunes of Mexican immigrants in the United States, Herrera-Sobek examines how, for these artists, barbed wire has become a central metaphor for an art concerned with the quest for social justice.

Herrera-Sobek's identification of a strong religious subtext in many of the works she examines paves the way for Catherine Leen's analysis of the use of religious iconography in Chicana and Irish art. Leen traces the ways in which the image of the Virgin, in particular, has played a key role in the creation of national or community solidarity and pride on both sides of the Atlantic, while this icon has also been interpreted as problematic and even oppressive by feminist artists. The ways in which Chicana artists such as Ester Hernández, Yolanda López, and Alma López, and Irish artists Constance Short and Rita Duffy, reimagine and reappropriate religious iconography in their work to relate to the lives of contemporary women, and the controversy that such postmodern reworkings of images traditionally seen as Catholic have at times resulted in, are discussed.

To return to the notion of Chicana/o art's place in the "master's house" represented by the mainstream U.S. art world, not only have the artists mentioned in this section claimed a place in that house but they have also, like Sandra Cisneros's protagonist in *The House on Mango Street* (1991), redefined the idea of the house to also create their own spaces of creativity and activism. Whether through the embracing of nontraditional genres such as installation, the use of barbed wire in a practice that Herrera-Sobek identifies as aesthetic activism, or the reimagining of religious icons, these artists have created work that has inscribed itself into the consciousness of viewers both in and far beyond the United States, continuing and redefining the ways in which Chicana/o art can produce resistance.

WORKS CITED

Cisneros, Sandra. *The House on Mango Street*. New York: Vintage, 1991.

Gaspar de Alba, Alicia. *Chicano Art Inside/Outside the Master's House: Cultural Politics and the CARA Exhibition*. Austin: University of Texas Press, 1997.

Goldman, Shifra M., Marcos-Sanchez-Tranquilino, David R. Maciel, Harry Gamboa, Amalia Mesa-Bains, Victor A. Sorell, and Jacinto Quirarte. *Chicano Art: Resistance and Affirmation, 1965–1985*. Los Angeles: Wight Art Gallery, UCLA, 1991.

Marin, Cheech. http://cheechmarin.com/chicano-art/. Accessed March 1, 2013.

Sperling Cockcroft, Eva. "From Barrio to Mainstream: The Panorama of Latino Art." In *The Handbook of Hispanic Cultures in the United States-Literature and Art* (192–217), edited by Francisco Lomelí. Houston: Arte Público Press, 1994.

Wilson, Thomas H. "Chicano Art: Three Encounters." In *Chicano Art for Our Millennium* (xi-xii), edited by Gary D. Keller. Tempe, AZ: Bilingual Press/Editorial Bilingüe, 2004.

8 The Construction of Justice in Chicana/o Art

From Recognition to Distribution and Counter-Hegemony

Cristina Elgue-Martini

I propose to approach the theme of the construction of justice in contemporary Chicana/o art from a philosophical and epistemological perspective that holds that reality is narratively construed and that justice is a dialogical construction that accounts for the pluralism inherent in the perception and interpretation of the world. Justice—as a norm—is the result of negotiation and consensus in a multi/intercultural context, which not only manifests differences in ethnicity, gender, class, and age, but creates fruitful exchanges among cultural groups. Drawing on the ideas of Jürgen Habermas, Richard Rorty, and Jacques Derrida, and exploring the Latina/o reinvention of the U.S. urban landscape, this chapter aims to analyze the rich potential of Chicana/o artistic practices to create a democratic ethos.

As stated, my research is grounded in the theories derived from the "linguistic turn" devised by Rorty. Rorty coined this expression to emphasize the central role that language acquired in the study of philosophy and epistemology when, from the middle of the twentieth century, it ceased to be regarded as a transparent medium to represent a reality with an existence of its own and began to be conceived as the foundation of that reality—a position shared by Jerome Bruner in his psychocultural approach to education when he puts forward his theory about the "narrative construal of reality" (Bruner 1997, 130). From Rorty's perspective, the debate about realism and antirealism has come to an end because we are approaching a new conception of language and thought. Rorty urges us to accept the idea that reality is in most cases indifferent to the descriptions we make of it and that the self, instead of being adequately or inadequately expressed by a lexicon, is created by the use of a lexicon (Rorty 1991, 27).[1] From Habermas's partially coinciding point of view—despite his essentialist reminiscences—realism today has become a realism without representation (74), epistemological realism, that has as a correlative a moral constructivism (84), an issue that leads to the central problematic of my research: justice.

From the 1960s, after the emergence of the Chicano Movement, the population of Mexican origin established in the United States began to call itself Chicana/o. In opposition to Mexican American, the term that was used by the middle-class Mexican immigrant who was not involved in political processes, Chicana/o has a strong political content: it means ethnic and cultural awareness and social activism. In this context, the hybrid character of Chicana/o culture is projected in hybrid linguistic and plastic forms with an unquestionable political dimension: not only language, but also sculpture, painting, posters, murals, and more recently video works and room-sized installations have contributed to strengthen the democratic ethos of the Movement.

This chapter analyzes specifically the changes undergone in Chicana/o art from the 1960s onwards. As stressed in the CARIDAD (Chicano Art Resources Information Development and Dissemination) project, part of the CEMA (California Ethnic and Multicultural Archives) program of the University of California in Santa Barbara, Chicana/o art is "a public art to serve the Chicano social revolution" (CEMA 2005, n.p.). The first part of the chapter deals with twentieth-century artistic production, which broadly responds to this point of view—as reflected in the works of César A. Martínez, John Valdez, Luis Jiménez, Yolanda López, Luis Tapia, among others—and is mainly concerned with recognition. The second part analyzes the developments of the new millennium, which have distribution as a main goal and are opening the way toward what Portuguese theorist Boaventura de Sousa Santos has termed "counter-hegemonic globalizations" (2009, 229–231). These changes are evident in a new generation of Chicana/o artists, such as Adrián Esparza and Juan Capistrán, who have assimilated the artistic inheritance of the United States, resignified on many occasions as intertexts of their productions. Another group of artists, with Margarita Cabrera as an outstanding representative, not only denounces the exploitation of Chicanas/os in the United States but examines issues concerning unbridled consumerism and material waste in the border areas, the human relation to the natural world, and the changing nature of industry and power—that is, themes that are being addressed by emerging young artists of different national or ethnic affiliations on the globalized scene.

THE DIALOGICAL CONSTRUCTION OF JUSTICE: EPISTEMOLOGICAL IMPLICATIONS

As has been noted, my approach to Chicana/o art is based on the hypothesis that the concept of justice is not a universal one. Accepting that the promises of equality and freedom of the enlightenment/modernity project have been only partially fulfilled, Habermas proposes to dispense with the paradigm of conscience and subordinate reason to intersubjectivity (Sadivan 2004, 10): the Kantian paradigm of subjectivity is then replaced by the paradigm of communication. In his ethics of discourse, Habermas seeks to establish an intersubjective and rational foundation for norms based on the consideration of the pragmatic presuppositions of language (Sadivan 2004, 11).

According to Habermas, as soon as we perceive history and culture as the sources of an overwhelming variety of symbolic forms, and of the singularity of individual and collective identities, we become aware too of the challenge implicit in epistemic pluralism (Renaut, cited in Habermas 2004, 23).

Cultural pluralism also means, then, that the world is perceived and interpreted globally in different ways from the perspective of different individuals and different groups. There exists a sort of interpretative pluralism that affects the vision of the world and our comprehension of our own self, and this multiplicity of interpretative perspectives calls for the dialogic elaboration of practical truth. Practical discourse demands the adoption of a mutual perspective, a progressive decentering of the ego/ethnocentric comprehension of ourselves and of the world, which, according to Habermas, is a process based on reason. It is from this point of view that the two pragmatic conditions of his ethical discourse result: every participant in discourse is free, but epistemic authority must be exercised according to the pursuit of a reasoned agreement (Renaut 2004, 24).

Consensus is also essential for Rorty, although he does not assign a central role to reason. According to Rorty, democracy is one form among others, and it does not have to do with rationality but with shared beliefs (Mouffe 1996, 20). It is necessary then to think of strategies to convince people to achieve a more inclusive community and to create a democratic ethos. What matters are the way democracy functions and the liberal democratic subject's conditions of existence. We must think in terms of practices; we must create a "we." Derrida, on the other hand, refers to democracy as a "democracy to come" (1996, 161). For him, persuasion and discussion always imply the coexisting presence of force and violence. When one admits the irreducibility of violence, rules and conventions become necessary to stabilize power (Derrida 1996, 162). Conventions, institutions, and consensus are then means of stabilizing something that is chaotic and instable. Politics exists and ethics is possible precisely because stability is not natural, essential, or substantial (Derrida 1996, 163).

These philosophical changes have been accompanied by radical debates in the field of epistemology. For the discussion in this area I have given priority to de Sousa Santos's approach. In order to supersede modern knowledge and law, which he sees as the most consummate manifestations of what he calls "abyssal thinking," de Sousa Santos has proposed the category of "post-abyssal thinking." As the theorist explains:

> The understanding of the world by far exceeds the Western understanding of the world. Northern epistemologies draw abyssal lines between zones of being and zones of non-being, thereby committing epistemicide and wasting social experience in a massive scale. Mapping the lines is as much a search for absent knowledges as it is a search for absent beings. Knowing otherwise is also being otherwise. Knowing and being in a post-abyssal way involves a constant exercise of intercultural translation. (de Sousa Santos 2012, n.p.)

The new paradigms, from de Sousa Santos's point of view, aim for a global cognitive justice as the foundation of a global social justice (2009, 12). On the basis of an ecology of knowledges, global cognitive justice aspires to a total knowledge, to supersede the distinction between subject and object; it tends towards methodological transgression, discursive toleration, and union with nature. It throws light on the aesthetic dimension of science and, ultimately, it encourages the translation of knowledges and practices and the restitution of common-sense knowledge. The aim of the translation of knowledges is to create a cognitive justice on the basis of epistemological imagination. The aim of the translation of practices is to create the conditions for a global social justice on the basis of democratic imagination. The construction of a counter-hegemony will only be possible on the condition of reciprocal intelligibility and the consequent possibility of aggregation of nonhegemonic knowledges (de Sousa Santos 2010, 11–44).

As I have already stated, it is my purpose to consider the potential of Chicana/o artistic practices to build the democratic ethos (Rorty), to construct the "democracy to come" (Derrida), and to create the conditions for global justice and reciprocal intelligibility (de Sousa Santos).

CHICANA/O CULTURE

Chicana/o culture began to develop in the Southwest of the United States in mythical Aztlán, the place of origin, thousands of years ago, among the Cochise people, the ancestors of the Aztecs. The Aztecs left Aztlán in 1168 A.D. Guided by the god Huitzilopochtli, they settled in the place where an eagle with a writhing serpent in its beak perched on a cactus, where they founded the future capital of Mexico. Mexico was conquered and colonized by the Spaniards in the sixteenth century, and the Spaniards expanded their conquered territories to the North, that is, they occupied Aztlán. By this time, the process of the mixing of the races had already begun, however, and as Gloria Anzaldúa states: "For every gold-hungry *conquistador* and soul-hungry missionary who came north from Mexico, ten to twenty Indians and *mestizos* went along as porters or in other capacities" (1987, 5). In this context, the conquest meant for the Indians a return to their homeland, and these Indians and *mestizos* coming from Mexico intermarried with North American Indians, thus furthering the *mestizaje*.

In the nineteenth century, Anglos began to migrate illegally into Texas and gradually drove the *tejanos* from their lands. Wars followed, and in 1848 the United States imposed the Treaty of Guadalupe-Hidalgo, which left about 100,000 Mexican citizens in what had become U.S. territory. The guarantees that the treaty conferred on them were never honoured by the North Americans and the *tejanos* were inhumanly dispossessed of their lands and rights: "*Con el destierro y el exilio fuimos desuñados, destroncados, destripados*—we were jerked out by the roots, truncated, disembowelled, dispossessed and separated from our identity and our history" (1987, 7–8), as Anzaldúa states.

In the twentieth century, and as a consequence of the structural economic crisis that affected Latin America at that time, hundreds of thousands Mexicans migrated toward the Southwest of the United States and from there to other important urban centres. In Anzaldúa's words: "*En cada Chicano y mexicano* [that migrates], *vive el mito del tesoro territorial perdido.* North Americans call this return to the homeland the silent invasion" (1987, 10).

CHICANA/O ART

The hybridity of Chicana/o culture has been expressed in blended linguistic forms, as seen in the examples from Anzaldúa. Without questioning the central role played by articulate language in the process of identity building, I want to highlight in this chapter the potential of the plastic arts—murals, posters, paintings, sculptures, contemporary multimedia installations—as a medium for the expression of the processes of denunciation, resistance, and struggle that take place on the frontier—a term that involves not only the geographic borderland, that is, the Texas-U.S. Southwest/Mexican border, but all the spaces in which Chicana/o culture has developed. As stated by Anzaldúa:

> In fact, the Borderlands are physically present wherever two or more cultures edge each other, where people of different races occupy the same territory, where under, lower, middle and upper classes touch, where the space between two individuals shrinks with intimacy. (1987, viii)

According to my hypothesis, while the aim of Chicana/o art in the twentieth century was mainly recognition, in the twenty-first century the emphasis has shifted to distribution and more universal concerns, such as the human relationship to the natural world, consumerism, material waste, outsiderism, and cultural stereotypes. Thus approached, the works of Chicana/o artists are contributing to the creation of a counter-hegemony, as characterized by de Sousa Santos, which is a consequence of the conditions for global justice based on democratic imagination and reciprocal intelligibility.

THE TWENTIETH CENTURY: RECOGNITION

The Chicano Movement emerged as ethnic awareness in the 1960s, and beyond the achievement of civil rights and the preservation of the Spanish language, which were then its main goals, it aimed at the construction of an identity on the basis of a distinctive ethnic and cultural inheritance that interacted with a new space. In the 1970s, the Movement consolidated through its antiwar manifestations: those Chicanos who did not go to fight in Vietnam proposed changing the system that oppressed them, and they also vindicated the right of their people to self-determination. This context saw the birth of several groups of Chicana/o artists: The Royal Chicano Air Force, Toltecas de Aztlán [Toltecs from Aztlán], Con Safos [With Sappho], Mujeres Muralistas [Women Muralists], Los Four, and the United Farmworkers Union, among others. The joint action of the different groups achieved important changes in the field of federal politics and the implementation of new programs of education. The Bilingual Education Act of 1968, which provided federal funding to school districts to develop bilingual education programs, was one of the most significant achievements in this sense. It was the first federal legislation to address the unique educational needs of students with limited English-speaking ability and led the way for further legislation regarding the equality of educational opportunity.

Toward the end of the 1980s, the Chicana/o artist was accepted in art galleries and museums, and, as is the case with Chicana/o writers, some of them were already in the process of attaining canonical status. The themes that prevailed in the twentieth century in this pluralistic and heterogeneous art aimed mainly, as already mentioned, at recognition, that is, the construction of justice was centred, first, on visualizing the group within the Anglo community, which meant at the same time putting the symbolic potential of artistic languages in the service of the process of identity building. Thus, one of the central topics was the barrio and its characters, the tradition of religious art, and pre-Columbian roots. Following Derrida, however, in the face of the irreducibility of violence and its conventions, institutions and consensus are only means of stabilizing something that is chaotic and instable; thus violence was also expressed in the early forms of Chicana/o art: the violence of experiencing the crossing of the frontier and the violence of life in the big cities of the Southwest of the United States; the violence of U.S. institutions against Chicana/os, and the violent reactions of the latter to situations where they lived as unfair. In terms of a form of expression, Chicana/o art incorporated murals, posters, prints, photography, drawing, acrylic and oil painting, and sculpture. With regard to their poetics, Chicana/o artists expressed themselves through a diverse range of tendencies, including neoexpressionism, neoregionalism, folk and naïf, neosurrealism, minimalism, abstract and conceptual art.

Of the different expressive media above mentioned, because of its strong didactic potential, the mural was at the beginning the most innovative genre of this public art at the service of a political program. The murals that Chicana/o artists began to produce toward the end of the 1960s were the expression of the Movement of the communities of the Third World, which aimed to awaken the awareness of the people about their social conditions and to help in the process of identity construction. The murals painted on the walls of big buildings and along the highways of North American cities were conceived as a militant art, as a strategy of the Chicana/o struggle for civil rights. In those first murals, pre-Columbian motifs or Chicana/o characters, whose strong stylization turned them into stereotypes, predominated. In 1993, Sylvia Gorodezky commented on the prevalence of these murals:

> In the Northwest of the United States there are 88 murals that have been produced by minority communities; 86 among them have been the work of Chicano artists. . . . But the biggest production is in the American Southwest where there are more than one thousand. (1993, 73)

As has been noted, a distinctive motif in the building of the Chicano identity in those days was the inhabitant of the barrio. In the acrylic paintings of César A. Martínez, a San Antonio artist, the barrio dweller has been immortalized as *El Güero* [*The Foreigner*] and *Bato² con sunglasses,* compositions that show a distant young man with a calculated indifference and a potential for violence. In *Hombre que le gustan las mujeres* [*The Man who Likes Women*], John Valdez presents, in an ironic way, the stereotypical image of the Chicano macho: a vigorous Chicano with an impressive drawing of the Virgin of Guadalupe tattooed on his breast and of two comparatively smaller girls on each arm: one of them, sensual and naked, the other one, its dichotomous version, the traditional Mexican wife. By way of contrast, in his composition *La Butterfly,* Valdez creates a paradigmatic version of the contemporary Chicana; the title points to a small tattoo on her breast, which the girl, with heavy makeup on and around her eyes, shows off with a defiant attitude.

Luis Jiménez's paintings expand the gallery of Chicana/o stereotypes: *El Chuco* [a shortened form of the *pachuco*] tells about the strong attraction women exert on the Chicano: it shows the *pachuco* with a bandana wrapped around his head walking casually, accompanied by a Chicana in very light clothes, just as he turns his head, attracted by another woman. Another group of his works responds to a more strongly political conception. In the sculpture *El aullido del coyote desafiante* [*The Defiant Howl of the Coyote*], made of fiberglass and lacquer, with the paradigmatic animal performing the action referred to by the title, Jiménez expresses another variant of the unyielding attitude characteristic of his Chicana/o characters. On the other hand, *Cruzando el Río Bravo* [*Crossing the Rio Bravo*] is one of his strongest testimonies of the frontier motif: a determined Mexican is crossing the river carrying a woman on his shoulders; the woman presses her baby against her breast while sadly looking backward toward the homeland she is leaving behind. In Gorodezky's opinion, "his works are a mixture of God Huitzilopochtli: the warrior ready for battle and the modern machine-man" (1993, 45–46).

Luis Tapia, a descendant of the first settlers of New Mexico, pays homage to his origins through a naïf art that resignifies the old tradition of polychromatic religious images. *Reredos,* an altarpiece of carved wood painted in vibrant reds and greens playing with the effect of Whites and Blacks, is an outstanding example of his art. Tapia rejects both the status of local artist and of craftsman. He describes his creative philosophy: "I believe in tradition, I am this tradition, but tradition is not to copy, what I do to preserve my heritage is to innovate it, watering it as if it were a plant that is growing" (cited by Gorodezky 1993, 39). Leo Limón, who was born and still lives in East Los Angeles, has been called the "Alley River Cat Artist" by former Los Angeles Mayor Richard Riordan. The appellative makes reference to the fact that Limón has become known as a painter of cat faces on the cement walls channeling the Los Angeles River. Limón's work on paper deals mostly with the sacred role played by the heart in indigenous cultures and makes use of many Aztec symbols. In a similar mode, the work of Carmen Lomas Garza is decidedly naïf. Her gouache *Barriendo de susto . . . [Sweeping from Surprise . . .*] depicts a scene from the everyday life of a Chicana/o family: the action takes place in a bedroom, protected by the Virgin of Guadalupe, who presides over the scene from a portrait on a chest of drawers. A woman lying on a mantlepiece on the floor, with candles at the four corners, either unconscious or dead, is the object of a ritual by a *curandera [healer]*; another two women pray, and the master of the house, who has only one arm, carries his hat in his hand in an attitude of grief and respect; through the glass of the door the viewer can see a boy playing outside, indifferent to the ritual that is taking place. *Nopalitos frescos . . . [Fresh Cactus . . .]*, another gouache, shows, with humour and irony, a big cactus and two hands, which cut a succulent leaf with a knife and fork to offer it as if it were a *tamale* [steamed corn wrap].

If the works above mentioned exemplify one aspect of Chicana/o art, the adherence to its Mexican origins in an attempt to preserve one of the components of its hybridity, the production of Yolanda López, instead, has a more avowedly political content. This political message is directed, in some of her compositions, at an expanded ethnic group, pointing to the developments of the twenty-first century. In the drawing *Quitándosela y poniéndosela: Unión con las mujeres de Centroamérica [Taking It Off and Putting It On: Unity with the Women of Central America]*, the majority of the canvas is occupied by a large woman's face. The woman is putting on and taking off a mask. Half the background of the composition features rifles and the other half roses. This dichotomy is repeated on the frame of the drawing. The composition puts emphasis on a feminist interpretative perspective, which calls for a dialogic elaboration of new practical truths—in this case, the contemporary roles performed by women in new lived and imagined spaces. Yolanda López also produced performances and installations in which she appeared as a character. *La artista como la Virgen de Guadalupe [The Artist as the Virgin of Guadalupe]*, for example, is a parody of one of the founding myths of Chicana/o culture and one which is discussed in detail by Catherine Leen elsewhere in this volume. In the central place where the myth locates the Virgin, the artist places herself wearing shorts and tennis shoes, her hands together not in prayer but holding her brushes. In her deconstruction of the myth, the artist is keeping and even strengthening it as an ingredient of Chicana/o identity, but at the same time she is expanding and extending its scope, answering artistically the challenge implicit in the epistemic pluralism posed by Habermas: she is contributing to the progressive decentering of the ethnocentric comprehension of ourselves and of the world.

Other works of the period are more explicit in their demand for justice. Rupert García's serigraphy *Cesen deportación* [*Stop Deportation*] shows, on a brilliant red background, the imperious request ¡CESEN DEPORT-ACIÓN! which is written in yellow. Parallel to this emphatic exhortation, three thick threads of barbed wire cross the whole width of the rectangular composition. This work is discussed further by María Herrera-Sobek in the next chapter of this volume. Together with this kind of poster production, Carlos Almaraz's oils, such as *Europa y el jaguar* [Europe and the Jaguar], in a style with powerful allegoric impact, show the collision between the European and the *mestizo—Civilización y Barbarie* [*Civilization and Barbarism*], the dichotomy that organized Latin America's approach to culture and nationhood from the Romantic movement up to the middle of the twentieth century. Almaraz, together with another three artists, formed the collective Los Four, and Almaraz's great mural "Boycott Gallo," situated at All Nations' Center in the Eastern area of Los Angeles, achieved the status of a historical monument for the community until its destruction at the end of the 1980s. Another artist who created an emblematic icon with powerful recognition content was Charles "Chas" Bojórquez, who in 1969 produced a symbol that represented him as a stylized skull called *Señor Suerte* [*Mr Luck*], which became a street image representing protection from death.

I have already mentioned that in the decade of the 1970s, in the context of the Vietnam War, the Chicano Movement participated in antiwar protests. Even if these protests were peaceful, there were some violent protests in Los Angeles at this time. In 1972, after one such demonstration, there were incidents that led to a confrontation with the police on Whittier Boulevard. The event was represented by Frank Romero in his epic oil, *The Closing of Whittier Boulevard*, where the protagonists are the low riders, large cars from the 1950s painted with popular motifs of Chicana/o culture. The low rider was one of the most representative icons of urban Chicana/o culture, the object onto which the young Chicano projected his dreams and fantasies in brilliant lacquer and shining chrome. The paradigmatic expression of the meaning of the Low Rider is perhaps Gilbert Luján's art-objet, *Our Family Car*, where the car is acknowledged as an object of recognition of Chicana/o identity.

By the end of the twentieth century, works by Chicana/o artists were already being exhibited in museums and art galleries, and, as happened with Chicana/o writers, some plastic artists were also in the process of becoming canonical. This change of status in Chicana/o culture was noted by *Time* magazine in a special issue of July 11, 1988, which featured Chicano actor Edward James Olmos on the cover with the legend ¡MAGNÍFICO!

[MAGNIFICENT!] printed in letters almost the same size of the name of the publication. The cover included a significant comment: "Hispanic culture breaks out of the barrio" (*Time* 1988). It is worth mentioning that in 2000, Edward James Olmos was the seventh person to be honored with a plaque on Whittier Boulevard, which by that time had become known as the Latino Walk of Fame.

Another central name of the Movement was García, who achieved great public recognition and who produced a memorable portrait of Che Guevara above the slogan "Right on." Melesio Casas' *Humanscapes* are also notable as instances of the reaffirmation of a Chicana/o identity, because they show scenes of Chicana/o life, but, as Rubén C. Cordova remarks, they are also important in their incorporation of new techniques:

> The 153 paintings that San Antonio-based artist Mel Casas calls Humanscapes were inspired by a glimpse of a drive-in movie screen. . . . Marshall McLuhan's *Mechanical Bride* (1951) deeply influenced the analysis of media imagery and technology that is evident in these paint-ings. In addition to contemporary cultural influences, the early phase of the Humanscape series also drew on the same artistic influences, namely surrealism and Dada, that shaped the work of other pop artists. By the end of 1967, Casas included parts of signs within his paintings. These signs led to freestanding, independent texts that doubled as subtitles. By juxtaposing punning texts and images, Casas broke from the explicit cinematic setting. (2011, 51)

Of the many groups of Chicana/o artists, East Los Streetscapers, a collective that included artists such as David Botello, Wayne Healy, George Yepes, and Rudy Calderón, deserves special mention. The group produced murals for their neighborhood, and, in the case of Botello and Healy, their works achieved a much greater impact in the region and were also a significant presence in the states of Washington and California.

I would like to finish this part of the chapter with a reference to one of the most representative exhibitions covering the first two decades of the Movement: the national tour *Chicano Art: Resistance and Affirmation 1965–1985,* curated by the Wight Art Gallery at UCLA, which toured muse-ums and art galleries of the United States in those two significant decades and led to the publication of a book bearing the same name, which was published in conjunction with the exhibition, with a catalogue of 128 works in various media and 54 murals. The book, edited by Richard Griswold del Castillo, Teresa McKenna, and Yvonne Yarbro-Bejarano, represented a milestone in the study of Chicana/o art at the time. In one of its chapters, Jacinto Quirarte makes reference to "Exhibitions of Chicano Art: 1965 to the Present." Philip Brookman also considers the development of Chicana/o art chronologically in "Looking for Alternatives: Notes on Chicano Art, 1960–90," while the panorama is completed by Holly Barnet-Sanchez and

Dana Leibson in "The Contexts of Chicano Art and Culture: A Selected Chronology." The book contains an appendix with information on artists' spaces and theaters, artists' biographies, a glossary of Chicana/o terms, and a bibliography. The exhibition included works by some of the artists already mentioned, such as Yolanda López and César Martínez, and highlighted the collective ASCO. The group was started by Patssi Valdez, the photographer Harry Gamboa, Jr., and the artists Willie Herrón and Gronk. Taking their name from the Spanish word for revulsion and nausea, ASCO used performance, public art, and multimedia to respond to social and political unrest in Los Angeles from 1972 to 1987, the period during which the group was active. Their contribution to Chicana/o art and their social impact became clear when the Los Angeles Museum of Art (LACMA) organized the exhibition *Asco: Elite of the Obscure, a Retrospective, 1972–1987.*

The exhibition *Chicano Art: Resistance and Affirmation* was reedited and toured again between 1990 and 1993. The impact of the tour was on this occasion examined by Alicia Gaspar de Alba in her study *Chicano Art Inside/Outside the Master's House: Cultural Politics and the CARA Exhibition* (1998). I have placed special emphasis on the *CARA* exhibitions not only on account of their scope and impact, but because the title itself points to problematics that in the new millennium have been referred to as problematics of recognition—that is, the CARA exhibitions have highlighted that, in its pragmatic effect, twentieth-century Chicana/o art aimed mainly at the ethnic, social, and cultural recognition of the Chicanos. Yet, much of this art, in its construction of different belief systems, in its affirmation of the pre-Columbian heritage, and in the light it throws on *mestizo* culture, is already paving the way for what de Sousa Santos has termed "post-abysmal thought," which he defines as "learning from the South through an epistemology of the South" (2010, 32), a kind of thought that, as already stated, aims at an ecology of knowledges.

I have mentioned that most Chicana/o artists achieved recognition before the end of the twentieth century and that their works were exhibited in mainstream museums and galleries in the United States. Yet, it is interesting to note that the 1999 edition of the renowned *American Art Book* by Phaidon does not include a single instance of Chicana/o art, and the Chicano Movement is not mentioned in the list of movements that appears at the end of the book.

THE TWENTY-FIRST CENTURY: DISTRIBUTION AND COUNTER-HEGEMONY

In order to consider the changes introduced by the new millennium, I will concentrate my analysis on the exhibition *Apariciones fantasmales. Arte después del movimiento chicano/Phantom Sightings: Art after the Chicano Movement,* organized by LACMA. The exhibition was curated by Rita

González and Howard Fox, from LACMA, and Chon Noriega, director of the Chicano Studies Research Center of UCLA and adjunct curator of Chicano and Latino Art of LACMA. After being shown in Los Angeles, the exhibition was displayed in the Museo Tamayo de Arte Contemporáneo de México, with the support of the U.S. Embassy, from October 2008 to January 2009, after which it travelled to Texas and New York.

I have chosen to analyse the works in this exhibition, first, because it shows the state of Chicana/o art at the beginning of the twenty-first century, and, secondly, because it coincided with an evaluation on the part of the new generations of artists both on the position of Chicana/o culture in U.S. culture and on the heritage of Chicana/o art after the Civil Rights Movement of the 1960s and 1970s. *Apariciones fantasmales. Arte después del movimiento chicano* explores the last twenty years of Chicana/o production from the perspective of the twenty-first century, and focuses on conceptual and urban art. In the words of Ramiro Martínez, director of the Museo Tamayo, it is "the first extensive revision—after twenty years—that explores the development of the current production of American artists of Mexican descent" (Museo Tamayo 2008, n.p.). This means that the contexts of the works of more than 30 artists represent a local crossroads that has experienced the effect both of global migrations and transnational movements. Moreover, the title of the exhibition renews the debate on the status of Chicana/o culture and seems to imply that it continues to be a phantom culture, ignored by the vast majority of U.S. society.

The name of the exhibition pays homage to Harry Gamboa, Jr., who in 1981 stressed that the media had relegated Chicana/o culture in Los Angeles to a phantom culture. As stated in *Arte Nuevo* on the occasion of the opening of the exhibition in Mexico City:

> The influence of ASCO on the youngest generation is seen in the ephemeral urban forms that prevail in the installations of Arturo Romo-Santillano, Scoli Acosta, Shizu Saldamando, Mario Ybarra Jr. y Cruz Ortiz. These practices are a form of urban activism that show the presence in real life of an apparently "phantom" culture. (López 2008, n.p.)

In the context of this discussion, it is important to mention that many of the artists participating in the exhibition no longer consider that they are producing Chicana/o art; instead they state their critical position both at local and global levels and, as has been the case since the emergence of cultural studies, they blur the line between elite and popular art. Following this tendency, the exhibition includes painting and sculpture but also film, photo, installation, multimedia, collage and bricolage, and performance practices. Much of it is an art made of found materials, and, as a whole, it amounts to a sort of anthropology of the present.

As an introduction to the analysis of artistic production, it is relevant to mention some data taken from the field of education that provides evidence to infer the status of Chicana/os in U.S. society in this century so as to justify the implied reference to their culture in terms of a phantom culture, as indicated by the name of the exhibition. In the chapter that Mike Davies devotes to education in his book *Magical Urbanism. Latinos Reinvent the U.S. City* (2001)—using information provided by the population census of 2000—the author notes that in 1997 President Clinton recognized the 30 percent dropout rate among Latina/o high school students (versus 8 percent for whites and 13 percent for African Americans). Davies adds:

> In an economy where all good jobs (even for police officers and plumbers) seemingly demand at least fourteen years of education, nearly half of Spanish-surname residents aged twenty-five or older in New York City lack a high school diploma, as do 55 percent of adult Latinos in Massachusetts and 58 percent of Mexican immigrants in Los Angeles. (2001, 132)

The low degree of integration of Latinas/os was made evident by Harvard University's Civil Rights Project, according to which "Nationwide, nearly 70 percent of Black students and 75 percent of Latinos attend schools that are predominantly black, Latino and Native American" (cited by Davies 135). According to the same source, from 1970 to 1997, as the school population shifted from an Anglo majority to a Latina/o plurality, "spending per pupil in California fell more than 15 percent relative to spending in the rest of the country" (quoted by Davies 2001, 135).

It is precisely in the urban space that I have been referring to, from San Francisco and Los Angeles to San Antonio and New York, where the production of the artists participating in the exhibition is placed, a space that at the turn of the millennium is comprised of Chicana/o migrations, but at the same time of transnational groups from different ethnic and cultural backgrounds in the context of a globalization that the practices of these artists turn into a counter-hegemonic one.

On the occasion of the exhibition, the Museo Tamayo organized the Symposium *Sitio, presencia y ausencia: Apariciones y estrategias del arte después del movimiento chicano* [*Place, Presence and Absence: Appearances and Strategies of Art after the Chicano Movement*]. As Luis Reyes explains in *La Jornada*, a Mexican national newspaper, "in the session devoted to *Sitios*, the discussion was centered on the conceptual 'sites' and on how the artist—with a binational and transitory perspective—changes his/her focus" (Reyes 2008, n.p.). Daniela Pérez summed up the main difference from the earlier generations of Chicana/o artists when she explained that in the 1960s and 1970s Chicana/o artists looked for iconographic referents, such as Pancho Villa or the Virgin, "that point to the Chicano identity, yet, the exhibition that we are showing does not necessarily make use of such traditional iconography, but of certain conceptual strategies" (Reyes 2008, n.p.). Yet, the participants also underlined that during that early phase of the Movement, artists struggled against racism, and fought for civil rights, and "they performed actions in public spaces through underground mechanisms, they addressed economic topics and they called international attention to the major thematics of the frontier and the exploitation of the workers, as it occurs today in the Tamayo" (Reyes 2008, n.p.).

Sharing the contemporary interest in the critical category of space, which in the practices of these borderline artists becomes doubly significant, they question not only the concept of monuments, but they aim to bring to the heart of the debate the silences of official history and institutions about their stories as minority ethnic groups. Like their twentieth-century precursors, they use public spaces for their interventions, but put more emphasis on social absence than on the ethnic peculiarities of their culture.

There is, at the same time, a determination on the part of several artists to assert their presence not only in the geographic space of the new nation, but in its cultural history. To achieve this purpose they assimilate and transform texts from the history of U.S. painting through the use of parodic, transcultural, and hybrid practices. Adrian Esparza in *One and the Same* unweaves the fabric of the traditional Mexican *sarape* [shawl] and uses part of the material to elaborate an abstract composition that evokes the mural paintings of Sol Lewitt. In *White Minority,* Juan Capistran pays homage to a landmark of the American School, Frank Stella's *Black Paintings* of the 1960s and 1970s; yet, as noted in *Arte Nuevo,* "many viewers will more easily recognize in his compositions the four vertical panels of the device of the punk hardcore group Black Flag" (López 2008, n.p.). The homage is not only achieved through the refunctionalization of cultural artefacts, that is, through the use of parody as a strategy. Carlee Fernandez creates self-portraits that include photographs of the people that have influenced his personal and professional history: artists, writers, and his own father. Although these works are examples of the use of strategies traditionally termed as intertextual, the different cultural traditions that they put into contact contribute to create what de Sousa Santos has termed a cognitive justice, based on epistemological imagination. Michael Govan, president and director of LACMA, asserts:

> These artists do not identify themselves as regional, and, maybe, some of them do not consider themselves Chicanos first. They have assimilated the mainstream American culture in the same way that the American culture has assimilated their diverse and divergent demography. If they appear here integrated as a group of artists inspired by the Chicano movement, it is not as a result of their own free will or consensus. This is an artificial museographic product, a means to reflect and speculate on interests and themes confronted by contemporary Chicano artists. (quoted by Lebenglik 2008, n.p.)

The exhibition opens with a yellow Volkswagen, a work by Margarita Cabrera, which, because of its high potential for denunciation and the power of its form, has become a sort of symbol of the exhibition, since it has been reproduced in most press and Internet articles on the show. Its name is *Vocho (1974)*, which is the nickname of that popular Volkswagen car in Mexico. The car is almost completely made of cloth. As stated by Lebenglik: "The artist has replaced with cloth all the parts of the car in whose processes of fabrication or ensamblado participate workers of Mexican origin, with the worst working conditions: what remains of the original car if we take away the vinilo cloth, the padding and the thread—is extremely small" (2008, n.p.). If this work has been acknowledged as the icon of the exhibition, it is clear that the central aim of Chicana/o art in the new century has turned from recognition into an interest in working conditions and retribution in the industrial scene of the urban centers, which in a certain sense points to a new form of traditional class politics. In their dialogical construction of the concept of justice, Chicanas/os are putting emphasis on what twenty-first century theorists have termed "distribution."

Waste and found materials, abandoned things, and the uninhabited urban landscape play a major part in the exhibition, just as the processes that have transformed into fetishes some of the new objects that have been integrated into Chicana/o culture in the new lived space. As observed in *Arte Nuevo:*

> The work of Christina Fernández is centered on the revealing waste that is left in a deserted urban landscape. Delilah Montoya's photographs, on the other hand, show the things abandoned by the illegal immigrants on their journey through the Arizona desert. Margarita Cabrera, Gary Garay, Julio César Morales and Jason Villegas conceptually remake the manufactured objects that are related to the North America Free Trade Agreement and the crossing of the frontier, whereas Eduardo Sarabia approaches as fetishes the luxury articles of the narcoculture. (López 2008, n.p.).

I mentioned that one of the purposes of the artists participating in the exhibition was to destabilize the monument. This is the aim of Sandra de la Loza's *Pocho Research Society.* It is a piece of conceptual installation art placed within a specially built precinct in the main room of the museum which, through videos, light boxes, maps, and documents, produces a rededication to Fort Moore Pioneer Memorial (in downtown Los Angeles) with the purpose of giving another version of the history of the war between Mexico and the United States that the monument commemorates. The space, a third space with social and temporal density, is resignified through the imagination using as a strategy the enumeration by the artist of the different uses of the place throughout history, thus achieving a new history, told through maps, old newspaper articles, and videos that aim to problematize the grand narratives.

CONCLUSION

As stated in the introduction, this brief review of the main forms in which Chicana/o art has evolved, of its recurrent motifs and predominant media and styles, both in the twentieth and in the twenty-first centuries, had as its aim the construction of meanings with the purpose of assessing its contribution to the dialogical construction of justice in the borderlands.

Chicana/o art was born as "a public art to serve the Chicano social revolution" and continues to be a critical and engaged art. As an instance of intercultural discourse, it is an art of tensions, where negotiations do not always occur in a harmonious way; it is an art that shows that culture is always a process that involves struggles between competing sets of practices, inexorably tied up with relations of power, and that these struggles are more significant in hybrid spaces. As a political art representing the resistance of a minority ethnic group, it has embraced a mission to denounce the institutional violence exerted on the group and the silences of official history in order to create more inclusive ways of perception and expression. On this basis, its potential to build the democratic ethos and its role in the contemporary processes involving the dialogic construction of justice are of vital importance. Its epistemical contributions to a counter-hegemonic globalization, working on the basis of reciprocal intelligibility and the consequent possibility of aggregation of nonhegemonic knowledges, are also crucial.

NOTES

1. All translations into English from the bibliography in Spanish are the author's.
2. Gorodezky defines the *bato* as: "a young Chicano from Los Ángeles, who walks carefree in the streets wearing a *bandana* wrapped around his head and tattoos on his body" (1993, 19).

WORKS CITED

Anzaldúa, G. *Borderlands/La Frontera. The New Mestiza.* San Francisco: Aunt Lute Books, 1987.
Bruner, J. *The Culture of Education.* Cambridge, MA: Harvard University Press, 1997.
CEMA (California Ethnic and Multicultural Archives). *Arte Chicano. Una Guía Informativa.* http://cemaweb.library.ucsb.edu/chicanoArtSpanishVersion.html. Accessed October 19, 2005.
Cordova, R. C. "The Cinematic Genesis of Mel Casas's Humanscape, 1965–1967," *Aztlan: A Journal of Chicano Studies* 36, no. 2 (Fall 2011): 51–87.
Davies, M. *Magical Urbanism: Latinos Reinvent the U.S. City.* New York: Verso, 2001.
Derrida, J. "Notas sobre deconstrucción y pragmatismo." In *Deconstrucción y pragmatismo* (151–170), edited by Chantal Mouffe. Translated by Marcos Mayer. Buenos Aires, México y Barcelona: Paidós, 1996.

de Sousa Santos, B. *Una epistemología del Sur: La reinvención del conocimiento y la emancipación social.* Buenos Aires: Clacso, 2009.

———. *Para Descolonizar Occidente. Más allá del pensamiento abismal.* Buenos Aires: Clacso, 2010.

———. "Boaventura de Sousa Santos in conversation with Shiv Visvanathan, Suely Rolnik and Sarat Maharaj. Chaired by Brenna Bhandar." *Spaces of Transformation: Epistemologies of the South. Reinventing Social Emancipation.* Tate Modern, Starr Auditorium, April 28, 2012, 14.00–16.30. http://www.tate.org.uk/whats-on/tate-modern/talks-and-lectures/spaces-transformation-epistemologies-south. Accessed December 18, 2012.

Gaspar de Alba, A. *Chicano Art Inside/Outside the Master's House: Cultural Politics and the CARA Exhibition.* Austin: University of Texas Press, 1998.

Gorodezky, S. M. *Arte Chicano como cultura de protesta.* México: Centro de Investigaciones sobre Estados Unidos de América; Mexico: Universidad Nacional Autónoma de México, 1993.

Griswold del Castillo, R., Teresa McKenna, and Yvonne Yarbro-Bejarano, eds. *Chicano Art: Resistance and Affirmation 1965–1985.* Los Angeles: Wight Art Gallery, UCLA, 1991.

Habermas, J. *La ética del discurso y la cuestión de la verdad.* Barcelona: Paidós, 2004.

Lebenglik, F. "Estéticas en estado de tensión." *Página* 12, December 9, 2008. http://www.pagina12.com.ar. Accessed October 20, 2011.

López, M. "Apariciones fantasmales. Arte después del movimiento chicano." *Arte Nuevo,* November 9, 2008. http://arte-nuevo.blogspot.com.ar/2008/11/apariciones-fantasmales-arte-despus-del.html. Accessed September 28, 2012.

Mouffe, C. "Deconstrucción, pragmatismo y la política de la democracia." In *Deconstrucción y pragmatismo* (13–33), edited by Chantal Mouffe. Translated by Marcos Mayer. Buenos Aires, México y Barcelona: Paidós, 1996.

Museo Tamayo. "Boletín de Prensa." México D.F., October 14, 2008. http://www.museotamayo.org/assets/boletines/2008-exposiciones/081016Aparicionesfantasmales.pdf. Accessed November 28, 2012.

Renaut, A. "Coloquio con Jürgen Habermas." *La ética del discurso y la cuestión de la verdad* (15–67). Buenos Aires: Paidós, 2004.

Reyes, L. "Realizan amplia revisión sobre el movimiento chicano en el arte actual." *La Jornada,* November 8, 2008. http://www.jornada.unam.mx/2008/11/08/index.php?section= cultura&article=a05n3cul. Accessed October 20, 2011.

Rorty, R. *Contingencia, ironía y solidaridad.* Translated by Alfredo Eduardo Sinnot. Barcelona: Paidós, 1991.

Sadivan, P. "Introducción." In *La ética del discurso y la cuestión de la verdad* (9–14). Buenos Aires: Paidós, 2004.

9 Barbed Wire Iconography and Aesthetic Activism

The Borderlands, Mexican Immigration, and Chicana/o Art

María Herrera-Sobek

Something there is that doesn't love a wall,
That sends the frozen-ground-swell under it,
And spills the upper boulders in the sun;
And make gaps even two can pass abreast

Robert Frost, "Mending Wall," 1914

Chicana/o cultural art production exploded in the 1960s as part of the political upheaval commonly known as the Chicano Movement. This art movement, therefore, has its roots deeply entrenched in revolutionary articulations and as a response to social, economic, educational, and political concerns of the Mexican American population, which viewed itself as marginalized and occupying a second-class citizen status in U.S. society. One area of particular emphasis in Chicana/o contestatory art has been the subject of immigration. In this study I center my attention on Chicana/o art and the use of barbed-wire iconography within its creative space and posit that it is inscribed as a semiotic sign specifically designed to encode concepts of dehumanization, oppression, racism, pain, brutality, exclusivity, and suffering as they relate to Mexican transnational migratory movements. I explore the use of barbed wire in the works of such visual artists as Rupert García, Malaquías Montoya, Manuel Unzueta, Consuelo Jiménez Underwood, Adriana Yadira Gallego, and Daniel Márquez. Furthermore, my analysis makes use of the theoretical paradigm I have developed and titled "aesthetic activism" or the use of art, that is, the beautiful, for social transformation—specifically in the quest for social justice.

BARBED WIRE: A HISTORICAL OVERVIEW

The history of barbed wire evidences its connections to issues of pain and suffering even when not related to immigration. The Wikipedia entry for "Barbed Wire" defines it as:

a type of fencing wire constructed with sharp edges or points arranged at intervals along the strand(s). It is used to construct inexpensive fences and also on walls surrounding secured property. It is also a major feature of the fortifications in trench warfare. A person or animal trying to pass through or over barbed wire will suffer discomfort and possibly injury. (2012, n.p.)

Barbed wire was patented in 1874 by Joseph F. Glidden and he later mass produced it with Isaac Ellwood in 1876 in De Kalb, Illinois. "The Devil's Rope," as it soon came to be known by religious groups (Krell 2004), proved to be both popular and controversial. It was popular because it was an inexpensive way to keep cattle and other animals enclosed as well as to prevent both wild and domesticated animals from damaging agricultural lands. Nevertheless, the success of barbed wire in keeping animals out was through the process of inflicting pain. Reviel Netz in his perceptive book *Barbed Wire: An Ecology of Modernity* conceptualizes barbed wire as an ecological equation: "whose main protagonists are flesh and iron" and links it to violence over flesh in an attempt to control both space and motion or mobility (2004, xii). He further perceives barbed wire as having a "defining characteristic of a certain period of history" encompassing the years 1874–1954 and further asserts that the "Age of Barbed Wire" is "the period of the coming of modernity" (Netz 2004, xii). Olivier Razac's equally fascinating study *Barbed Wire: A Political History* (2003) similarly conceptualizes barbed wire as having a tremendous effect on world civilization. He points to three historical periods of barbed wire influence: (1) the settling of the North American prairie at the turn of the nineteenth century, (2) World War I trenches, and (3) World War II in Nazi concentration camps (Razac 2003, 3). The colonization and settlement of the Western United States implied the partitioning off of lands in small parcels. Barbed wire was used to parcel out these lands, which in turn impinged on the Prairie Indians' ability to continue living their traditional mode of life. It therefore can be perceived as a cultural weapon that subjugated the Indians, who were accustomed to living and traveling in the Plains area freely for generations. Furthermore, it also limited the space in which buffalo and bison roamed in search of pasture lands and thus decimated their numbers. These were the two animals on which the Indians depended for their livelihood and lifestyle, and this additional setback contributed additionally to their decline. Barbed wire enjoyed tremendous success in the nineteenth and early twentieth centuries all over the United States, but particularly in the Midwest and West; later its use began to spread to Europe also.

The employment of barbed wire first appeared in bellicose encounters in America during the Spanish-American War in 1898 and among Europeans in concentration camps during the Boer War in South Africa, also in 1898 ("Barbed Wire," 2012, n.p.). It proved effective in that conflict and, when World War I exploded in Europe, barbed wire began to be perceived as a powerful weapon. The utilization of barbed wire to enclose people during wartime continued to underscore its use as a painful and powerful instrument of control. Prisoners of war were enclosed in concentration camps that were surrounded by barbed wire. World War II greatly contributed to making concentration camps, with their barbed wired fences, even more symbolic of humanity's capacity to inflict pain and suffering on each other.

Although both Netz's and Razac's book-length studies on barbed wire are excellent excursions on barbed wire and European and Asian cultures' use of it, they do not touch upon this technology and its use on the Mexican-U.S. border. My intervention precisely focuses on barbed wire and its use in the visual artistic expression of the Mexican-U.S. borderland's cultural production as it relates to border politics and the Mexican immigrant experience. I want to underscore that this area of cultural production encompasses within its purview conceptualizations and representations of the border and immigration. It is a politically engaged art, and the artists producing it participate in what I denominate as "aesthetic activism."

MEXICAN IMMIGRATION TO THE UNITED STATES

The Mexican-U.S. border is a porous one and has been the site of migratory movements since the Spanish Colonial Period (1492–1821), when Europeans, mainly from Spain, began their explorations dating back to the year Christopher Columbus set foot in what was to the explorers a "new" land in 1492. Expeditions to all parts of the American continent began in earnest and groups of Spaniards with their black slaves and Indian serfs in tow initiated their journeys to the lands north of Mesoamerica, and of course to the southern American hemisphere now known as Central and South America. Much of the land in North America eventually became part of the United States: the Deep South, the Midwest, the Southwest, and the Northwest including the land in Alaska. Names such as Francisco Coronado, Fray Marcos de Niza, Alvar Núñez Cabeza de Vaca, Fray Junípero Serra, Capitan Juan de Anza, Father Kino, and numerous other colonizers have left their names indelibly chiseled in these lands (see *Norton Anthology of Latino Literature,* 2010).

Migrations did not cease after the Spanish Colonial Period, which had witnessed intensive migratory movements from what was then known as New Spain. After the Mexican Independence Movements (1810–1821), the Mexican Period (1821–1848) continued to bring new settlers and new migrations of people. Anglo-American immigration began to proliferate during this time period, particularly in the states of Texas and California. Later, the U.S.-Mexico War (1846–1848) ended with a defeat for Mexico and the loss of almost half of its territory. The United States acquired the lands that now make up the states of California, Arizona, New Mexico, Colorado, Utah, Nevada, Oregon, and Texas; this territory had been part of the Mexican nation and was lost under the terms of the Treaty of Guadalupe Hidalgo, signed in 1848 after Mexico's defeat in the war.

Serious immigration, especially from Mexico to the United States, began soon after 1848 due to the Gold Rush in California and the expansion and development of the newly acquired lands. Experienced miners from Chile, Peru, and Mexico arrived in California to work in the mines, although they were not welcomed and conflicts arose between the new arrivals, the recent Anglo-American immigrants, and the more established Californios, who were also perceived as foreigners by the new Anglo settlers. This has been amply written about in Leonard Pitt's book, *The Decline of the Californios: A Social History of the Spanish-Speaking Californians—1864–1890* (1966).

Mexicans also migrated to Texas since they were experts in cattle raising, and the new cattle drives emanating from South Texas, which required them to travel with hundreds of cattle to the stockyards of Chicago, needed their expertise. These cattle drives were initiated by Anglo-Americans settling in Texas from 1860 to 1900. Equally important in stimulating Mexican immigration to the United States was the building of the railroads in the Southwest during this same time period. The railroads connecting the Eastern Seaboard with the Western states, particularly California, were instrumental in the opening and expansion of the Southwest. Mexican labor, together with Chinese labor (although the Chinese were prohibited from coming to the United States after the Chinese Exclusion Act of 1882) became highly instrumental in building railroads, irrigation projects, dams, canals, and roads, as well as agricultural fields throughout the Western states.

Mexican immigration to the United States exhibits a cyclical pattern, both in the number of immigrants and in the response the U.S. population has towards these immigrants. In times of need, the United States encourages Mexican immigrants to come to work in the agricultural fields, railroads, and other areas of employment. Conversely, in times of economic depression, this country mounts a concerted effort to get rid of immigrants through deportations or by other means such as repatriations. For example, in the 1860s through the 1890s, during the building of the railroads and opening of the Western territories, Mexican immigration was encouraged and indeed recruiters went into the different states in Mexico to try to lure workers in *enganches* (literally hooks), more officially known as contracts, to come to work in the United States. This state of affairs continued throughout the 1890s through the World War I period and up until the late 1920s. When the great economic depression hit the United States in the 1930s, there were immense deportation and repatriation drives, and millions of Mexican and U.S. citizens of Mexican descent were deported or forced to leave. However, when the United States entered World War II in 1942, the nation once again needed Mexican labor, and the U.S. government convinced Mexico, after much negotiating, to allow Mexican workers to come and work in the fields, factories, and railroads. Great migratory waves took place during what is popularly known as the *Bracero* Program in effect from 1942 to 1964. The term *bracero* is derived from the Spanish word *brazos* or arms—that is working arms—and is similar to the Guest Worker Programs initiated in Europe in the 1960s. The *Bracero* Program was the accord signed by both Mexico and the United States to import Mexican labor in order to help the World War II war effort. U.S. recruitment centers were set up throughout large Mexican cities, and thousands of Mexican workers migrated to the United States under the auspices of this bilateral agreement. After the *Bracero* Program ended in 1964, undocumented immigration increased due to various factors, including an economic boom from the 1970s to the 1990s and the ease of finding employment in the United States. It is specifically this last migratory movement, in particular taking place in the last five decades, that has been immortalized in film, literature, song, and art.

AESTHETIC ACTIVISM AND CHICANA/O UNDOCUMENTED IMMIGRANT ART

I define "aesthetic activism" as an ideological political position held by artists in all areas of artistic expression who use what people consider aesthetically beautiful techniques, that is, the arts, such as film, literature, visual art, photography, theater, and so forth, in the pursuit of social justice. Montoya, an artist of the early Chicano Movement, has eloquently articulated this sentiment when he stated in an essay he wrote for the journal *Puentes* regarding his views on art:

> Through our images we are the creators of culture and it is our responsibility that our images are of our times—and that they be depicted honestly and promote an attitude towards existing reality; a confrontational attitude, one of change rather than adaptability—images of our time and for our contemporaries. We must not fall into the age-old cliché that the artist is always ahead of his/her time. No, it is most urgent that we be on time. (2010, 199)

Montoya firmly believes that artists should use their art as "A voice for the voiceless" (2010, 199). This sentiment of social responsibility will be expressed and reiterated by other artists featured in this essay.

The earliest works of art that I have identified related to Mexican immigration to the United States are two woodcuts by the famous Mexican artist José Guadalupe Posada (1852–1913). Posada was a graphic artist from Aguascalientes, Nuevo León, Mexico, who specialized in woodcuts and prints. His body of work is famous the world over and he became known for his depiction of Mexican everyday life, mostly in a satirical manner. His art attacked the hypocrisy extant in all strata of society: from the most humble tortilla and tamale vender in the streets or marketplaces to the most aristocratic denizens of society. No one was saved from Posada's razor-sharp humor via his images that were sometimes accompanied by equally satirical verses. In this manner Posada also touched the lives of the immigrant, who he depicts as being "hooked" [*enganchado*] to emigrate to the United States by what he perceived to be rapacious U.S. corporations (mostly railroad and agricultural concerns in the 1890s–1910s). Two of these woodcuts are titled, *No vayas al gringo* [*Don't Go Where the Anglo-Americans Are*], meaning don't go to the United States, appearing in 1910 (Keller 2002, 224), and *Casa de enganches: Contratas voluntarias* [*Contracting Office: Voluntary Contracts c. 1895–1910*]. The latter refers to these *Casas de Contratas*, which were the contracting centers established by U.S. companies to recruit Mexican workers (see Berdecio and Appelbaum 1972).

With respect to the latter half of the twentieth and the early twenty-first centuries, an explosion of artwork appeared in the 1960s with the inception of the Chicano Movement in 1965. García from central California is one of these early artists who manifested in his artwork a strong responsibility toward articulating a social protest against unjust immigration laws. Barbed wire iconography has been a particularly effective strategy used by these artists to denounce unfair and oppressive immigration laws that force immigrants wanting to emigrate and work in the United States to take dangerous actions in their attempt to cross the border. In his silkscreen poster featuring barbed wire titled *¡CESEN DEPORTACION!* [*CEASE DEPORTATION!*], which is dated 1972, García presents a painting startling in its simplicity yet extremely effective in conveying his message, which is also discussed in the

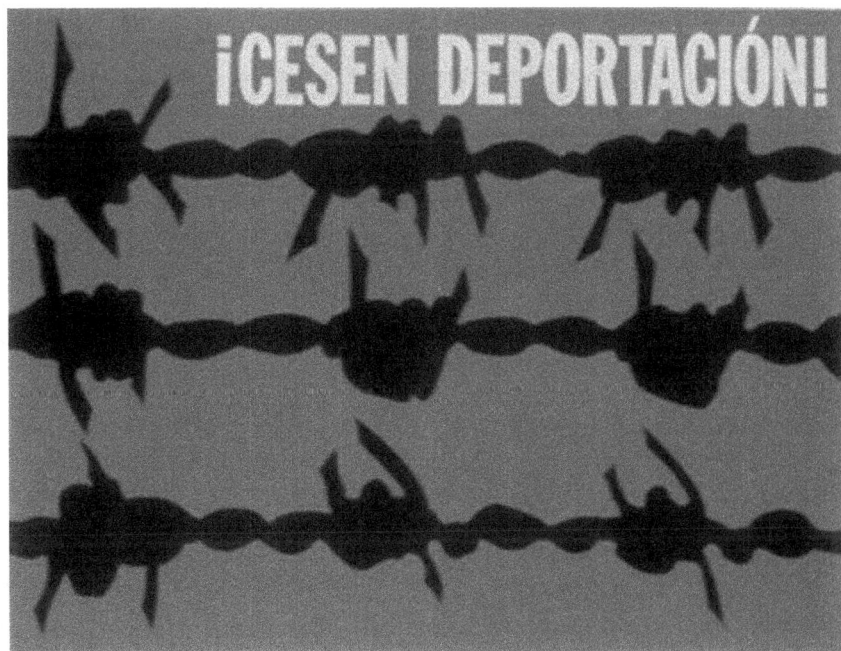

Figure 9.1   *¡CESEN DEPORTACION!* © 1972 Rupert García; Rena Bransten Gallery, SF, CA; Magnolia Editions, Oakland, CA; Thomas Paul Fine Art, Los Angeles, CA.

previous chapter of this volume. The work immediately attracts the viewer due to the eye-catching, bright red paint used as background and the imagery of barbed wire painted black on the red background. In spite of its simplicity, the powerful message conveyed through the image of sharp-pointed steel barbed wire, stranded from left to right in a background of bright red with the exclamatory words of "¡CESEN DEPORTACION!", encodes a powerful statement advocating social justice for the undocumented immigrant worker.[1] The message, inscribed in yellow letters near the sharp points of the barbed wire, points to the human anguish and torture experienced by those whose only crime is to seek work in the United States. The red implies the bloodshed by those who die while trying to migrate to this country. The red color attracts the attention of the viewer and holds it. In addition, it is associated with the Farm Workers Union flag, which bears the colors of red and black.

García, like numerous other Chicana/o artists, has explicitly articulated his ideological stance regarding art and political activism. Montoya firmly adheres to the philosophy related to political activism and artistic expression. In his "Artist's Statement" he amplifies:

> It is important to note that my other "voice" is the poster/mural. I am much more articulate and able to express myself more eloquently through this medium. It is with this voice that I attempt to communicate, reach out and touch others, especially to the silent and often ignored populace of Chicano, Mexican and Central American working class, along with other disenfranchised people of the world. This form allows me to awaken consciousness, to reveal reality and to actively work to transform it. What better function for art at this time? "A voice for the voiceless" . . . As a Chicano artist I feel a responsibility that all my art should be a reflection of my political beliefs—an art of protest. The struggle of all people cannot be merely intellectually accepted. It must become part of our very being as artists otherwise we cannot give expression to it in our work. (Montoya 2010, 199)

That Montoya is indeed a politically engaged artist can be seen in his powerful artwork depicting the suffering and travails of the common people, especially the Mexican immigrant. He consistently utilizes the barbed-wire motif in his paintings to indicate the pain and oppression of his people. A cursory overview of forty-five of Montoya's silkscreens displayed on his gallery website (http://www.malaquiasmontoya.com/prints0php) shows that eleven of these silkscreens/lithographs exhibit the barbed-wire motif. Those works depicting the barbed wire icon include: *Scholarship Activism Justice* (2004), *Abajo con la Migra* [*Down with Border Patrol*] Silkscreen (1981), *Undocumented* Silkscreen (1981), *Yo Vengo del Otro Lado* [*I Come From the Other Side*] Silkscreen (1994), *Untitled* Silkscreen (2002), *La Cruzada* [*The Crossing*] Silkscreen (1994), *Abriendo Brecha Conference* [*Widening the Gap Conference*] Print (2004), *El Hombre Sin Paíz* [*The Man Without a Kountry*] (sic) Lithograph (2005), *Tierra Nuestra* [*Our Land*] Silkscreen (2004), *La Madre* [*The Mother*] Silkscreen (2000), and *The Oppressor* Silkscreen (1989). These eleven pieces of artwork are mostly silkscreens and include his most famous art piece titled *Undocumented* dating from 1981. He duplicated this painting in acrylic paint in 2003 using a different male figure under the same name with the same narrative—that is, a male figure caught in the strands of barbed wire.

Montoya also has 20 paintings done in acrylic and, of these, six feature barbed wire within the artwork's narrative. Those acrylic paintings featuring the barbed-wire motif include: *Migration* acrylic painting (2004), *Undocumented* acrylic painting (2003), *An Immigrant's Dream, the American Response* acrylic painting (2003), *Migration* acrylic painting (2002), *Virgen Campesina* [*Peasant Virgin*] acrylic painting/collage (2001), and *Cristo Campesino* [*Peasant Christ*] acrylic painting (1999).

In addition to the silkscreens and acrylic paintings, Montoya also has drawings that are featured on his website. There are twenty-nine images of the drawings in this category, and out of these twenty-nine pieces of art, four bear the motif of barbed wire: *Long Before Long After* charcoal (1992), *Untitled* oil stick on paper (2003), *Untitled* charcoal (1996), and *Untitled* charcoal (1996).

The earlier 1981 silkscreen of *Undocumented* depicts a Christ-like male figure attempting to cross the border and getting trapped, stuck on the six rows of barbed wire strung across the frame of the painting from left to right and which the viewer assumes to be the border. The word "Undocumented" is plastered across the canvas, leaving no doubt that this refers to the remnants of an undocumented immigrant.

Montoya has articulated his vision of social injustice for the undocumented immigrant via this limp, male figure crucified on a barbed-wired fence. The figure lacks hands and his head is bowed and faceless—there are no distinguishing features except for a flash of brown paint and an outline of a nose, thus the artist highlights a dehumanized figure. There seems to be blood dripping from his head, as demonstrated by red splotches of liquid flowing down from the man's head to his feet down to the bottom of the frame. Nevertheless, the male figure seems to be powerful because he was able to break through some of the barbed wire—at least at the heart level and below the waist—and also the head has managed to smash through the dangerous barbed-wire barrier. The most striking elements of the figure are the powerful legs and feet, which perhaps convey a feeling of victory and not total defeat. There is a strong sense of movement and energy; it is a dynamic painting with the man's huge legs and feet overcoming the barbed wire.

The barbed-wire motif and undocumented Christ-like figure are reiterated in another one of Montoya's silkscreens titled *Cristo Campesino* (2010, 198). In this painting we have the face of a farm worker, in a frontal view from the neck up, with a red farm worker's handkerchief tied around his neck. The farm worker's hat on top of his head and face occupy the whole space of the

Figure 9.2   Undocumented, Silkscreen © 1981 Malaquías Montoya.

canvas. The brim of the hat extends beyond the canvas. The Christ-like face has his eyes almost, but not completely, shut and his mouth evidences a slight grimace since the lips are half open, displaying a row of perfectly straight, white teeth. Unlike Christ, the farm worker has a mustache but no beard, this detail unmistakably associating him with Mexican men. The color of his face is an ashen gray, depicting Christ-like suffering and near death similar to Christ dying on the cross. What links this figure with both Christ and a farm worker is the crown he wears on his forehead. The crown is made of huge, spiky, painful-looking thorns and intertwined with these is barbed wire. Splashes of what appears to be blood are spattered across his forehead, around the eyebrows and the top of his eyelids. Some of the red blood seems to be flowing downward on each side of the nose. The red handkerchief highlights and accentuates the red splashes of blood since the color red ties them together. In the background, light green agricultural fields can be seen against a gray-blue sky, and five figures march in a row whilst carrying the farm worker's red flag. Those carrying the flags are not visible; only the flags on

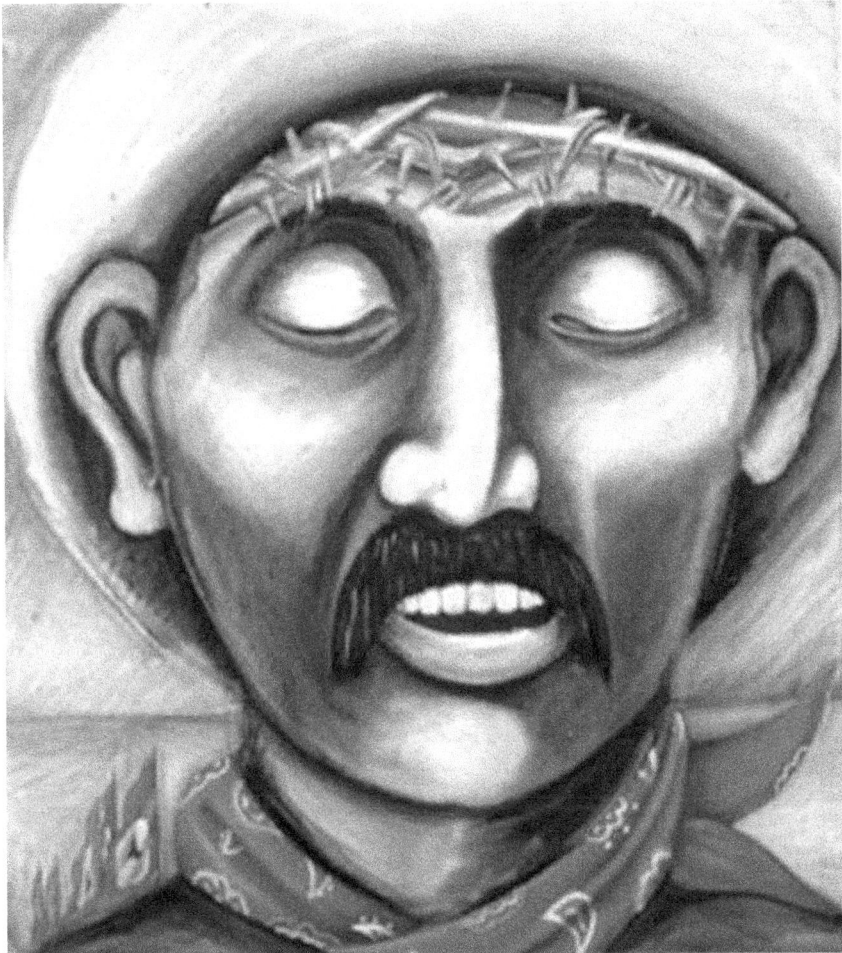

Figure 9.3 *Cristo Campesino*, Acrylic Painting © 1999 Malaquías Montoya.

their poles can be seen. The group of five walk in a procession in the lower left-hand side of the farm worker's face. The red handkerchief tied around the neck of the central Christ-like figure and the red blood blotches are all linked together and round up the composition.

The painting provides a powerful image of a suffering people. The crown of thorns and barbed wire on the forehead of the man brilliantly conflate Christ with immigrant workers crossing the border.

A second artist who conflates the image of Christ with the undocumented immigrant is Unzueta from Santa Barbara, California. Unzueta is a muralist as well as an artist who paints in other mediums. His painting *Jesús en la frontera* [*Jesus at the Border*] is absolutely stunning in its overall composition as well as the use of color. The incorporation of different shades of red—from bright red to light pink—dominates the composition, which features at its center a huge cross placed slightly off center to the right of the viewer. A Christ-like figure hangs from the cross. I say "hangs" because the outstretched arms are not nailed or bound to the cross but are held up high, almost in supplication. They also help reiterate the cross motif since the figure holds his arms outstretched, that is to say, the figure itself forms a cross with his body. The ethnicity of the Christ-like figure is communicated in shades of brown and black (lengthwise half of the figure is in brown and half in black). The hair and the face of the kneeling figure hint at the figure being of indigenous background. The man is depicted kneeling, arms outstretched, head bowed. The fingers of both hands are extended and slightly curled, conveying pain and anguish. A pink shroud serves as a background for the cross and a white cloth is intertwined between the Christ-like figure and the cross, linking them together. The white shroud or sheet signifying death is the shroud in which the figure will be covered upon burial, as Christ was.

The barbed wire appears in the composition of *Jesús en la frontera* as thorns in dark navy blue—almost black. This strategy repeats the hue found in the kneeling figure. The thorns resemble, or are meant to be, a visual metaphor for barbed wire since the strands of the thorns (images resembling barbed wire) are painted along the border of the pink cloth or shroud that serves as a backdrop for the painting. There are approximately seven strands of thorns/barbed wire along the border of the cloth toward the bottom of the painting, and these are interrupted in the middle by the cross. Hope is depicted via a green plant at the right of the canvas. Also, throughout the painting roots seem to be sprouting everywhere—a common motif in Mexican and Chicana/o paintings signifying life emanating from death.

Unzueta reiterates the theme of barbed wire as a metaphor for the border, as well as for the pain and suffering experienced by Mexican undocumented immigrants, in his beautiful painting titled *Sarape Alambrista* [*Border Crossing Shawl*]. *Alambrista* is a term given to undocumented immigrants who attempt to cross the Mexican-U.S. border where there are steel wire fences, as opposed to crossing where there is a river (the Rio Grande in Texas) or the desert in Arizona. These wire fences exist mostly in California. Chicano critic Francisco Lomelí expounds on Unzueta's preoccupation with the suffering and social injustices visited on human beings in an essay titled "*Una imagen con dos voces*" ["An Image with Two Voices"], focusing on the Santa Barbara artist as these political views are expressed in his artwork. Lomelí states:

> In his [Unzueta's] paintings and murals are embodied his anxieties and preoccupations regarding humankind. Immersed in such ambiguities the artist searches, almost blindly, for a meaning to our existential disparities such as injustice, war, poverty and the abuses leveled at immigrants. (2009, 5) [my translation]

In the painting, *Sarape Alambrista,* what appears to be a beautiful red and blue, flower-decorated shawl is slung over or wrapped around a two-strand string of barbed wire. The shawl and barbed wire are painted over a black background with a circle (the moon?) on the upper right side of the frame of the painting. The beauty of the shawl, which appears to be of fine, soft fabric, possibly silk or fine cotton, contrasts with the hard, sharp steel barbs of the two strands of the wire, which run across the upper half of the painting. The fringes at both ends of the soft cloth reiterate the sharp spines of the barbed wire.

As pointed out earlier, women visual artists also incorporate barbed-wire iconography in their works. Jiménez Underwood, as well as Rosa M., Jacalyn López García, and others make ample use of barbed-wire imagery as a metaphor for issues of social injustice related to the harsh politics of immigration and the laws and policies emanating from them (see Herrera-Sobek 2006, 66–70). Yadira Gallego is yet another woman artist concerned with the plight of the Mexican immigrant and border suffering. She too incorporates barbed-wire icons into her paintings and adheres to the notion that the artist has a social responsibility to advocate for social justice via artwork. In her "Artist's Statement," appearing in Volume 7 of the journal *Puentes,* she elucidates:

> My artwork is forged from ideals about equality and understanding rooted in the Civil Rights and Feminist movements, with sensibilities born out of my upbringing alongside the US/Mexico border. Growing up in Nogales, Arizona-Sonora, I learned early on that *la línea* stretched beyond geographic boundaries; that in fact, its effects resonated deeply as impressions in the human spirit and psyche. These early observations on border phenomena led to an examination of power and duality through my work, reconciling spiritual consciousness with physical reality and social constructs. (2009, 151)

She further amplifies her political ideological stance and details how she uses paint in her artworks to depict social protest and through the beauty of her art articulates her political activism. In this manner, she affirms my central thesis of how artists use beauty as a form of aesthetic activism. Gallego states:

> I go about charting the many dimensions and possible interpretations of border phenomena via two concurrent bodies of work. One trajectory exposes psychological ramifications of human rights violations manifested through fragmentation, scarring and stagnations. Heavy layers of paint build up the scars while the sanded surface reveals the grittiness and tension co-existing within the border subjects. These bodies remain fragmented elements that speak of political, spiritual and cultural divisions. (2009, 151)

Yadira Gallego's political activism is evident in her painting titled *Con piedras en los pies, cruzó* [*With Stones on Her Feet She Crossed*]. The artwork presents a headless woman, perhaps representing the anonymity of all immigrant women who attempt to cross the border and are successful in spite of all the odds against them. The figure of the headless woman sits on an old, blue wooden chair. The blue paint is peeling and the different older layers come through and have left the chair speckled with white and red. The chair is placed at the left side of a rectangularly shaped canvas. The headless woman is portrayed sitting on the chair; her nude torso, hips, thighs, and legs are all visible to the spectator. On her lap sits a huge maguey plant bearing five enormous, opened, green leaves. The maguey covers her face and can be perceived as a metaphor for Mexicans, since the maguey plant is inextricably linked to Mexico and Mexicans. One can instantly recall the ubiquitous curio figure of a Mexican male sitting and sleeping, using the maguey plant to lean against. A huge yellow sun serves as the background for the sitting nude figure. The reddish-brown barbed wire is prominently displayed since it is strategically placed around her toes, circling the inside soles of the figure's feet, clasping and binding her feet together. The barbed wire continues to travel upward around the woman's ankles, then her legs— the binding of the feet and legs ends right above her knees. One strand of barbed wire is depicted as floating up from the figure's knees toward the green plant and continues upward, ending at the edge of the big yellow round sun featured as a background for the image. The barbed wire bears a reddish-brown tint, thus evoking blood and pain. There is a general reddish-brown-black hue predominating in the background of the painting. Perhaps the only optimistic tones conveyed in the painting, whose principal subject is pain and suffering, are the lush green maguey plant and the bright yellow sun, although it too bears a reddish color on the left edge of the circle. The title is also affirmative since it states: *Con piedras en los pies, cruzó*, which can be translated as *With Stones on Her Feet, She Crossed*. That is to say, in spite of all the obstacles placed in the way of this woman's search for a better life, she was still able to accomplish her goal.

Adriana Yadira Gallego, *Con piedras en los pies, cruzo*, 1998
Oil on canvas, 60" x 40"

Figure 9.4 *Con piedras en los pies, cruzó* © 1998 Adriana Yadira Gallego.

Jiménez Underwood is another woman artist, who recently retired from California State University, San Jose. Jiménez Underwood works with different mediums: textiles, prints, silkscreens, as well as installations. In all cases she makes use of barbed wire to denote the hardships associated with crossing the border. She also has articulated what I have denominated as aesthetic activism, since she views the role of the artist and political activism as not exclusive from each other. In an artist's statement appearing in *Contemporary Chicana and Chicano Art: Artists, Works, Culture and Education*, she argues that "aesthetic elegance and political bluntness exist in tandem, yet do not collide; rather, they mesh perfectly, one sustaining and reinforcing the other, much like the warp and weft of woven textiles" (Keller 2002, 44). There are many pieces of artwork done by Jiménez Underwood that focus on the border and incorporate barbed-wire iconography. One powerful image painted by Jiménez Underwood and utilizing the imagery of barbed wire is titled *La Virgen de los Nopales* [*The Virgin of the Cactus Plant*].

Jiménez Underwood's silkscreen dating from 2003 depicts a desert scene with strings of barbed wire "raining" on the green cactus plants in an otherwise empty desert landscape. The barbed wire is rendered in black, and on the background, barely visible to the eye, are the outlines, finely penciled in white paint, of several ghostly figures of the Virgin of Guadalupe. While the painting expresses pain and suffering through the metaphor of the cactus's

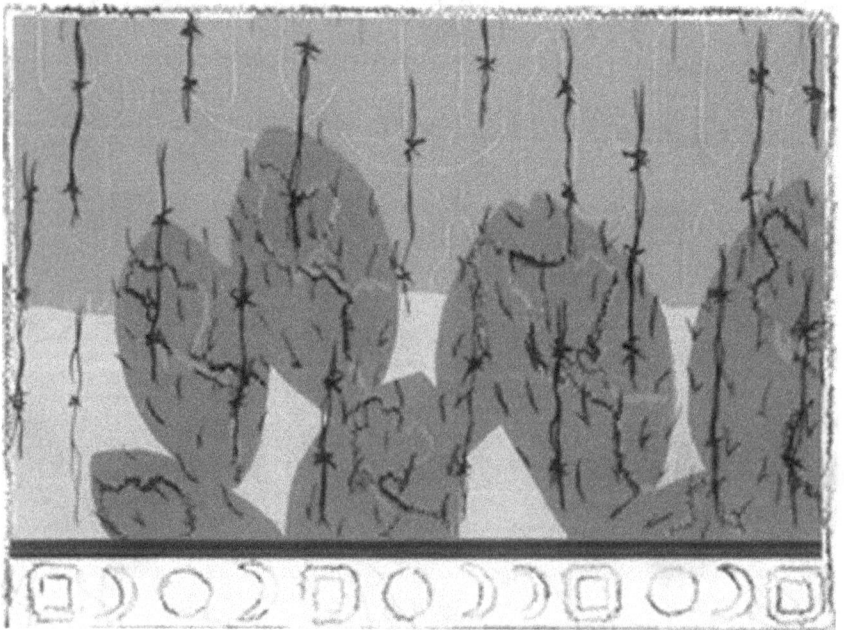

Figure 9.5   La Virgen de Los Nopales, Silkscreen © 2003 Consuelo Jiménez Underwood; photo by Keay Edwards.

sharp spines and the spikes of the barbed wire, the fact that the Virgin is watching over the immigrants articulates hope for the safety of would-be immigrants daring to cross the dangerous desert.

The amazing creativity displayed by Chicana/o visual artists in their rendering of the barbed-wire icon as a metaphor for pain and suffering experienced by undocumented immigrants attempting to cross the border and for the mean-spirited border politics as a whole seems to be infinite. Márquez is another border artist who employs barbed wire in some of his paintings related to *La Frontera*. Born in San Pedro de las Colonias, Coahuila, Mexico, in 1954, he now makes his home in the Los Angeles, California area. He has two paintings, both dating from 1994, that are stunning in their conceptualization and execution related to the undocumented Mexican immigrant experience titled *Travesías—El Reptil* [*Crossing—The Reptile*] and *Travesías—La Cerca de Picos*. [*Crossing—The Barbed Fence*]. The paintings form part of the California Ethnic Multicultural Archives Collection housed at the University of California, Santa Barbara.

The first painting, *Travesías—El Reptil,* portrays a male immigrant figure who is drawn as half-human, half-reptile slithering under a barbed-wire fence, hence the title. The man's complexion is green, like a reptile's skin, and his body has the outline of a reptile, such as a lizard or a frog. There are six rows of barbed wire strung diagonally across the canvas, which features a black backdrop indicating nighttime. The message is clearly articulated via the horrible image of a man who has been forced to transform himself into a reptile while attempting to cross the border under the steel barbs of the barbed-wire fence. The message inscribed in the painting clearly denounces the dehumanization of human beings who are transformed into animals in their quest for economic survival.

The second painting in the series, *Travesías—La Cerca de Picos,* reiterates the scene first observed in Montoya's silkscreen titled *Indocumentado,* that is, the figure of a man trying to cross the barbed-wire fence and being caught in it. Both the Montoya and Márquez renderings convey the image of a crucified Christ figure in the guise of an undocumented immigrant. Márquez's painting is rendered in a huge rectangular frame with fifteen rows of barbed wire fence strung in a diagonal manner. There is also a top layer of barbed wire looped around the steel bar holding the barbed wire fence—the loops of wire clearly show the steel spikes almost floating upward in the air. The man's ghostly body is stuck on the barbed wire—his head at the top facing the first two rows of wire; his torso and legs are between the third and tenth row of steel wire with the prickly steel points trespassing the body. The man's right foot is planted between the ninth and eleventh rows and the left foot lies at the twelfth and fourteenth rows near the edge of the right side of the rectangular canvas. The background is again rendered mostly in black, at the top one-third of the frame and then at the bottom half of the painting, which is rendered in dark navy blue—almost black. There is a band of purple hue possibly designating the night sky and next to it a swathe of reddish brown, no doubt as a metaphor for blood. These bands of purple and reddish-brown color are at the level of the man's chin and waistline.

CONCLUSION

All of the visual artists analyzed in this study focusing on their use of barbed wire iconography demonstrate a strong sense of responsibility for exposing social injustices. In the artworks analyzed above, they specifically articulate their views on unreasonable immigration policies, which cause extensive human suffering. Nevertheless, in spite of their concern and portrayal of undocumented Mexican immigrants' pain and suffering, these visual artists encompass an optimistic view of life and hope for a better future where artificial borders will not matter. Yadira Gallego expresses this general view in her "Artists' Statement" cited previously:

> Conversely, the interstices of the border also allows for movement and exchange, for more porous relationships between different nations and cultures. This perspective facilitates a link between border ebb and flow, and the nature of dance as a conduit for human expression. (2009, 151)

This chimes with Gloria Anzaldúa's much cited statement that the border is *"una herida abierta* [an open wound] where the Third World grates against the first and bleeds. And before a scab forms it hemorrhages again, the life-blood of two worlds merging to form a third country—a border culture"—a statement that aptly describes the nature of the Mexican-U.S. border and the anguish, pain, and suffering it produces (1987, 3). Chicana/o artists' sensibilities and open political commitment to make evident this suffering through the iconography of barbed wire is a brilliant strategy for opening the minds and hearts of U.S. society. It is safe to say that upon viewing the figures of people strung along the border on steel spikes piercing human flesh in Chicana/o artwork, one is likely to never forget it and hopefully this will lead to constructive action.

NOTE

1. I am grateful to Salvador Güereña, Director of CEMA (California Ethnic Multicultural Archives) at the University of California, Santa Barbara, for providing me with the following image: García ¡*CESEN DEPORTACION!* (1972).

WORKS CITED

Anzaldúa, Gloria. *Borderlands/La Frontera: The New Mestiza.* San Francisco: Aunt Lute Press, 1987.

"Barbed Wire." Wikipedia. http://en.wikipedia.org/wiki/barbed_wire. Accessed November 29, 2012.

Berdecio, Roberto, and Stanley Appelbaum, eds. *"Casa de enganches. Contratas voluntarias"* [Recruitment office. Voluntary contracts. Broadside, 1895–1910]. In *Posada's Popular Mexican Prints: 273 Cuts by José Guadalupe Posada.* New York: Dover, 1972. Available through CEMA (California Ethnic and Multicultural Archives), University of California, Santa Barbara.

Gallego, Adriana Yadira. "Artist's Statement." *Puentes* 7 (otoño 2009): 151–152. See www.adrianaclaudio.com.

Herrera-Sobek, María. "Border Aesthetics: The Politics of Mexican Immigration in Film and Art." *Western Humanities Review* Fall (2006): 60–71.

Keller, Gary, Mary Erickson, Kaytie Johnson, and Joaquin Alvarado, eds. *Contemporary Chicana and Chicano Art: Artists, Works, Culture, and Education,* Vols. 1 and 2. Tempe, AZ: Bilingual Press/Editorial Bilingüe, 2002.

Krell, Alan. *Devil's Rope: A Cultural History of Barbed Wire.* London: Reakton Books, 2004.

Lomelí, Francisco. *"Manuel Unzueta: Una imagen con dos voces." Ventana Abierta* (primavera 2009): 5.

Montoya, Malaquías. "Artist's Statement." *Puentes* 8 (invierno 2010): 199.

———. www.malaquiasmontoya.com. Accessed November 16, 2012.

Netz, Reviel. *Barbed Wire: An Ecology of Modernity.* Middleton, CT: Wesleyan University Press, 2004.

Posada, José Guadalupe. *Posada's Popular Mexican Prints: 273 Cuts by José Guadalupe Posada.* New York: Dover, 1972.

Razac, Olivier. *Barbed Wire: A Political History.* New York: New Press, 2002.

10 *Virgen* Transatlantic
Religious Iconography in Irish and Chicana/o Art

Catherine Leen

The success of the comedy series *Father Ted,* a satire about the Catholic Church in Ireland first broadcast in April 1995 on Britain's Channel 4, was indicative of the waning influence of a church whose authority had not been questioned by many Irish people up to the twentieth century. The series centred on the eponymous Father Ted, who, after embezzling church funds to pay for a holiday to Las Vegas, is exiled to the grim, isolated Craggy Island, a thinly disguised Ireland, together with a young, dim-witted priest called Father Dougal and an older, violently alcoholic priest called Father Jack. In Episode Three of Series One, entitled "The Passion of St Tibulus", the priests are ordered by the tyrannical Bishop Brennan to protest against their local cinema's screening of a film that the Catholic Church has deemed blasphemous. Bishop Brennan explains the need for the protest as follows:

Bishop Brennan:	His Holiness has banned it, but because of some loophole the bloody thing is showing on this godforsaken dump.
Father Dougal:	Oh yes, that's right. Is it any good, do you know?
Bishop Brennan:	I don't care if it's any good or not! All I know is that we have to be seen to be making a stand against it.

This exchange says much about the nature of the Catholic Church's protests against works of art that represent religious subjects in a manner considered to be contrary to its interests. Despite not having seen the film and clearly exhibiting a complete lack of interest in engaging with it, the bishop instructs the priests to "make the Church's position clear" by organising a protest. This episode of *Father Ted* recalls real-life protests against films such as Martin Scorsese's *The Last Temptation of Christ* (1988), which proved controversial internationally because of its suggestion that Christ may have had sexual thoughts, and Mexican director Carlos Carrera's *El crimen del Padre Amaro* (2002), which again raised the ire of the Catholic Church by featuring a scene in which a priest made love to a woman draped in the

Virgen de Guadalupe's cape. A more recent exhibition in 2011 involving the work of Chicana artist Alma López also led to condemnation by the Catholic Church in Ireland, as we shall see later in this chapter, thus highlighting the fact that the representation of religious topics in art remains a contentious issue for the church.

Throughout history, paintings and other artworks that engage with religious iconography have been met with censorship, protests, and criticism that often overlook the artists' intentions in favour of stirring up the strong feelings inextricably linked with images that seem to question or critique religious faith. While controversies in recent years about depictions of the Muslim community in the media make it clear that censorship of religious art is not the exclusive preserve of the Catholic Church, the art that will be examined here has met with sometimes hostile receptions because of its engagement with imagery traditionally associated with the Catholic Church. Irish and Chicana/o artists have employed this religious iconography in their work in very different ways. There are many similarities in the histories of these images in both communities, nonetheless, and their use by contemporary artists raises complex questions about the continuing efforts of the Catholic Church to deny artists the freedom to interpret them in ways that depart from its standard depictions. This chapter examines the place of religious art in the construction of national identity in Ireland and in the Chicana/o community with reference to the works of Chicana artists Alma López, Ester Hernández, and Yolanda López, and the Irish artists Constance Short and Rita Duffy, and considers their reception.

IRISH AND CHICANA/O RELIGIOUS ART AND NATIONAL IDENTITY

Ireland emerged from centuries of British rule at the turn of the twentieth century to create an independent republic that sought to foster a distinctive new national identity. Up to the early eighteenth century, Ireland was essentially a colony of the United Kingdom, with the result that Catholics were forced to practice their religion in secret. The passage of the Catholic Emancipation Act in 1829 led to a gradual decline in religious persecution, however. This change was first reflected in Irish art in the increase of crucifixion scenes on tombstones (Harbison 2000, ix). While the Irish Literary Revival promoted a unique identity made famous far beyond Ireland's shores through the works of renowned writers such as W. B. Yeats and J. M. Synge, visual emblems, especially those associated with Catholicism, were also a key component of the new republic.

John Turpin observes that the figure of the Virgin Mary became central to this new Irish identity, and devotion to her was promulgated through pictures hanging in the home, publications of various kinds, or church art and altars (2003, 68–79). This veneration of the Virgin and other saints did not mark an entirely seamless or complete transition from pre-Catholic spiritual beliefs, however. Long before the arrival of Catholicism in Ireland, the native people venerated Celtic Gods and Goddesses, many of whom, such as the Goddess Brigid, were polysemous, as were the pre-Columbian deities worshipped by Mexicans before the Conquest (Watson 1915, 264). In fact, K. Theodore Hoppen notes that well into the nineteenth century, popular religious practices, such as the evil eye, curses, and celebrations of harvests survived in Ireland in tandem with the Catholic worship regulated by the church (Hoppen 1999, 71).

As part of a drive to replace such traditional beliefs with church-sanctioned icons, the Catholic Church became an important patron of the arts, commissioning works even from Protestant artists, such as Jack B. Yeats (Pyle 1986, 10). Like another renowned Irish artist, Louis le Brocquy, Yeats' interest in religious subjects emphasized the social over the devotional. Le Brocquy's conflation of the traditionally Catholic subject of the nativity with a depiction of a traveller family in his 1945 pen-and-ink drawing *Nativity, Connemara*, provides an interesting alternative to the omnipresent figure of the Virgin Mary (Scott 2006, 17). Peter Harbison confirms that in recent decades religious subjects have generally proved of little interest to Irish artists, going so far as to comment on "a strong tendency away from religious representations in art," but he commends the Catholic Church for continuing to be an important patron to the small number of artists who are interested in pursuing religious themes in their work (Harbison 2000, ix). In her study of the relationship between the new Irish Republic and Catholicism in Ireland, Síghle Bhreathnach-Lynch interprets the church's patronage of the arts, and particularly its insistent Marianism, as decidedly less positive, however:

> [I]n the drive to construct the ideal Irish woman, politicians received wholehearted support from the Church. The hierarchy, whose patriarchal views were identical to those of the men running the country, agreed that women should be denied access to the public arena. The Madonna proved the perfect exemplar. . . . What resulted were stereotypes of Irish women as either pure, chaste virgins, or mothers who had done their duty by their country in ensuring the continuation of the race. (Bhreathnach-Lynch 2007, 96)

Moreover, she observes that even devoutly Catholic artists have often faced interference in their interpretations of religious icons. In the 1920s, sculptor Michael Shorthall's design for a statue of Saint Anthony was rejected by the church hierarchy, ironically, because he sought to achieve an authentic depiction of the saint that reflected his peasant Portuguese heritage. Shorthall's dark-complexioned, stocky figure departed radically from the "popular effete, graceful painted plaster images" favoured by the Catholic Church (Bhreathnach-Lynch 2007, 111). The church's desire for relentlessly conformist images is also notable in commissions featuring the Virgin Mary. The standard image of the Virgin is very similar to that apparently witnessed in the small Co Mayo town of Knock in 1879: "life size . . . clothed in white robes, which were fastened at the neck. . . . She wore a brilliant crown on her head, and, over the forehead, where the crown fitted the brow, a beautiful rose" (Hoppen 1999, 166). This prototype of the Virgin was relentlessly reproduced around the country, with the only variation being that at times her robes, or a sash at her waist, were blue in colour. Mary's heavenwards gaze confirms her role not as an important figure in her own right but as an intermediary between the Irish people and God, while the robes, which cover every inch of her body except her face and hands, suggest that, despite being a model of maternity, she is an utterly asexual figure.

The church's prescriptive and proscriptive standards for religious iconography met with the approval of the heroes of the 1916 Rising, which led to the establishment of the new Republic. Patrick Pearse, a key figure in the Rising, had warned of the folly of artists highlighting the humanity of the Virgin in their work, saying: "I often fancy that if some of the Old Masters had known rural Ireland, we should not have so many gross and merely earthly conceptions of the Madonna as we have" (Foster 1989, 449). The church's insistence on preserving a standardised, bland image of the Virgin met with a different reaction from writer W. B. Yeats, who lamented the censorship by a Galway convent of a 1905 design for a stained-glass window by artist Sarah Purser "because of the personal life in the faces and in the attitudes, which seemed to them ugly, perhaps even impious" (Meaney 2011, 8). Purser was instructed to abandon her design and to copy "an insipid German chromo-lithograph, full of faces without expression or dignity, and gestures without personal distinction" (Meaney 2011, 8).

Clearly, the lesson here was that imitation was preferred to innovation, and that a very limited range of models was to form the basis for the iconography of the Virgin Mary in church-sponsored art. Matters changed little after the establishment of the Irish Republic, as Minister of Fine Art Count Plunkett declared that religious art was to "give free voice to a Catholic community . . . to deal with the intellectual commonplaces of Catholic life, while recognizing Theology in its relations with the ordinary incidents of civilization" (Benson 1992, 22). As the twentieth century unfolded, the church's influence on Irish society gradually unravelled. Although Pope John Paul II's triumphant visit to Ireland in 1979 drew crowds of up to 1.2 million people to the Phoenix Park in Dublin, it masked the reality that the church's overarching control of Irish society was waning:

> Already in 1979, after roughly two decades of rapid economic growth, openness to the outside world, and fairly sweeping cultural change, the Catholic church in Ireland was in serious trouble. The indications of its malaise included the steep fall in religious vocations, the worrisome decline in Mass attendance among adolescents and young adults, and a

dramatic loss of moral credibility owing to its rigid stance on artificial contraception. (Donnelly 2000, 12)

Recent revelations of the widespread and systematic cover-up of child sexual abuse by the clergy, especially those cases revealed in the 2009 Report of the Commission to Inquire into Child Abuse (commonly known as the Ryan Report), dealt a further blow to the church's influence and credibility. Changes in society and particularly the exposure of the hypocrisy of the church meant that, with notable exceptions that will be examined in the next section, few Irish artists dealt with religious imagery in their work for much of the late twentieth and early twenty-first centuries. Those who did, such as Patrick Pye or Mainie Jellett, were devout Catholics whose work is clearly devotional. The one notable exception to this rule in the Republic of Ireland is David Godbold, whose work approaches religious themes in an irreverent and iconoclastic manner, often picturing religious images as cartoons set against incongruous texts so that his work, like Francis Bacon's famous Pope paintings, "responds to Catholicism in purely aesthetic terms," treating the source material as art-historical rather than religious references (Carrier 2005, 12). Thus, there is little in twentieth-century Irish art that can be considered a tradition of political religious painting and even those artists who intermittently engage with the topic approach it in very diverse ways, so that it is difficult to identify a unique visual language comparable to that created by contemporary Chicana artists who have responded to their own Marian tradition.

The decline in the church's all-encompassing control of everyday life and the conflation of the image of the Virgin Mary with a national ideal that has been rejected by women as repressive and unrealistic are issues that are also relevant to Mexican and Chicana/o art. Unlike Ireland, however, where a pantheon of saints was celebrated in ecclesiastical art alongside the Virgin, the worship by the faithful in Mexico, and later by the Chicana/o community in the United States, has been utterly dominated by Marianism through the figure of the Virgen de Guadalupe. No other religious image has been as central to the history and culture of Mexico. Ilan Stavans observes that the Catholic Church in Mexico attempted to destroy the belief system they encountered through means of brute violence and the substitution of European deities for pre-Columbian gods and goddesses:

> Spanish missionaries, characterizing natives as idolatrous, decapitated the religions they found, replacing aboriginal gods with "civilized" European objects of worship. Quetzalcóatl and Coatlicue became Jesus Christ and the Virgin Mary. (2001, 111)

Ana Castillo sees the conflation of pre-Columbian and Catholic deities somewhat differently, noting that the adoption of the new icons may well have been a survival mechanism for the indigenous people of Mexico, particularly with regard to their apparently enthusiastic devotion to the Virgen de Guadalupe:

> On the very hill of Tepeyac where Tonantzin was said to have been worshipped, Juan Diego, a recently converted Catholic Nuhua, witnessed the visitation of the brown virgin who was eventually named the Virgin of Guadalupe by the Church. Speculation may be that converting the mother goddess, Tonantzin, into the Virgin Mary as Guadalupe, the brown virgin, was the Mexic Amerindian people's way of attempting to hold on to their own beliefs. (Castillo 1995, 111)

While the Catholic Church, in close allegiance with the conquistadores, undoubtedly did not hesitate to impose their faith by force, Castillo's opinion has merit in that the Virgin of Guadalupe has always been seen as a particularly Mexican icon and as a defender of the poor. The fact that she appeared to a poor shepherd means that throughout the centuries her image has been invoked in a wide range of sometimes conflicting situations by those who are oppressed and seek justice. The priest Miguel Hidalgo y Costilla raised her image as he declared Mexico's independence from Spain on September 16, 1810, a moment still commemorated in Mexico (Shorris 2004, 127). During the Mexican Revolution, her image was held aloft by rebel armies as they went into battle. As Carlos Monsiváis observes, displays of devotion to the Virgin are as fervent and diverse today as they have been since the time of the conquest:

> Year after year, on the evening of 11 December, popular faith gathers in its thousands at the Basilica of Guadalupe. If devotion to the Virgin of Guadalupe ['Guadalupismo'] is not exactly the national essence [. . .] it is the most extraordinary expression of our religious life, manifesting itself in the communal efforts of many—trade unions, families and street gangs. (Monsiváis 1997, 36)

In his study of the vagaries of the use of the image as an expression of devotion since 1492, Serge Gruzinski notes that when the Conqueror of Mexico, Hernán Cortés, asked the Aztec emperor to install a cross and an image of the Virgin and Child in the Templo Mayor, the most sacred site in what is today Mexico City, his request was roundly refused and he was forced to compromise:

> His project for installing images on the sanctuary and his words, considered "blasphemous," brought jeering from the native priests and Montezuma's scandalized refusal. The sovereign then repented of having exposed his gods to the stranger's gaze and offered an expiatory sacrifice, Cortés presented his apologies, and was content with erecting a chapel in Montezuma's palace, with his blessing. (Gruzinski 2001, 36)

The irony here is evident, as it seems that blasphemy is in the eye of the beholder and that the seemingly inappropriate use of religious icons was not only condemned by the Spanish. After the short-lived initial period of accommodation and compromise that marked the early days of the conquest had passed and as the Catholic Church's domination of religious life in Mexico was consolidated, the clergy, as in Ireland, were careful to exercise strict control over the ways in which the Virgin was depicted. European models were imported and imposed as the standard, while strict vigilance was exercised over those who produced the images (Gruzinski 2001, 163).

In the 1970s, as Chicana/o communities in the United States sought to foster a unique identity to counter generations of marginalization and racism, the Virgin became both a galvanizing and a divisive symbol. On the one hand, as in previous political movements in Mexico, her image was frequently used to communicate solidarity and ethnic pride, especially during the United Farm Workers' strikes. On the other, Chicanas increasingly saw that the image of the Virgin, as in Ireland, was not just one of nationalistic pride but one of oppression. As Anzaldúa confirms, the church has sought to use the symbol of the Virgin "to make us docile and enduring," but she adds that this attempt has not succeeded as "the *indio* and the *mestizo* continue to worship the old spirit entities (including *Guadalupe*) and their supernatural power, under the guise of Christian saints" (Anzaldúa 2007, 53).

Precisely because the symbol has always been polyvalent, it has led to the creation of a specific genre among artists who have engaged with and reimagined the symbol since the era of the Chicano Movement. As Tey Marianna Nunn, the curator of a groundbreaking exhibition in Santa Fe in 2001 that was to bring the conflicting reactions to the image to the fore, confirms: "Reimagining La Virgen is now so common in the community that it has become an established tradition in the Chicano and Latino art historical canon" (Nunn 2011, 29). While Nunn's assertion is undoubtedly true, the long tradition of reappropriating the image of the Virgin in Chicana/o art is far from accepted by many, particularly those who continue to claim the image as unambiguously Catholic. The debate surrounding the exhibition curated by Nunn was reflected in a more recent controversy about the work of Chicana artist Alma López in Cork, Ireland, in 2011.

BLASPHEMOUS RUMOURS: IRISH AND CHICANA RELIGIOUS ART AND ITS DISCONTENTS

The reaction in Ireland to Alma López's 2011 exhibition *Our Lady and Other Queer Santas* suggests that strong feelings are still evoked by the use of religious imagery, though it also raises questions about how controversies can be engineered and manipulated by special-interest groups. This exhibition was part of an international conference entitled "Transitions and Continuities in Contemporary Xicana/o Culture," which was held at

University College Cork, from June 23 to 25, 2011.[1] The conference was accompanied by two art exhibitions featuring the work of Celia H. Rodríguez and Alma López, respectively. The latter exhibition provoked strong criticism from the Bishop of Cork and Ross, who considered one of its images, *Our Lady*, to be offensive to Catholics. Dr. John Buckley was moved to proclaim that: "Respect for Mary, the mother of God, is bred in the bones of Irish people and entwined in their lives. It is regrettable and unacceptable that this exhibition seeks to portray the mother of God in such an offensive way" (English 2011, n.p.). While the bishop's confidence in his ability to speak for all Irish people and his firm belief that this image is so central to contemporary Irish life are highly debatable, what is notable about this comment is the tacit implication that a non-Irish artist has no right to present such an image in case that local sensibilities would be offended, despite the fact that, as Nunn has noted, the Virgen de Guadalupe is a defining symbol of Mexican and Chicana/o culture and López's work is part of an established tradition among contemporary Chicana/o artists. The objection voiced here recalls the censorious tones of previous church authorities in Ireland, who believe that it is their right to determine how religious icons are portrayed and who do not hesitate to denounce images that they believe depart from their standards. This territorial attitude to the image is also reflected in the bishop's willful oversight of the facts that this exhibition took place in the secular space of a university building and that the artist was there to launch her book, *Our Lady of Controversy: Alma López's Irreverent Apparition,* coedited with Alicia Gaspar de Alba, which is itself a reflection on censorship, church intervention into artistic practice, and the interests behind demonstrations against supposedly blasphemous art.

Although the protests against the exhibition in Cork were on a very small scale, with no more than twenty people assembled outside the university on any given day and mainly local press coverage of the event, the organisers in the Department of Hispanic Studies at UCC were subjected to harassment in the form of abusive anonymous calls. This was notwithstanding the fact that before the exhibition opened, they had sought legal advice that clarified that the show was not contrary to the recently enacted legislation on art and blasphemy. This controversial law, passed on January 1, 2010, states that blasphemy is a crime and that anyone who "publishes or utters matter that is grossly abusive or insulting to matters held sacred by any religion, thereby causing outrage among a substantial number of the adherents of that religion" will face a fine of up to €25,000 (Office of the Attorney General 2009, 26). As Mary Cremin and Oonagh Young, the curators of a 2010 show entitled *Blasphemy* note, it has set a dangerous international precedent and "Ireland's legislation is being used to legitimise the proposals of Pakistan and the OIC (Organisation of Islamic Conference) to establish defamation of religion as a principle of international law" (2010, n.p.).

Although the Irish blasphemy law was cited as one reason why López's work should not be on show in Cork, it quickly became apparent that the protest was far from organic, and that the local church authorities had been alerted to the exhibition by a group called America Needs Fatima, which had previously denounced López's work in the United States. America Needs Fatima seized on the opportunity of the exhibition at UCC to further condemn López, attempting to disrupt the conference by jamming its website and suggesting that her work was in breach of the recent antiblasphemy law. This action was the latest in a decade-long campaign against López, which has previously included other dubious protests (López 2011, n.p.). Together with its affiliate, the American Society for the Defense of Tradition, Family, and Property (TFP), America Needs Fatima has also been responsible for many other questionable actions intended to cause controversy, such as a campaign urging Notre Dame University to prevent President Obama speaking at a commencement address and receiving an honorary doctorate because they claim that he is a "manifestly pro-abortion president" (America Needs Fatima 2009, n.p.).

A key point about objections to López's image *Our Lady,* both in Ireland and elsewhere, is the persistent misreading of the work, which overlooks its subtleties and complex engagement with pre-Columbian history and Chicana identity. The image, which has been dismissively and inaccurately referred to as the "bikini Virgin," is in fact a contemporary rendering of the traditional image of the Virgin featuring performance artist Raquel Salinas swathed in roses and gazing directly at the viewer (Gaspar de Alba 2011, 2). Instead of being held aloft by a cherub, she is supported by a bare-breasted winged woman, while her cloak of stars had been replaced by an image of the pre-Columbian Goddess Coyolxauhqui, who could well be the *Our Lady* who gives the work its name. López has countered accusations that the image is offensive as follows:

> I know that many churches, in Mexico and Europe and the United States, house images of male angels and most prominently, a Crucifixion practically naked except for a skimpy loincloth. When I see *Our Lady* as well as works portraying La Virgen by many Chicana artists, I see an alternative voice expressing the multiplicities of our lived realities. I see myself living a tradition of Chicanas who, because of cultural and gender oppression, have asserted our voice. I see Chicanas creating a deep and meaningful connection to this revolutionary cultural female image. I see Chicanas who understand faith. (López 2011, 14)

Just as she had responded to the controversy surrounding the reaction to the image in Santa Fe, while in Ireland López persuasively defended her piece, explaining that she sought to reimagine the icon, in a nonreligious way as "a symbol of Mexican and Chicano culture and as a tribute to women" (McLysaght 2011, n.p.). She roundly denied that the image was blasphemous and suggested that her sexuality was the real issue that motivated America Needs Fatima to inform the bishop and local politicians about her exhibition: "I am queer," she said. "I think these protests are about racism, sexism and homophobia" (McLysaght 2011, n.p.). While this is undoubtedly the case, in the Irish context the protests also represented an attempt on the part of the church to reassert its authority at a time when it has been greatly eroded. The protests also failed to acknowledge that López's work, as she herself highlights, is part of a Chicana artistic tradition that seeks to unpack the multilayered meanings of the image of the Virgin of Guadalupe while making it relevant to contemporary women.

The precursor of this genre is Ester Hernández, a pioneering feminist Chicana artist who in 1974 joined Las Mujeres Muralistas, a San Francisco–based collective of Chicana and Latina artists seeking to bring their perspective to the art being produced by the Chicano Movement. As Kaytie Johnson asserts:

> Through her images of women, Hernández explores and celebrates the Latina mystique. Strong, confident, and aggressive, the female figures that populate her work challenge the roles normally assigned to Mexican American women and demolish stereotypes, defying and calling into question the patriarchal nature of the Chicano community and art movement. (2002, 24)

In *I Love Lupe,* the accompanying DVD to López and Gaspar de Alba's book, Hernández reflects on her engagement with the image of the Virgin de Guadalupe. It began in 1974, when she produced a small monochrome pen-and-ink drawing entitled *La Virgen de Guadalupe Defendiendo los Derechos de los Xican@s [The Virgin of Guadalupe Defending the Rights of the Chicanos].*

This drawing conflated the traditional image of the Virgin—framed by rays of divine light and wearing a cloak of stars while perched atop a winged cherub—with an image of a contemporary woman, dressed in a martial-arts outfit and performing a karate kick that seems to break though the rays. This small piece encapsulates a number of key ideas that would inform the use of the image of the Virgin of Guadalupe by Chicana/o artists. She is depicted as a modern, assertive woman whose active stance departs dramatically from the conventional static pose of the Virgin. Her body is further celebrated through an acknowledgement of her strength and independence, represented by her practice of martial arts, which also suggests her openness to other cultures and her self-reliance. The traditional framing devices of the cloak and divine rays have not been abandoned, however, thus paying homage to her roots and heritage. It is also an intensely personal image that incorporates a self-portrait.

In conversation with Yolanda López and Alma López, Hernández explains that a number of influences inspired the piece. On one level, it was a reaction to the fact that when her grandmother, who was a very independent, earthy woman, died a few years before she made the image, she felt

Figure 10.1   La Virgen de Guadalupe Defendiendo los Derechos de los Xican@s [The Virgin of Guadalupe Defending the Rights of the Chicanos] © 1975 Ester Hernández.

that the traditional mass cards bearing the image of the Virgen de Guadalupe did not represent her. It also recalls a period in the 1970s when she was taking a martial-arts class, a pivotal time for Chicanas, who were, as Hernández explains, "opening ourselves up to the world and finding our inner strength." The artist also comments that her upbringing was not strictly Catholic, although she considers herself a Guadalupana, and so she did not anticipate that the image would be seen as problematic:

> Some people who were very, very Catholic and very traditional were extremely offended. Some, like men, for example, said that this was obviously the anger toward them, anger toward the Church, anger toward virginity . . . People kind of read into it wherever they were coming from and from their own background and experiences. So, to me, that took me by surprise, because again I didn't have all that legacy, I didn't have all that luggage like a lot of people did. If anything, I thought it was funny, but certainly I got a lot of support from the Chicanas and from some of the guys who were much more open-minded. They loved it.

This work by Hernández finds striking parallels in an image by the Irish artist Constance Short, *Jumpin' the Border,* which also generated a great deal of controversy for its perceived irreverence towards the Catholic Church. Short, a founding member of the gallery and theatre space Project Arts Centre in Dublin, has opposed patriarchal and other forms of oppression throughout her career. Her interest in overturning the traditional position of women in the art world as passive subjects painted by male artists is suggested by her participation in an exhibition at the Project in 1975, where a group of six women artists showed nude portraits of male sitters: "our irreverent idea was to give men a bit of exposure during International Women's Year" (Watson 2007, 96).

Short produced *Jumpin' the Border* for a solo exhibition of her work at SoHo 20 Gallery in New York in 1996, which combined a series of works on dance with images of women freeing themselves from oppression. Seeking to create a piece that would link the two series, Short had an epiphany that was inspired by a personal experience. Just before the New York show, she visited her mother, who was living in a retirement home that she liked but still complained of as "the cross she had to bear" (Short 2011, n.p.). Her mother's comment ultimately became the catalyst for the creation of her most controversial work: "I said to myself would she ever get off that cross, and it was a eureka moment. I went home and took out a little piece of lino six inches by four and I cut it in half an hour. I think I called it *Jumpin' the Border,* you know, moving on" (Short 2011, n.p.). This linocut portrays a naked woman high-kicking off a large cross that would more usually be associated with Christ, in a joyful attitude that suggests liberation from oppression. This image was made into a much larger site-specific piece, seven by five feet in dimension, for the New York show.

Figure 10.2   Jumpin' the Border © Constance Short; photo by Deirdre Behan.

Shaped like a large Crucifix composed of nine of the smaller images, this work was badly received by conservative Catholic Irish Americans when it was shown at SoHo 20 Gallery in February 1996 (Short 2011, n.p.). The very fact that a naked woman rather than an almost naked man, a staple of church art as López has observed, was depicted on the cross was enough for some gallery visitors to demand that the show be cancelled. The controversy really began, however, when the piece was shown in Germany at the Frauenmuseum, Weisbaden, in February 1997. Following its purchase by the Weisbaden Local Authority, the piece was to be put on permanent exhibition at the Museum Wiesbaden, a decision that outraged the local Republican Party, who sought a ban on exhibiting what they judged to be a "blasphemous work" (Fehlinger 1997, 8). There followed an intense debate in the local media on the right to artistic expression and freedom of speech. An article entitled "Klare Absage für ein Kunst-Verbot" ["Clear Rejection of Art Ban"], summarises the opposing arguments about displaying the work as follows:

> While the women politicians in Wiesbaden are generally pleased with this gesture, the right wing in the parliament were incensed about the supposedly blasphemous nature of the piece, which they feel represents the destruction of Christian values. They suspected that the artist had an obscene intention when she portrayed on the cross a naked womanly body, which in the Bible is a parable for sin. (Fehlinger 1997, 7)[2]

This horror at the depiction of a Crucifixion in a manner that is not typical of Catholic iconography, and the contiguous distaste at the representation of a naked female body, recall the Irish Church hierarchy's earlier attempts to control any image that they believe falls within its ownership. While Short's work clearly rejects the church's attempts to control and confine women, it is above all a joyful piece that expresses liberation and a break with the past, rather than presenting a lascivious "sinful" scenario, as the Republicans' description of the piece suggests. Ultimately, the effort to ban the work was rejected by the other local parties and the piece remained on show, but the Republicans' pointed lack of engagement with the artist's message here is clear and recalls Hernández's belief that those who view a work of art very often interpret it solely in the light of their own agendas.

While the work of López and Short may be known as the result of the controversies they have provoked, other Chicana and Irish artists, most notably Yolanda López and Rita Duffy, have also reimagined religious iconography in their work in complex and diverse ways. Throughout her career, Duffy has been at the forefront of the artistic engagement with religious iconography in Northern Ireland, where she lives and works. As Northern Ireland remained a part of the United Kingdom after the rest of the island became a republic, religious iconography became even more dominant in this part of the country, though often as much as a badge of Nationalist or Unionist allegiance as an expression of faith. Duffy has depicted subjects as diverse as surveillance watchtowers, the *Titanic* ship, and the Arctic Circle in her work, and her name remains intimately associated with the city of Belfast. Her works that deal with issues such as sectarianism and decommissioning of arms in a war-torn city are connected to her more intimate pieces by an enduring concern with justice and the assertion of human rights. As Sheila Dickinson puts it, even her seemingly mundane works that picture people going about their daily routines are "laden with meaning. These acts were known to be watched, surveyed from within (by overbearing religion) and from without (overbearing state). Duffy believes that as young as three years old she could tell that there was trouble in the place she knew as home" (Dickinson 2012, 10). Although it would seem that religious iconography would be a natural topic for artists growing up in a city divided along religious lines, Duffy found when she studied at art college in Belfast that this was not the case:

> When I arrived at art school a lot of students spent their time in the library looking up art magazines to see what was going on in London and New York and I remember thinking everything's going on all around us right here . . . here I was in art school and the place was going up in flames around us. . . . I really had that feeling of "to thine own self be true." What you are experiencing is as valid as anyone flinging yellow paint around a canvas in London or New York. So when I started my work it was very much about what I was physically and personally experiencing and responding to and thinking about. It was inevitable that I started thinking about this religious stuff. (Duffy 2012, n.p.)

Duffy's early works from the 1990s directly rejected the patriarchal control of the Catholic Church, through images such as *Dictator,* which features an oversized cardinal on a huge stage preaching to a cowed and reverential crowd. She also reimagined iconic figures such as the Virgin Mary in paintings such as *Báidín Beag* [*Small Boat*], a wryly humorous work that pictures the Virgin hovering in the sky as though propelled by helicopter blades in a reference both to the constant surveillance endured by people in the North of Ireland during the troubles and to her Catholic education: "I went to convent school and the whole idea of being good as opposed to being bad was very important. . . . You had that sense that you are being watched" (Duffy 2012, n.p.). Another key image from this period, *Emerging from the Shamrock,* used the triptych framework of traditional Catholic altarpieces, in much the same way as Chicana artists employ the standard template of the Virgen de Guadalupe wearing a cloak of stars and surrounded by divine light, to present a radically new image of Irish womanhood far removed from the passive, desexualized image of the Virgin Mary.

Figure 10.3   Emerging from the Shamrock © Rita Duffy; photo by Chris Hill.

The woman at the centre of the piece commands the viewer's attention, as she boldly strides forward dressed in a basque and bridal veil and wearing high heels. Her sexuality is underlined in a manner that departs from Irish tradition and specifically from the extremely demure Irish beauty pageant the Rose of Tralee, which the image lampoons in having the figure emerge from a shamrock, as the contestants originally did when they walked onto the stage (Ferran 1998, 154). As she walks, the woman crushes underfoot lilies that may be a symbol of virginity, as Paula Murphy suggests, or of Republican allegiance. Murphy interprets this image as "woman, liberated from religious control and social constraints, walking independently and with confidence into the new century, with babies and bishops, politics and powerlessness confined to the side panels" (Murphy 1998, 90).

Another aspect of Duffy's work that parallels the work of Chicana artists is her representation of textiles and items of clothing. Yolanda López famously reimagined the Virgen de Guadalupe through a series of portraits that included images of her mother and grandmother seated at sewing machines, stitching the cloak of stars that adorns the Virgin's figure. By recasting the cloak in the domestic sphere of the seamstress, López simultaneously relates it to the lives of real women and celebrates female manual labour that is undervalued and often rendered invisible. López is among the artists mentioned by Laura Elisa Pérez in her study of the use of dress by

Chicana artists to comment on the discrimination Chicanas face because of their ethnicity, social class, and gender:

> Dress and body decoration in the Chicana art of the 1980s and 1990s call attention to both the body as social and to the social body that constitutes it as such, specifically through gendered and racialized histories of dress, labor (in domestic service and the garment industry), immigration, urban dwelling, academic discourse, art production, and religious belief. (Pérez 2007, 51)

Duffy's exhibition *Banquet* included a series of paintings of women's handbags that began with *Crucible*, an image of an animal-print bag shaped like St Patrick's bell that "was poking fun at this huge Christian artefact in Irish history" (Deepwell 2005, 47). This exhibition also featured the painting *Geansaí*, an Irish word for sweater, which paid homage to her mother's skill at knitting. Through humour and deft observation, Duffy transforms the everyday handbag, implicitly calling into question the right of the Catholic Church to intrude on every aspect of women's lives, while the sweater image pays tribute to a previous generation of women who were limited to expressing themselves by clothing their families, much as the Chicana seamstresses in López's work use their domestic skills to earn additional income. Duffy continued her exploration of dress in the 2006 series *Cloth*, which portrayed garments from clerical robes to judicial clothing to interrogate the structures of power in Northern Ireland :

> Removing the human body from these paintings . . . accentuates the processes by which these non-human objects and artefacts take on meaning only within their relations with us and with other objects. The pomp and ceremony that cloaks legal process in rituals of deference, are seen here from another angle. (Bell 2007, 8)

One arresting example of this radical decontextualization is *Mantle*, a painting of a cardinal's scarlet robe that seems to hover against a vivid red, streaked backdrop, which is strongly suggestive of blood, violence, and trauma.

While Duffy has bravely and unstintingly opposed the damage caused by a repressive, patriarchal church throughout her career, she has also recognised that the education she received from the nuns at her convent school empowered her and led her to believe that she could have a career in a society where she was doubly marginalised by being Catholic and female. Her latest project pays tribute to these women by producing a series of portraits of elderly nuns, whose own achievements have been relegated to a footnote in the history of the church:

> The nuns were kept in their proper place as regards the church. They were servants and service providers. I wanted to do a project that's all

Figure 10.4   *Mantle* © Rita Duffy; photo by Chris Hill.

about giving a face to those women who dedicated their entire lives. Surely the life of one nun from Killeshandra who went out and spent years and years in the wilderness of Nigeria is at least as worthy as one of these paedophile priests who they tried to protect. (Duffy 2012, n.p.)

Like the Chicana artists whose work relates religious iconography to the lives of contemporary women, Duffy does not ignore the influence of the church on her work and the society she forms part of, but rather reflects on this heritage in ways that celebrate women without shrinking from an often searing critique of the terrible damage done by church authorities who used their positions of power to tyrannise others. Her work, like that of Short and the Chicana artists mentioned in this chapter, reinterprets the legacy of the Catholic Church to forge a new identity that does not discard the past but incorporates it into a vision of a future where women can live their lives free of the rigid control of a patriarchal, oppressively religious society.

HEAVEN HELP US ALL: SOME CONCLUSIONS

As this study suggests, church control over religious iconography and artists' rebellion against such constraints are not new issues. The portrayal of artists' attempts to interpret religious symbols in creative ways not dictated by the church as radical and new suggests something transgressive and even unnatural about such work, however. Ultimately, what constitutes an unacceptable or even blasphemous work of art is a slippery concept that can be used by various groups to assert their authority and quash any form of protest that they do not wish to acknowledge. S. Brent Plate's study on the subject of controversial religious art, *Blasphemy: Art that Offends,* provides a useful framework for considering why certain works of art provoke strong and even litigious reactions. He notes that: "No work of art is blasphemous in and of itself; it must be deemed so from within religious and/or political power structures" (2006, 50). Moreover, he adds that the power struggles over a work of art can reflect both the might of authorities who attempt to censor a piece and the use of a certain visual vocabulary by artists to subvert this control:

The differences and overlaps between political and religious authority are critical to take into account, even as they are ultimately impossible to separate. The power of images also works in the opposite direction, as people without social power (often in terms of race, class, and gender) utilise images in transgressive ways to assert power. (2006, 28)

This awareness of the power divisions in society is critical. In the Irish context, Short has noted that the art world continues to be male-dominated and that undoubtedly women are criticized more for engaging with religious art in a nondeferential manner (Short 2011, n.p.). Duffy, in turn, recalls that as a young, Catholic, working-class woman, she was not expected to have a career as an artist and was seen as something of an oddity. Any efforts by the Catholic Church in Ireland today to censor art that engages with religious symbolism must surely be seen in the context of its dramatically reduced influence on society and as an effort to reassert its power. As Duffy notes, however, the enduring influence of the Catholic Church on Irish society cannot be underestimated and needs to be addressed by artists:

> Even though we're watching the death knells and they're hammering the nails in the coffin as we speak, it's still a relevant thing to enquire. How do we sort this out? Where do the victims of abuse go? Do you just sweep all that to one side? In my experience the pendulum you move over swings back unless you do the hard, dirty difficult work of unravelling and dealing with, how was that? Why was that? (Duffy 2012, n.p.)

One unintended positive outcome of the now open acknowledgement of the church's abuse of its power is precisely that Irish artists have engaged more in recent years with religious iconography than they have in the past. A public art installation in Temple Bar, Dublin, entitled *Trespass and Forgiveness,* deals with the trauma suffered by survivors of sexual abuse by the church, while exhibitions such as *Blasphemy* at the Oonagh Young Gallery, Dublin, and *Blasphemous,* at the Irish Museum of Contemporary Art, both in 2010, suggest that, with time, Irish artists will begin to engage more with religious art in response to the blasphemy law.

Chicana artists, meanwhile, are continuing their struggle against the traditional roles imposed on women by a male-dominated society. It is clear that religious iconography continues to provide a rich and diverse source of inspiration to these artists. Alma López's most recent series *Queer Santas* celebrates saints, such as the virgin martyrs St. Wilgefortis and St. Lucia, whose rebellion against the social strictures of their times led to their deaths. López presents the saints in modern dress against jewel-coloured backdrops featuring symbols that explain their histories. By casting the saints as contemporary women, she underscores their relevance to modern society but also reminds the viewer that many of the women now revered by the Catholic Church were, paradoxically, celebrated originally precisely because of their nonconformist, rebellious natures. Hernández has continued to engage with the image of the Virgen de Guadalupe in her work though a recent poster that protested Arizona's racist SB 1070 law. Entitled *Wanted: Terrorist La Virgen de Guadalupe,* the poster imagines the Virgin, again depicted as a contemporary woman, in a police wanted poster. The clear inference here is that even this symbol of divine intervention is not safe from laws that racially profile all Mexicans or people of Mexican descent in the state. The vibrancy, diversity, and power of the work discussed here suggests that, far from being passé or clichéd, religious imagery remains a vital subject for artists to explore. Religious iconography provides Chicana and Irish artists with a means of reflecting a new identity whose multifaceted nature may be postmodern but which can communicate a message of resistance and female pride while paying homage to the ancient history of syncretic religious practices on both sides of the Atlantic.

NOTES

1. This conference was co-organised by Professor Nuala Finnegan and Niamh McNamara of University College Cork, Dr Ana Cruz of Cork Institute of Technology, Dr Niamh Thornton of the University of Liverpool, Professor Wilifried Raussert of the University of Bielefeld, and the author.
2. Sincere thanks to Claire Bermingham for translating this article from German.

WORKS CITED

America Needs Fatima. "Stop the Scandal at Notre Dame." April 15, 2009. http://americaneedsfatima.blogspot.ie/2009/04/stop-scandal-at-notre-dame.html. Accessed February 5, 2012.

Anzaldúa, G. *Borderlands/La frontera: The New Mestiza.* San Francisco: Aunt Lute Books, 2007.

Bell, V. "The Poetry of Cloth: Painting, Potentiality and Politics." In *Cloth: A Visual and Verbal Collaboration,* edited by Rita Duffy and Paul Muldoon (8–9). Portadown: Millennium Court Arts Centre, 2007.

Benson, C. "Modernism and Ireland's Selves." *Circa* 1, no. 61 (1992): 18–23.

Bhreathnach-Lynch, S. *Ireland's Art, Ireland's History: Representing Ireland, 1845 to Present.* Omaha, NE: Creighton University Press, 2007.

Brent Plate, S. *Blasphemy: Art that Offends.* London: Black Dog, 2006.

Carrier, D. "David Godbold's Recent Drawings." In *Once It Was a Lie, Now It's the Truth.* Dublin: Kerlin Gallery, 2005.

Castillo, A. *Massacre of the Dreamers: Essays on Xicanisma.* New York: Plume, 1995.

Cremin, M., and O. Young. *Blasphemy.* Dublin: Oonagh Young Gallery, 2010.

Deepwell, K. *Dialogues: Women Artists from Ireland.* New York: Palgrave Macmillan, 2005.

Dickinson, S. "Paint, Blood and Tears." In *Rita Duffy: Arctic Circus* (10). Banbridge: F. E. McWilliam Gallery and Studio, 2012.

Donnelly, J. S., Jr. "A Church in Crisis: The Irish Catholic Church Today." *History Ireland* 8, no. 3 (Autumn 2000): 12–17.

Duffy, R. Personal Interview with the author, Dublin, May 4, 2012.

English, E. "Cork Bishop Criticises 'Offensive' Mary Image." *Irish Examiner,* June 23, 2011. http://www.irishexaminer.com/ireland/cork-bishop-criticises-offensive-mary-image-158770.html. Accessed July 2, 2011.

Fehlinger, Von M. 1997. "Klare Absage für ein Kunst-Verbot." ["Clear Rejection of Art Ban."] *Frankfurter Rundschau,* June 27, 1997, p. 7.

Ferran, D. "Rita Duffy—Mid Term Report." *Irish Arts Review Yearbook* (151–161). Dublin: Eaton Enterprises, 1998.

Foster, R. F. *Modern Ireland 1600–1972.* London: Penguin Books, 1989.

Gaspar de Alba, A. "Our Lady of Controversy: A Subject that Needs No Introduction." In *Our Lady of Controversy: Alma López's Irreverent Apparition* (1–12), edited by Alma López and Alicia Gaspar de Alba. Austin: University of Texas Press, 2011.

Gruzinski, Serge. *Images at War: Mexico from Columbus to Blade Runner (1492-2019)*. Durham, NC: Duke University Press, 2001.

Harbison, P. *The Crucifixion in Irish Art: Fifty Selected Examples from the Ninth to the Twentieth Century*. Dublin: Columba Press, 2000.

Hoppen, K. T. *Ireland Since 1800: Conflict and Conformity*. Essex: Longman, 1999.

Johnson, K. "Ester Hernández." In *Contemporary Chicano and Chicana Art*, Vol. 2 (24–25), edited by G. D. Keller. Tempe, AZ: Bilingual Press, 2002.

López, A. "'Our Lady' Stalked by America Needs Fatima since 2001." July 11, 2011. http://almalopezblog.blogspot.ie/2011/07/our-lady-stalked-by-america-needs .html. Accessed May 5, 2012.

López, A., and Gaspar de Alba, A., eds. *Our Lady of Controversy: Alma López's Irreverent Apparition*. Austin: University of Texas Press, 2011.

McLysaght, E. "Artist Says She's Offended by UCC Blasphemy Controversy." June 28, 2011. http://www.thejournal.ie/artist-says-shes-offended-by-ucc-blasphemy-controversy-165510-Jun2011. Accessed April 15, 2012.

Meaney, G. *Gender, Ireland and Cultural Change: Race, Sex, and Nation*. New York: Routledge, 2011.

Monsiváis, C. *Mexican Postcards*. New York: Verso, 1997.

Murphy, P. "Madonna and Maiden, Mistress and Mother: Woman as Symbol of Ireland and Spirit of the Nation." In *When Time Began to Rant and Rage: Figurative Painting from Twentieth-Century Ireland* (90–101), edited by James Christen Steward. London: Merrell Holberton, 1998.

Nunn, Tey M. "It's Not about the Art in the Folk, It's about the Folks in the Art: A Curator's Tale." In *Our Lady of Controversy: Alma López's Irreverent Apparition* (17–43), edited by Alma López and Alicia Gaspar de Alba. Austin: University of Texas Press, 2011.

Office of the Attorney General, Irish Statute Book, Defamation Act 2009. http://www.irishstatutebook.ie/pdf/2009/en.act.2009.0031.pdf.

Pérez, L. E. *Chicana Art: The Politics of Spiritual and Aesthetic Altarities*. Durham, NC: Duke University Press, 2007.

Pyle, H. *Jack B. Yeats in the National Gallery of Ireland*. Dublin: National Gallery of Ireland, 1986.

Scott, Y. *Louis le Brocquy: Allegory & Legend*. Limerick: Hunt Museum, 2006.

Shorris, E. *The Life and Times of Mexico*. New York: Norton, 2004.

Short, C. Personal interview with the author. Dublin, September 18, 2011.

Stavans, I. *The Hispanic Condition: The Power of a People*. New York: HarperCollins, 2001.

Turpin, J. "Visual Marianism and National Identity in Ireland, 1920–1960." In *Art, Nation and Gender: Ethnic Landscapes, Myths and Mother Figures* (67–79), edited by T. Cusack and S. Bhreathnach-Lynch. Hampshire: Ashgate, 2003.

Watson, Grant. "Constant Spirit." *Irish Arts Review*, 24, no. 3 (2007): 96-97.

Watson, W. T. "The Celtic Church in Its Relations with Paganism." *The Celtic Review* 10, no. 39 (1915): 263–279.

Conclusion

The thematic, methodological, and geographical diversity and scope of the chapters in this volume clearly reflect the significance of Chicana/o Studies in an increasingly globalised world. As Arjun Appadurai has noted, however, there can be a serious gulf between academic discourse on globalisation and the concerns about global processes and markets among the public in general, especially among those who are socially and economically disenfranchised. Appadurai suggests that there is a danger that the disparity of ways in which globalisation is experienced in and beyond academia can lead to what he terms a "double apartheid," the first part of which is notable for the gap between academic and everyday discussions of the negative aspects of globalisation, while the second part concerns the gap between economically marginalised people and their representatives and national debates on the problems that stem from globalisation (Appadurai 2001, 2–3). He suggests that the solution lies in a reconceptualisation of place—a central theme of this volume—as academics must move toward seeing particular geographical areas as constantly evolving, rather than concrete and fixed. He also advocates the creation of research communities composed of scholars from diverse traditions and cultures in order to "create communities and conventions of research in which membership does not require unquestioned prior adherence to a quite specific research ethic" (Appadurai 2001, 14–16).

This openness to new ideas and approaches in a transnational and transcultural research environment recalls Anzaldúa's efforts to open up the investigation of Chicana/o culture and echoes her calls for an inclusiveness that can lead to healing, even after traumatic events such as 9/11. Indeed, her comments seem almost prophetic in the light of recent events that have been central to the experience of Mexican or Latina/o immigrants and to the Chicana/o community in the United States.

In the build-up to the 2012 U.S. presidential election, again there was much discussion about the concerns expressed in some quarters about the presence of the Mexican and Latina/o populations in the United States. Much of this discussion took the form of negative campaigning against supporters of immigrants' rights, with candidates vilifying opponents who called for the reform of harsh immigration laws through virulently racist advertisements, such as those approved by Nevada Republican Sharron Angle as part of her bid to win a Senate seat against Democrat rival Senator Harry Reid. Angle's advertisements claim that Reid supported "special tax breaks" and "social security benefits" for undocumented immigrants, who are referred to throughout as "illegal aliens". The voiceover that makes these allegations is accompanied by images of a group of men dressed as Latino gang members easily crossing through a chicken-wire fence that represents a border radically dissimilar to the almost impenetrable and heavily policed barriers raised over the past few decades to prevent undocumented immigrants entering the United States (goodganews 2010). Another of Angle's campaign advertisements criticised Reid for opposing Arizona's harsh anti-immigrant law, S.B. 1070, which, among other provisions, requires police to check people's immigration status if there is "reasonable suspicion" that they may be in the United States illegally (Scott Harr, Hess, and Orthmann 2011, 108). Although Arizona's laws have led to much public debate and criticism, they remain in force and have been followed by the enactment of strict new laws in Georgia, Utah, and Alabama. Alabama's HB 56 surpassed even Arizona's in its severity. It not only allows police to check a person's legal status in the country but also prevents undocumented immigrants from receiving state or local benefits, studying at public colleges, or working. It also criminalises the transportation of an undocumented person or the renting of a property to them, as well as the employment of an undocumented person rather than a documented one. One of the provisions of this law that has raised most concern is the requirement for every school district to report each year to the state education board the number of "presumed illegal immigrants" in their schools (Fausset 2011, n.p.).

A related recent controversy in Arizona centres on the banning of high school courses on Mexican American Studies. This prohibition stems from an atmosphere in which antipathy toward the Latina/o population has been notable for some time. In a comparative study between Texas, which allows undocumented high school graduates access to federal aid for in-state college tuition fees, and Arizona, which does not, the authors conclude that the situation in Arizona may not change because of the "continued strength of anti-immigration sentiment" in the state (Dougherty, Nienhusser, and Vega 2010, 165). This view would appear to be confirmed by the passage on December 31, 2010, of House Bill 2281 in Arizona, which prohibits the teaching to public school students of courses that:

1. Promote the overthrow of the United States government.
2. Promote resentment toward a race or class of people.
3. Are designed primarily for pupils of a particular ethnic group.
4. Advocate ethnic solidarity instead of the treatment of pupils as individuals (Arizona State Legislature 2010, 1).

The bill recognises the necessity of teaching about the Holocaust and of protecting courses for Native American students "required to comply with federal law." Mexican American Studies courses have enjoyed no such protection, however, and the Tucson Unified School District (TUSD) has removed them from the core curricula and now only offers them as electives, despite the fact that they were extremely successful (Cabrera, Meza, and Cintli Rodríguez 2011, 20). The bill has also led to teachers being prevented from teaching certain texts on threat of being fired and to the removal of banned books from high schools. According to Yolanda Soweto, a Chicana/o literature teacher in Pueblo High School, this bill has led to great disruption to carefully prepared curricula and fears among students that they will be prosecuted for finishing projects already in progress based on Chicana/o texts. She also observed that an American literature text she was given to replace some of the texts she was forbidden to use in her classes contained the seminal Chicano Movement poem "*Yo Soy Joaquín*" by Corky González, noting the irony that, "It's OK to teach it if it's in this book, but not in (a Chicano literature) class" (Herreras 2012, n.p.).

The election win by Obama in 2012 was seen by many as a reflection of the Democrats' appeal to the Latina/o vote and the Republican's failure to see the value of this constituency. Sixty-seven percent of the Latina/o vote went to Obama (BBC 2012, n.p.). Since then, there has been a dramatic change in the way the Republicans address this portion of the electorate. As for the Democrats, the ongoing debates over the partial introduction of the DREAM act by Obama's administration and the promises of access to education and health care for a limited number of undocumented migrants does not hide the fact that under Obama the number of deportations have reached record levels (Preston 2012, n.p.). This all makes Latinas/os central to many contradictory discussions at a national level. They are both to be wooed and to be contained.

The current context means that there is also a renewal of Chicana/o activism that is reminiscent of the foundational moment of the Movement. One such example is the *Librotraficante* [book smugglers] group led by Tony Diaz, which has challenged Arizona's HB2281 by "smuggling" banned books into Arizona, setting up ad hoc libraries, and travelling around giving readings from those books. The ban and the consequent activism are testimony to the centrality of culture to the struggle for civil rights in the United States.

The continuing debates on this and other issues pertaining to the racism and sustained exclusion endured by Chicanas/os and other Latinas/os in the United States make this volume an important contribution to a growing body of publications on Chicana/o Studies that features an international community of scholars who see Chicana/o culture as vibrant and enriching, rather than being the narrow, politically motivated field that Arizona's bill would suggest in their references to separatism and even sedition. While, undoubtedly, Chicana/o art, literature, and popular culture engage with the issues pertinent to the Chicana/o people in a way far removed from the elitist debates on globalisation cautioned against by Appadurai, the fact that it has become a part of university curricula in such diverse places far beyond the United States must surely suggest that it is the creativity and complexity of this culture that appeals to scholars worldwide rather than some imagined political agenda. The likelihood of courses on Chicana/o Studies outside the United States seeking to overthrow the U.S. government is surely remote, while the fact that the students who take courses on Chicana/o Studies outside the United States are unlikely to be Latinas/os means that the aim of these courses cannot be the privileging of a particular ethnic group over another or the fostering of racial or ethnic divisions. Indeed, the suggestion that Chicana/o Studies is solely motivated by political or ideological concerns is as reductive as arguing that James Joyce's *Ulysses,* a novel that depicts life in Dublin city in meticulous detail, could only be relevant to inhabitants of the Irish capital. The increasing international interest in Chicana/o Studies is rather motivated by an appreciation of a culture whose richness and diversity are reflected in the chapters of this volume. The vibrancy and constant evolution of Chicana/o Studies means that it appeals to scholars across disciplines and borders who seek to represent cultures in constant transition and to respect cultural diversity while acknowledging individual voices and experiences.

WORKS CITED

Appadurai, A. "Grassroots Globalization and the Research Imagination." In *Globalization* (1–22). Edited by A. Appadurai. Durham, NC: Duke University Press, 2001.

Arizona State Legislature. House Bill 2281. 2010. http://www.azleg.gov/legtext/49leg/2r/bills/hb2281s.pdf. Accessed February 27, 2013.

British Broadcasting Corporation. "US Election: Power of the Latino Vote." *BBC Online,* October 31, 2012. http://www.bbc.co.uk/news/world-us-canada-20153941. Accessed February 27, 2013.

Cabrera, Nolan L., Elisa L. Meza, and R. Cintli Rodríguez. "The Fight for Mexican American Studies in Tucson." *NACLA Report on the Americas* (November-December 2011): 20–24.

Dougherty, K. J., K. H. Nienhusser, and B. E. Vega. "Undocumented Immigrants and State Higher Education Policy: The Politics of In-State Tuition Eligibility in Texas and Arizona." *The Review of Higher Education* 34, no. 1 (2010): 123–173.

Fausset, R. "Alabama Enacts Illegal Immigration Law Described as Nation's Strictest." *Los Angeles Times,* June 10, 2011. http://articles.latimes.com/2011/jun/10/nation/la-na-alabama-immigration-20110610. Accessed February 27, 2013.

goodganews. "Sharron Angle's Race Baiting Ads Attacking Harry Reid." *YouTube.* October 7, 2010. http://www.youtube.com/watch?v=2qP3DBLUOeQ. Accessed March 1, 2012.

Herreras, M. "TUSD Banning Books/ Well Yes, and No, and Yes." *Tucson Weekly,* January 17, 2012. http://www.tucsonweekly.com/TheRange/archives/2012/01/17/tusd-banning-book-well-yes-and-no-and-yes. Accessed February 27, 2013.

Preston, J. "Record Number of Foreigners Were Deported in 2011, Officials Say." *New York Times,* September 8, 2012. http://www.nytimes.com/2012/09/08/us/us-deports-record-number-of-foreigners-in-2011.html. Accessed February 27, 2013.

Scott Harr, J., K. M. Hess, and C. M. H. Orthmann. *Constitutional Law and the Criminal Justice System.* Belmont, California: Wadsworth, 2011.

Guide to Further Reading

As this volume demonstrates, the richness and diversity of Chicana/o Studies mean that no guide to readings on the field can possibly be exhaustive. The suggestions that follow instead seek to direct readers to sources that expand on the topics highlighted in this volume, particularly Chicana/o theory, literature, popular culture, visual culture, and the borderlands. The resources provided also concentrate as much as possible on recent scholarship and works with a transnational and interdisciplinary focus, including several bilingual or Spanish-language texts.

PRINT RESOURCES

Aldama, Frederick Luis. *Spilling the Beans in Chicolandia: Conversations with Writers and Artists*. Austin: University of Texas Press, 2006.
———. *Your Brain on Latino Comics: From Gus Arriola to Los Bros Hernandez*. Austin: University of Texas Press, 2009.
———. *The Routledge Concise History of Latino/a Literature*. New York: Routledge, 2013.
Arredondo, Gabriela, Aida Hurtado, Norma Klahn, and Olga Najera-Ramirez, eds. *Chicana Feminisms: A Critical Reader*. Durham, NC: Duke University Press, 2003.
Blanco-Cano, Rosana, and Rita E. Urquijo-Ruiz. *Global Mexican Cultural Productions*. New York: Palgrave Macmillan, 2011.
Burton-Carvajal, Julianne, Patricia Torres, and Ángel Miquel, eds. *Horizontes del segundo siglo: Investigación y pedagogía del cine mexicano, latinoamericano y chicano*. México: Universidad de Guadalajara, 1998.
Cañero, Julio, ed. *Nuevas reflexiones en torno a la literatura y cultura chicana*. Madrid: Biblioteca Benjamin Franklin, 2010.
Concannon, Kevin, Francisco A. Lomelí, and Marc Priewe, eds. *Imagined Transnationalism: U.S. Latino/a Literature, Culture and Identity*. New York: Palgrave Macmillan, 2009.
Davidson, Miriam. *Lives on the Line: Dispatches from the U.S.-Mexico Border*. Tucson: University of Arizona Press, 2000.
Dear, Michael, and Gustavo Leclerc, eds. *Postborder City: Cultural Spaces of Bajalta California*. New York: Routledge, 2003.
Delgado, Richard, and Jean Stefancic, eds. *The Latino/a Condition: A Critical Reader*. New York: New York University Press, 2010.

Durán, Ignacio, Iván Trujillo, and Mónica Verea, eds. *México Estados Unidos: Encuentros y desencuentros en el cine.* México: Universidad Nacional Autónoma de México/Consejo Nacional Para la Cultura y las Artes/Instituto Mexicano de Cinematografía, 1996.

Edberg, Mark. *El narcotraficante, narcocorridos and the Construction of a Cultural Persona on the U.S.-Mexican Border.* Austin: University of Texas Press, 2004.

Espejo, Ramón, Juan-Ignacio Guijarro, Jesús Lerate de Castro, Pilar Marín, and María Angeles Toda Iglesia, eds. *Critical Essays on Chicano Studies.* Bern: Peter Lang, 2007.

Ezra, Elizabeth, and Terry Rowden, eds. *Transnational Cinema: The Film Reader.* London: Routledge, 2006.

Foster, David William, ed. *Chicano/Latino Homoerotic Identities.* New York: Routledge, 1999.

Fox, Claire. *The Fence and the River: Culture and Politics at the U.S.-Mexico Border.* Minneapolis: University of Minnesota Press, 1999.

Fregoso, Rosa Linda, and Cynthia Bejarano, eds. *Terrorizing Women: Feminicide in the Americas.* Durham, NC: Duke University Press, 2010.

Fuentes, Carlos. *The Buried Mirror: Reflections on Spain and the New World.* Boston: Houghton Mifflin, 1992.

Gerds, Heike. *Living Beyond the Gender Trap: Concepts of Gender and Sexual Expression Envisioned by Marge Piercy, Cherríe Moraga and Leslie Feinberg.* Aachen: Shaker Verlag, 2004.

Gómez-Peña, Guillermo. *Dangerous Border Crossers: The Artist Talks Back.* London: Routledge, 2000.

Gonzalez, Rita, Howard N. Fox, and Chon A. Noriega, eds. *Phantom Sightings: Art after the Chicano Movement.* Berkeley: University of California Press and Los Angeles County Museum of Art, 2008.

Gutiérrez, David C. *Walls and Mirrors: Mexican Americans, Mexican Immigrants and the Politics of Ethnicity.* Berkeley: University of California Press, 1995.

Habell-Pallán, Michelle. *Loca Motion: The Travels of Chicana and Latina Popular Culture.* New York: New York University Press, 2005.

Herrera-Sobek, María, ed. *Critical Insights: The House on Mango Street.* Pasadena, CA: Salem Press, 2011.

———, Francisco Lomelí, and Juan Antonio Perles Rochel, eds. *Perspectivas transatlánticas en la literatura chicana: Ensayos y creatividad.* Spain: Servicio de Publicaciones de la Universidad de Málaga, 2005.

———, and David Maciel, eds. *Culture across Borders: Mexican Immigration and Popular Culture.* Tucson: University of Arizona Press, 1998.

Iglesias Prieto, Norma. *Entre yerba, polvo y plomo: Lo fronterizo visto por el cine mexicano.* Tijuana: El Colegio de Frontera Norte, 1991.

———. *Beautiful Flowers of the Maquiladora: Life Histories of Women Workers in Tijuana.* Austin: University of Texas Press, 1997.

———, and Rosa Linda Fregoso, eds. *Miradas de mujer: Encuentro de cineastas y videoastas mexicanas y chicanas.* Tijuana: El Colegio de la Frontera Norte, 1998.

Kaplan, Caren, Norma Alarcón, and Minoo Moallem, eds. *Between Woman and Nation: Nationalisms, Transnational Feminisms, and the State.* Durham, NC: Duke University Press, 1999.

Keating, Ana Louise, ed. *Entremundos/Among Worlds: New Perspectives on Gloria Anzaldúa.* New York: Palgrave Macmillan, 2005.

Limón, José E. *Mexican Ballads, Chicano Poems: History and Influence in Mexican-American Social Poetry.* Berkeley: University of California Press, 1992.

Lomelí, Francisco A. *The Chican@ Literary Imagination: A Collection of Critical Studies by Francisco A. Lomelí.* Spain: Biblioteca Benjamin Franklin, 2012.

López, Marissa K. *Chicano Nations: The Hemispheric Origins of Mexican American Literature.* New York: New York University Press, 2011.

Noriega, Chon A., Terezita Romo, and Pilar Tompkins Rivera, eds. *L.A. Xicano.* Seattle: University of Washington Press, 2011.

———, and Wendy Belcher. *I Am Aztlán: The Personal Essay in Chicano Studies.* Seattle: University of Washington Press, 2004.

———, and Ana M. López. *The Ethnic Eye: Latino Media Arts.* Minneapolis: University of Minnesota Press, 1996.

Polk, Patrick Arthur. *Botánica Los Angeles: Latino Popular Religious Art in the City of Angels.* Los Angeles: UCLA Fowler Museum of Cultural History.

Ramírez Berg, Charles. *Latino Images in Film: Stereotypes, Subversion and Resistance.* Austin: University of Texas Press, 2002.

Stavans, Ilan, Edna Acosta-Belén, Harold Augenbraum, María Herrera-Sobek, Rolando Hinojoso, and Gustavo Pérez Firmat. *The Norton Anthology of Latino Literature.* New York: Norton, 2010.

Tatum, Charles. *Chicano and Chicana Literature: Otra Voz del Pueblo.* Tucson: University of Arizona Press, 2006.

———. *Chicano Popular Culture: Que Hable el Pueblo.* Tucson: University of Arizona Press, 2001.

Thornton, Niamh. *Revolution and Rebellion in Mexican Film.* New York: Continuum, 2013.

———. and Par Kumaraswami, eds. *Revolucionarias.* Bern: Peter Lang, 2007.

Urquijo-Ruiz, Rita E. *Wild Tongues: Transnational Mexican Popular Culture.* Austin: University of Texas Press, 2012.

Xavier Inda, Jonathan. *Targeting Immigrants: Government, Technology, and Ethics.* Massachusetts: Blackwell, 2006.

WEB RESOURCES

Alternative Publications: http://alternativepublications.ucmerced.edu/

Published by Manuel M. Martín-Rodríguez of the University of California, Merced, this forum provides a space for previously unpublished work, mainly by Latina/o authors, and features a virtual library archiving featured works. It includes fiction, nonfiction, plays, poetry, bilingual texts, and works in the Spanish language.

Bold Caballeros and Noble Bandidas in American Pop Culture: http://noblebandits .asu.edu/

This site, inspired by Eric Hobsbawm's idea of the social bandit, provides essays, bibliography, and information on conferences and events related to the Caballero and Bandit in U.S. and Latin American culture.

California Ethnic and Multicultural Archives: http://www.library.ucsb.edu/special-collections/cema

This extremely comprehensive site includes a vast collection of Digital Chicano and Latino Art, and Chicana/o and Latina/o Collections featuring items including the papers of Oscar Zeta Acosta, Ana Castillo, Bert Corona, and María Helena Viramontes. Some items, such as images by the Royal Chicano Air Force, can be viewed online.

Centro de Investigaciones Sobre América del Norte (CISAN): http://www.cisan .unam.mx/

The website of the only center in Mexico dedicated to the study of Mexican-U.S. relations, located at the Universidad Nacional Autónoma de México, features information on research, publications, and multimedia content, including podcasts on issues such as migration and human rights.

Ecozon@: European Journal of Literature, Culture and Environment: http://www
.ecozona.eu/index.php/journal/index.

This online journal is distinguished by both being interdisciplinary and providing
the first multilingual platform for ecocriticism. It combines scholarly articles with
visual art, creative writing, and book reviews.

FIAR: http://www.interamerica.de/

Online journal of the International Association of Inter-American Studies of the
University of Bielefeld, Germany. Features articles and podcasts on issues related
to multiculturalism and transnationalism, as well as information on conferences
and other events.

Instituto Franklin de Investigación en Estudios Norteamericanos: http://www
.institutofranklin.net/en

Located at the Universidad de Alcalá de Henares, Spain, this site features information on academic programs, research, events, and publications.

La Bloga: http://labloga.blogspot.ie/

Contains creative writing, essays, reviews, and links to the works of writers
including Alma Luz Villanueva, Dagoberto Gilb, John Rechy, and Gary Soto.

Latinopia: http://latinopia.com/

Created by filmmaker, writer, and activist Jesús Salvador Treviño, Latinopia is a
multimedia site dedicated to Latina/o art, film and television, food, history, literature, music, and theater, with links to numerous relevant blogs and social media.
Videos include a reading by poet Diane García and an interview with Luis Valdez
on his play *Zoot Suit*.

NAR: http://nuestraaparenterendicion.com/

Spanish-language website dedicated to raising awareness about violence on the
Mexican-U.S. border, through news articles, creative writing, blogs, and bibli-
ography on issues relating to the borderlands, including the femicides in Ciudad
Juárez and immigration.

Pew Hispanic Center: http://www.pewhispanic.org/

Statistics, news items, and reports on Latina/o and Chicana/o issues.

La Pocho Nostra: http://www.pochanostra.com/

Performer, filmmaker, and writer Guillermo Gómez-Peña's interactive and pro-
vocative site features performance and literary archives, a blog, videos, essays,
and news.

Self-Help Graphics: http://www.selfhelpgraphics.com/

Information about events, community programs, exhibitions, and workshops.

72 Migrantes: http://72migrantes.com/

A virtual altar commemorating, through writing, images, and music, seventy-two
migrants murdered on the Mexican-U.S. border in 2010.

United Farm Workers: http://www.ufw.org/

Information on issues such as immigration and agricultural workers' rights in
English and Spanish. The site includes details of activism, campaigns, conventions, and news and multimedia educational resources on key historical events
such as the Delano Grape Strike and Boycott.

VG/Voices from the Gaps: http://voices.cla.umn.edu/

Created by the University of Minnesota, Voices from the Gaps celebrates the work
of women artists and writers of color. It includes essays, interviews, bibliography,

and other materials on Chicana writers such as Julia Alvarez, Gloria Anzaldúa, Ana Castillo, Lorna Dee Cervantes, Lucha Corpi, Alicia Gaspar de Alba, Graciela Limón, Helena María Viramontes, and Bernice Zamora.

Women Make Movies: http://www.wmm.com/

This multicultural, multiracial, nonprofit media arts organization promotes the work of independent women filmmakers. The site provides resources such as filmographies, links to other media organizations, and an extensive catalogue of works by Chicana filmmakers such as Lourdes Portillo and Sylvia Morales.

SELECTED ARTISTS' WEB PAGES

http://almalopez.net/
http://www.constanceshort.com/
http://www.esterhernandez.com/
http://ritaduffystudio.com/

SELECTED WRITERS' PAGES AND BLOGS

Castillo, Ana. http://www.anacastillo.com/content/
Castillo, Mary. http://marycastillo.com/
Cervantes, Lorna Dee. http://lornadice.blogspot.ie/
Cisneros, Sandra. http://www.sandracisneros.com/
Elizondo Griest, Stephanie. http://stephanieelizondogriest.com/
Gaspar de Alba, Alicia. http://www.aliciagaspardealba.blogspot.ie/
Piñeiro, Caridad. http://www.caridad.com/
Serros, Michele. http://www.myspace.com/micheleserros
Valdés-Rodríguez, Alisa. http://www.alisavaldesrodriguez.com/ http://alisavaldesro-driguez.blogspot.ie/

Contributors

Cristina Elgue-Martini is a professor at the National University of Córdoba, Argentina. Her main areas of research are Comparative Literature, Cultural Studies, Anglophone and Latin American Contemporary Literatures, and Women's Studies. She is vice-president of the Argentine Association of American Studies and is the current editor of the *Argentinean Journal of Canadian Studies*. She is author and editor of numerous publications, most recently: "Arquitectura e identidad poscolonial," in *Primeras Jornadas Internacionales y Segundas Jornadas Nacionales de Cultura y Literatura en Lengua Inglesa*; Universidad Nacional de La Plata, "La presencia medieval en las culturas anglófonas: De la utopía moderna al pastiche posmoderno," in *VII Jornadas Nacionales de Literatura Comparada*, edited by Rolando Costa Picazo (BM Press, 2007); and "La presencia de *Ulysses* en la obra narrativa de Ricardo Piglia," in *Proust y Joyce en ámbitos rioplatenses*, Beatriz Vegh y Jean-Philippe Baranbé, coords. (Montevideo: Universidad de la República, 2007).

Nuala Finnegan is head of the Department of Hispanic Studies and director of the Centre for Mexican Studies at University College, Cork. She teaches in the areas of Latin American and Chicana/o culture including literature, cinema, and photography. Her research interests are Mexican contemporary culture including literature and film, Latin American women writers, Latino writers, border studies, Chicana/o culture, and Latin American film. She is author of *Ambivalence, Modernity, Power: Women and Writing in Mexico since 1980* (Peter Lang, 2007), and with Jane Lavery edited *The Boom Femenino in Mexico: Reading Contemporary Women's Writing* (Cambridge Scholars Publishing, 2010) and *Monstrous Projections of Femininity in the Fiction of Mexican Writer Rosario Castellanos* (Edwin Mellen Press, 2000).

Mario T. García is professor of Chicana/o Studies at the University of California, Santa Barbara. He is a twentieth-century historian with expertise in mass immigration from Mexico; the development of immigrant communities such as El Paso; the "Mexican-American Generation" from the

1930s to the early 1960s; emergence of new leadership among the U.S.-born generation; as well as the Chicano Movement Generation of the late 1960s and early 1970s. His research involves generational approaches, civil rights struggles, oral history, and even more recently, Chicano Catholic history. His recent publications include: Enhanced E-Book Version (with Sal Castro) of *Blowout! Sal Castro and the Chicano Struggle for Educational Justice* (Chapel Hill: University of North Carolina Press, 2012); *Católicos: Resistance and Affirmation in Chicano Catholic History* (Austin: University of Texas Press, 2008); and *Memories of Chicano History: The Life and Narrative of Bert Corona* (University of California Press, 1995).

María Herrera-Sobek is chair of the Chicana and Chicano Studies Department and holds the Luis Leal Endowed Chair in Chicano Studies at the University of California, Santa Barbara. She taught at the University of California, Irvine, for several years and has been a visiting professor at Stanford and Harvard Universities. Herrera-Sobek is the author of several books including *The Bracero Experience: Elitelore versus Folklore* (1979); *The Mexican Corrido: A Feminist Analysis* (1990); and *Northward Bound: The Mexican Immigrant Experience in Ballad and Song* (1993). In addition she is the editor or coeditor of numerous anthologies including *Beyond Stereotypes: The Critical Analysis of Chicana Literature* (1985); *Chicana Creativity and Criticism: Charting New Frontiers in Chicana Literature* (with Helena María Viramontes) (1988 and 1996); *Gender and Print Culture: New Perspectives on International Ballad Studies* (1991); *Reconstructing a Chicano/a Literary Heritage: Hispanic Colonial Literature of the Southwest* (1993); *Chicano Renaissance: Contemporary Trends in Chicano Culture* (with David Maciel and Isidro Ortiz) (2000); and *Santa Barraza: The Life and Work of a Mexica/Tejana Artist* (2001).

Catherine Leen is a lecturer in the Department of Spanish at the National University of Ireland, Maynooth, Ireland. Her teaching and research interests center on Mexican and Chicana/o literature and cinema and Argentine and Paraguayan cultures. In 2008, she received a Fulbright Scholarship to conduct research at the Chicana/o Studies Center at the University of California, Santa Barbara. Her recent publications include "The Silenced Screen: Fostering a Film Industry in Paraguay," in *Contemporary Hispanic Cinema: Interrogating the Transnational in Spanish and Latin American Film*, ed. Stephanie Dennison (Tamesis, 2013); "*Familia* Fictions: Writing the Family in Tomás Rivera's *. . . and the Earth Did Not Devour Him* and Sandra Cisneros' *Caramelo*," in *Critical Insights: Family*, ed. John Knapp (California: Salem Press, September 2012); and "The Final Frontier: Imagining Latinos in Guillermo Gómez-Peña and Gustavo Vasquez's *The Great Mojado Invasion (The 2nd US-Mexico War)*," in *Imagined Transnationalism: U.S. Latino/a Literature, Culture,* *and Identity,* ed. Francisco Lomelí, Kevin Concannon, and Marc Priewe (Palgrave Macmillan, 2009).

Francisco A. Lomelí is chair of the Department of Spanish and Portuguese at the University of California, Santa Barbara. His research interests include literary history, Chicana/o literature, New Mexico studies, and Latin American literature, especially the novel and regional studies on Central America, Mexico, and Chile. His recent publications include *The Chican@ Literary Imagination: A Collection of Critical Studies by Francisco A. Lomelí* (Spain: Biblioteca Benjamin Franklin, 2012); *Imagined Transnationalism: U.S. Latino/a Literature, Culture and Identity,* coedited with Kevin Concannon and Marc Priewe (New York, Palgrave Macmillan, 2009); and *Perspectivas transatlánticas en la literatura chicana: Ensayos y creatividad,* coedited with María Herrera-Sobek and Juan Antonio Perles Rochel (Spain: Servicio de Publicaciones de la Universidad de Málaga, 2005).

Imelda Martín-Junquera is an associate professor at the Department of Modern Languages, Universidad de León, Spain. Her fields of research and interest are Chicana/o and Native American literature and culture, border studies, ecocriticism and ecofeminism, and postcolonial studies. Her recent publications include *Las literaturas chicana y nativo-americana ante el realismo mágico* (Secretariado de Publicaciones de la Universidad de León, 2005); with Manuel Broncano Rodríguez, editor of *Sociedades Multiculturales: Identidad y discurso artístico* (Servicio de Publicaciones de la Universidad de León, 2006); "The Brick People and the Struggle for Survival" en José Antonio Gurpegui and Carmen Gómez Galisteo (eds.), *Interpreting the New Milenio* (Cambridge Scholars Publishing, 2008); "Ecocrítica, racismo medioambiental y Renacimiento chicano," in José Carlos González Boixo (ed.), *Tendencias narrativas en la literatura mexicana actual* (Vervuert/Iberoamericana, 2009).

Ellen McCracken is a professor in the Department of Spanish and Portuguese at the University of California, Santa Barbara. Her research interests include contemporary Latin American literature, Latin American cultural studies, U.S. Latina/o literature, literary theory, visual and verbal semiotics, mass culture, and women's writing. Her recent publications include *The Life and Writing of Fray Angélico Chávez: A New Mexico Renaissance Man* (University of New Mexico Press, 2009), *New Latina Narrative: The Feminine Space of Postmodern Ethnicity* (University of Arizona Press, 1999), and *From Mademoiselle to Ms.: Decoding Women's Magazines* (St. Martin's, 1993).

Niamh Thornton is a senior lecturer in Hispanic Studies and Film at the University of Liverpool. Her primary area of research is contemporary Latin American and Mexican narrative and film, and she is currently completing a monograph on the war story in Mexican film, *Revolution and Rebellion in Mexican Film* (Continuum, 2013). Her recent publications include *Women and the Novela de la Revolución in Mexico* (Edwin Mellen Press, 2006); with Kathy Bacon, editor of *The 'Noughties' in the Hispanic and Lusophone World* (Cambridge Scholars Press, 2012); *Transcultural Encounters: Film, Literature, Art,* coedited with Pat O'Byrne and Gabriella Carty (Cambridge Scholars Press, 2010), and *Revolucionarias: Gender and Revolution in Latin America,* coedited with Par Kumaraswami (Peter Lang, 2007). In addition, she has previously coedited a special section for the *Bulletin of Latin American Research.* She has also published several chapters on film, literature, and digital cultures, as well as articles in journals such as the *Bulletin of Latin American Research; Bulletin of Hispanic Studies, Film and Film Culture;* and *Transnational Cinemas.*

Tatiana Voronchenko is the director of the Research Institute of Philology and Cross-Cultural Communications, and a professor in the Department of Journalism and Public Relations, Zabaikalsky State University for Humanities, Chita, Russia. Her research interests include American studies, ethnic studies, translation, and Chicana/o literature. She is the author of the first Russian-language book on Chicana/o literature: *На перекрестке миров: мексикано-американский феномен в литературе США* [*On the Crossroads of the World: the Mexican-American Phenomenon in American Literature*], 1998. Her recent publications include "The Writer's Landscape: Epiphany in Landscape," *Translator* (2001): 46–52, and the edited volume *Materials of the International Symposium, The Open World: Multicultural Discourse and Intercultural Communication as Part of the International Conference on Transborderland in the Changing World* (Chita: Zabaikalsky State Pedagogical University Press, 2006).

Index

For Product Safety Concerns and Information please contact our EU
representative GPSR@taylorandfrancis.com
Taylor & Francis Verlag GmbH, Kaufingerstraße 24, 80331 München, Germany

9 781138 097841